T0316399

The New Olive Branch (1820)
and Selected Essays

Economic Ideas that Built America

The Anthem **Economic Ideas that Built America** series aims to reconstruct the development of American political economy as seen through the eyes of its principal architects and interpreters. It will furthermore work to overcome the ideological nature of recent historiography. The volumes in the series – contextualized through analytical introductions and enriched with explanatory footnotes, bibliographies and indices – will offer a wide selection of texts inspired by very different economic visions, and will stress their complex consequences and interactions in the rich but often neglected history of American economic thought.

The New Olive Branch (1820) and Selected Essays

By Mathew Carey

Edited by Lawrence A. Peskin

ANTHEM PRESS

Anthem Press
An imprint of Wimbledon Publishing Company
www.anthempress.com

This edition first published in UK and USA 2014
by ANTHEM PRESS
75–76 Blackfriars Road, London SE1 8HA, UK
or PO Box 9779, London SW19 7ZG, UK
and
244 Madison Ave #116, New York, NY 10016, USA

British Library Cataloguing-in-Publication Data
A catalogue record for this book is available from the British Library.

Library of Congress Cataloging-in-Publication Data
Carey, Mathew, 1760–1839.
The new olive branch (1820) and selected essays / by Mathew Carey ;
edited by Lawrence A. Peskin.
pages cm. – (Economic ideas that built America)
Includes bibliographical references and index.
ISBN 978-1-78308-155-4 (hbk)
1. Tariff–United States. 2. Free trade–United States. 3. Protectionism–United States. I.
Peskin, Lawrence A., 1966– II. Title.
HF1754.C36 2014
382'.7097309034–dc23
2014028893

Portrait of Mathew Carey by J. Thomson, Historical Society of
Pennsylvania portrait collection.

ISBN-13: 978 1 78308 155 4 (Hbk)
ISBN-10: 1 78308 155 4 (Hbk)

This title is also available as an ebook.

CONTENTS

ACKNOWLEDGEMENTS

Even a relatively small project like this one creates a web of intellectual debt that needs to be acknowledged. I am grateful to Albrecht Koschnik and participants of the "Ireland, America, and the Worlds of Mathew Carey" conference sponsored by the McNeil Center for Early American Studies, the Library Company of Philadelphia, the Program in Early American Economy and Society (PEAES), and the University of Pennsylvania Libraries in 2011 for their comments and criticism on a related Carey presentation. Cathy Matson, director of PEAES, provided helpful advice on an earlier Carey project as well as on this one and has been a superb, if unofficial, mentor. James N. Green of the Library Company of Philadelphia is, in my opinion, the greatest living Carey expert, and I am very grateful for his occasional guidance. Perhaps the most rewarding aspect of working on this project has been my introduction to the Reinert family of Norway and Cambridge. Sophus Reinert of Harvard University provided excellent advice and conversation. Erik Reinert generously took the time to give the manuscript a thorough reading and offer incisive criticism. Most importantly, Francesca Viano, who invited me to edit the Carey volume of my choice, offered a great deal of encouragement and useful advice without which this volume would never have been completed.

INTRODUCTION

Mathew Carey has never quite been a forgotten name in America's collective memory. Born a baker's son in Dublin in 1760, he had a way with words that led him to work as a printer and, soon after, a newspaper publisher. He was forced to make a hasty exit from Ireland after being accused of libeling Parliament in his newspaper in 1784. Having forged connections with Benjamin Franklin and the Marquis de Lafayette, he was able to set himself up as a printer in Philadelphia, where he quickly rose to prominence in post-Revolutionary America.[1] He became the new nation's leading bookseller and publisher and one of its most important Catholic citizens. He wrote a prodigious amount of material printed in magazines, newspapers, pamphlets and books on subjects ranging from American politics to yellow fever and the history of Algeria. In recent years, there has been a revival of interest in his role as the new nation's leading bookseller/publisher and his position as a leading Irish Catholic. But can Mathew Carey be considered an influential economist? For that matter, was he an economist at all? These are crucial questions for understanding Mathew Carey's writings and his place within American economic history.

Carey's Influence Then and Now

Despite his influence on contemporaries, Carey's economic ideas have been largely ignored by posterity.[2] Carey was a key theorist in the tariff disputes of the 1820s and, along with his compatriot Hezekiah Niles, arguably the best-read economic writer in the early national United States. His economic essays frequently appeared in newspapers in Philadelphia, the nation's largest media market, and were reprinted throughout the country. His magazine, *The American Museum*, a forum for economic writing that was congenial to his point of view, was among the most important early national magazines and was widely distributed in the United States and abroad. Although his economic books and pamphlets were not big sellers, Carey strategically distributed them throughout the United States in an effort to get them into the hands of his influential contacts. Despite this influence and the vast extent of his publications, there have only been three reprints of any of his economic publications since his death in 1839.[3] The only monographic study of his economic thought was published in 1933. He receives only a couple of sentences of discussion in the most authoritative contemporary study of early American political economy, compared to his contemporaries John Taylor and Daniel Raymond who receive complete chapters.[1] Taylor and Raymond never sold more than a few thousand copies of their books during their lifetimes and, although their ideas gained influence among a well-educated elite, the vast majority of Americans had no idea who they were.

Posthumous obscurity is no doubt a common fate for popular writers. Like today's newspaper columnists, Carey provided a crucial service for contemporaries who needed to understand rapidly changing current events. Such work, however, rarely has a long shelf life given that it is written on short deadlines and without much regard for broader contexts or larger theoretical constructs. Nevertheless, if one wants to understand political economy as it happened, rather than as historians and economists have constructed it, it could be easily argued that Carey's work was far more important to his contemporaries than that of Raymond or Taylor, whose posthumous reputations have surely been greater than their contemporary influence. Also, like modern journalists, Carey's longer books can have a bit of a slapdash quality to them as the author revisits ideas that he has expressed frequently before in shorter, more ephemeral form. Such books, including *The New Olive Branch*, are particularly useful in allowing readers to view all at once opinions and attitudes that were developed piecemeal in various newspapers, pamphlets and other essays. In this sense, they are more useful to posterity than they were to contemporary readers who had been exposed to the ideas and debates in which Carey was engaged as they actually unfolded.

There have been at least three additional obstacles to Carey's posthumous reputation. The first is that Carey does not fit the Whiggish story of the supposed progression toward the embrace of classical economics and laissez-faire in the nineteenth century after the fortuitous publication of Adam Smith's *The Wealth of Nations* in the same year as the Declaration of Independence. Far from being a classical economist, Carey explicitly rejected Adam Smith and in fact mocked him as a purveyor of fanciful European theories that lacked factual foundation. Carey, therefore, may seem to be out of the main line of development of nineteenth-century American economics, provided of course that progress is defined as the movement toward full adoption of contemporary economic theories. While classical economics has provided a powerful tool for understanding human behavior, teleological models are rarely useful in understanding history, and it makes sense to pay closer attention to Carey's work to gain a more thorough understanding of the actual history of American economic thought, whether or not his ideas remain useful or compelling in our contemporary context.

Rather than pushing him to the margins of nineteenth-century society, Carey's persistent mercantilism and his rejection of Smith put him in a mainstream, if not *the* mainstream, of popular economic thought. As a younger man, Carey was near the center of a nationalistic effort to promote American manufacturing, which completely eschewed free-market doctrine in favor of a program of tariffs and government supports that was frankly emulative of the British mercantile system. In the generation following the American Revolution, American artisans and small manufacturers (blacksmiths, carpenters, shoemakers and the like) were particularly supportive of such a program. As a printer and baker's son, Carey fit right into this demographic. Manufacturing supporters, like Carey, also tended to be economic nationalists who, paradoxically, sought to use lessons learned from British mercantilism to free America from its dependence on British manufactures. Even President Jefferson, an agrarian southerner, began to see the utility of protecting manufacturing and instituting restrictions on trade. By the 1820s the promanufacturing movement had come to be dominated by larger manufacturers on the verge of becoming recognizable as capitalists. Smaller artisans, though by no means free-market supporters, had become disillusioned with the larger capitalists and were now more interested in securing protection from exploitative industrialists than protection for American manufactures.[5] Despite some discomfort in associating with wealthy capitalists, Carey remained at the center of this movement and was a leading light of the Philadelphia Society for the Promotion of National Industry, which lobbied for promanufacturing tariffs in the 1820s and for which Carey wrote a series of essays, two of which are printed in this volume.

The second obstacle to Carey's long-term reputation is that, setting aside the theoretical underpinnings of his work, Carey does not fit the modern definition of an economist. He was first and foremost a business man, and secondly a political operative. He was not well educated, nor was he a man of leisure, and he certainly was not associated with any university or academic elites in the way that Adam Smith, David Ricardo or even Thomas Malthus had been. Far from an objective or disinterested scholar, he was frequently a propagandist at the center of political economic struggles. Because most economic history today is written and read by academics, scholarly credentials can become important in evaluating the importance of historical subjects like Carey. But this is a view that would be difficult for an eighteenth-century reader to accept. The fact is that in the eighteenth century economic thinkers had just as frequently (if not more so) resembled Mathew Carey as Adam Smith. Influential eighteenth-century

British economic thinkers such as Malachi Postlethwayt, Adam Anderson and Joshua Gee were usually businessmen and often associated with the Board of Trade or state monopolies such as the Royal African Company or the East India Company. Similarly, German economic thinkers known as cameralists were government employees seeking to maximize tax revenues. Alexander Hamilton, arguably the most important economist of America's founding generation, was similarly employed by the state as secretary of the treasury. The model of the scholar-economist was just beginning to emerge in the nineteenth century, and it would be extremely anachronistic to exclude Carey from the list of economists merely because of his position in society or his lack of formal training.

A third obstacle was partly of Carey's own making. He was simply not as gifted a writer or as supple a thinker as contemporaries such as Daniel Raymond, let alone Adam Smith. Carey was well aware of this shortcoming, and he frequently apologized for the repetitiveness of his essays. He wrote his work extremely quickly, often completing books in a matter of weeks. The most comprehensive list of his economic writings includes roughly 200 items ranging from books and pamphlets to shorter newspaper essays.[6] His style, discussed in more length below, could also be off-putting, particularly to the modern reader. Most irritating today is his tendency to cut and paste complicated statistical tables and long excerpts from authoritative publications into his arguments. For modern readers, accustomed to seeing such items in little read footnotes or appendices, this habit can be particularly bothersome. In order to make Carey's work easier for modern readers, the present edition relegates many of these extracts into appendices. But the very opacity of Carey's style makes it important to understand. Far from viewing his cutting and pasting as a liability, Carey saw it as a strength. It was evidence of the scientific, factual basis of his thinking. Carey was not alone. Many other American economic writers, including Alexander Hamilton, adopted a similar style. Although they seem hopelessly antiquated today, from the perspective of the late eighteenth and early nineteenth century they should be seen as a forward looking group seeking to bring statistical rigor to what would today be considered the social sciences.

If we put aside modern notions of economics and economists, it is possible to see Mathew Carey as one of the most influential economic thinkers of his generation. The fact that his ideas may seem to be wrong-headed to most modern readers, that his style may seem a bit archaic, and that he was often on the losing side of political-economic battles, makes it all the more important to understand his thought if history is not to be written solely by the winners and, as Leopold von Ranke insisted, is to be remembered as it really happened.

Carey's Earlier Economic Thought

Carey's nationalistic and Anglophobic economic views were formed during a period in which Ireland struggled under British mercantilism. These tensions stretched back at least to the 1699 Woolens Act, which prohibited Ireland from exporting woolen goods outside of Britain and Ireland. The general understanding was that this act would prevent Irish competition with the important English woolen industry while rechanneling Irish manufacturing into linens by tacitly providing Ireland with a monopoly in the latter branch. English manufacturers and others appear to have continually feared that Irish manufacturers were subverting this act, and the restrictions certainly created discontent within Ireland. On the Irish side, Carey's own newspaper, *The Volunteer's Journal* (1783–84) accused the British government of undermining the 1699 act by allowing linen manufacturing to flourish in Scotland. As a very young man during 1780, Carey worked in Benjamin Franklin's printing shop while Franklin was serving as the rebelling United States' minister to France in Passy, near Paris. Franklin is the first luminary quoted in the front matter of *The New Olive Branch*. While in France, Carey also struck up an acquaintance with the Marquis de Lafayette, who would later help him become established in Philadelphia. These experiences may well have opened his eyes to the Americans' protests against British restrictions and the economic boycotts of the 1760s and 1770s.[7]

A close reading of *The Volunteer's Journal* certainly shows that he was aware of the political economy of the American Revolution occurring across the ocean and that it influenced his early positions. Carey's paper excoriated the government in London for its failure to protect Irish manufacturers and ran numerous articles supporting tariffs on imported manufacturers while lauding the "consumption of our own manufactures." Its columns warned repeatedly that if Britain did not support Irish manufactures, skilled craftsmen would desert its shores for the new nation. In words that strongly presage arguments in *The New Olive Branch*, he predicted that "America, destitute at present of manufactures, will with eagerness open her arms to our artists, and facilitate their passage, and thus the advantage of a free commercial intercourse with other nations will avail us little, if the manufacturer, so essential to this end, seduced by a flattering prospect of greater emolument, or driven by necessity should migrate from us for ever."[8] Echoing American Revolutionaries, *The Volunteer's Journal* began printing numerous articles calling for Irish patriots to wear homespun goods and use only domestic made manufactures, rather than consuming English goods, in order to send a message to the crown that they resented their economic dependence on England. Further echoing American patriots, *The Volunteer's Journal* called on "the men of Ireland" to enter "into a non-consumption agreement, respecting foreign manufactures, that must operate immediately, to the relief of thousands of our unemployed poor."[9] Eventually, incensed by the government's failure to implement protective duties, Carey ran a satirical article telling of the hanging of the responsible government official by "a numerous body of starving manufacturers." Carey imagined that as he stood on the gallows the official apologized for his corruption and for "the business of the protecting duties for which I so deservedly suffer this ignominious death, as the just reward of an ill spent life." This bit of satire was the final straw that prompted Parliament to charge Carey with printing seditious libel, thereby forcing him to flee Ireland for Philadelphia.[10]

Carey's economic nationalism and Anglophobia fit perfectly into the political climate of Revolutionary and post-Revolutionary America. Like many Americans, Carey's anger at British mercantile restrictions would not push him toward Adam Smith's version of free trade. Beginning with the nonimportation and nonconsumption movements of the 1760s, protecting domestic manufacturers had become a patriotic imperative for many Americans. Mechanics and those interested in founding new manufacturing ventures were buoyed by this development and a modest manufacturing boom that began during nonimportation and the Revolutionary War. After the war, as Carey was arriving in Philadelphia, American mechanics were outraged by the influx of British goods that flooded into the American market. They organized at the state and national level to try to implement protective tariffs. They supported the new constitution because it would give the federal government the power to lay tariffs on imported goods, and they railed against the British and British goods. Eventually, in 1789, the first US Congress passed a tariff that was, at best, mildly protective.

Carey took part in this movement, utilizing arguments developed in Ireland that foreshadowed, to a remarkable extent, the economic ideas he would express in *The New Olive Branch* and other publications of the 1820s. In 1785, shortly after his arrival in the United States, he wrote in his newspaper, the Pennsylvania *Evening Herald*, that it gave him "the highest degree of pleasure to find the legislatures of the different states turning their attention to every object that can check the progress of importations, and tend to the promotion of domestic manufactures." In a proimmigration pamphlet written in 1790 he introduced several lifelong themes, including Anglophobia and the need for skilled immigration to the United States together with promanufacturing protectionism. "During the connexion of this country with Great Britain," he wrote, "we were taught to believe that agriculture and commerce should be the only pursuits of the Americans: but experiments and reflexion have taught us that our country abounds with resources for manufactures of all kinds."

This passage could easily have been included 30 years later in *The New Olive Branch*, in which Carey argues that it is time for the United States to establish manufacturing on an equal footing with farming and agriculture. In a letter to his family in Ireland, he lauded the new nation's government and, striking a theme that he would repeat innumerable times, noted that "in the promotion of national misery or happiness, governments are omnipotent."[11]

Carey also furthered his knowledge of American political economy and widened his circle of influence as publisher of *The American Museum*. During its five year run (1787–92), *The American Museum* became one of the most influential magazines in the new nation and catapulted its publisher into national fame, including a favorable review from George Washington. Carey distributed it widely, even sending copies to Germany. Although *The American Museum* included literature and politics as well as political economy, Carey took great care to provide voluminous promanufacturing and protectionist contributions from the first issue onward. In addition to essays by important American economic writers, he included state papers related to manufacturing and tariffs. *The American Museum* also served as a sort of clearing house for the publications turned out by the numerous mechanic and manufacturer-led societies that were emerging to promote manufactures in the new nation's cities. The April 1789 issue was quite typical: it offered economically oriented readers "Three Letters on the Trade and Commerce of America"; the constitution of the New York Manufacturing Society; a circular letter "from the corresponding committee of the tradesmen and manufacturers of the town of Baltimore to the mechanics and manufacturers of the city of Philadelphia"; and extracts from an essay entitled "What Labour is Profitable and What Unprofitable." Carey was particularly fond of material written by Alexander Hamilton and Tench Coxe, both of whose state papers on manufactures would influence much of *The New Olive Branch*. As publisher, Carey got to know many of these writers when he solicited their work, and he even toyed with the idea of offering Coxe a partnership in the magazine.[12]

As a book publisher, large bookseller and printer, Carey straddled the line between the mechanics who had promoted manufacturing during the Revolution and larger scale capitalist-manufacturers who began to come to prominence in the late eighteenth and early nineteenth century. In his own business, he occasionally employed the same sort of protectionist, promanufacturing tropes that would appear in his later economic works. In 1801, for example, in an effort to promote a national book fair, he wrote his fellow booksellers, "The patriotic spirit of fostering domestic arts and manufactures, which, to the honor of our country, is rapidly spreading among our citizens, demands, from all persons interested in those arts and manufactures, suitable exertions to extend and improve their respective branches." During the early years of the nineteenth century he also became more involved in the effort to create new banks to provide credit to manufacturers and others. In a pro-bank pamphlet addressed to Dr. Adam Seybert, he wrote, "The genuine cause of the scarcity of money is, the importing beyond the amount of our exports: and the consequence is the diminution of specie, and inability of the banks to discount as much as usual." The anti-import sentiment, the balance of trade argument and the call for increased credit would remain hallmarks of protectionist arguments made by Carey and others for decades. Seybert, too, would remain an important figure for Carey, who would cite his work numerous times in *The New Olive Branch*.[13]

Carey's *The New Olive Branch*

The New Olive Branch, published in 1820, is overshadowed by the *Olive Branch*, or, as Carey called it in the tenth edition (1818), the "Political Olive Branch." The political *Olive Branch* has been described by Edward C. Carter II, an eminent Carey scholar, as "the most influential piece of political writing published on this side of the Atlantic during the War of 1812" and as Carey's "greatest single sustained literary effort." It went through ten editions and, according to Carter, sold more copies "than any other political book in the history of the United States before 1820 – more than 10,000 copies."[14] *The Olive Branch*, subtitled "Or, Faults on Both Sides, Federal and Democratic," first published in 1814, was Carey's attempt to rein in the intense political partisanship of the war years, which culminated in the infamous Hartford Convention of 1814, where some believe the New England Federalists came close to leaving the union or even prompting a civil war. Carey described his book as "an appeal on the necessity of mutual forgiveness and harmony," and, although the Federalists come in for the bulk of his criticism, it should probably be read as a sincere attempt to elicit political harmony among what today might be termed the moderate middle. He notes that "the mass of mankind [...] of all parties, and in all ages, have meant well [...]. And little more is necessary to produce harmony between them, than to understand each other correctly."[15]

The New Olive Branch, similarly, attempts to create harmony among the three great branches of the economy: agriculture, commerce and manufactures. To some extent, it also continues Carey's political mission from the *Olive Branch* in that it frequently admonishes Congress for its partisanship and inability to act on basic legislation without specifically targeting any party. Unlike its more famous predecessor, *The New Olive Branch* is barely mentioned by Carey scholars today. In fact, several scholars with whom I discussed early stages of this Anthem edition initially confused it with the political *Olive Branch*. Carey himself called it "in many respects [...] one of the best of my writings" on the subject of protecting manufactures, and in this assessment, if anything, he was unusually modest. He wrote it in seven weeks and published 1000 copies and two editions.[16] He also included it in his collection *Essays on Political Economy*, other portions of which are included in this Anthem volume as well.

Reissuing *The New Olive Branch* today serves at least three purposes. First, it is arguably Carey's most sustained, coherent, clearly organized work of political economy and the most succinct and accessible introduction to his economic thinking. Second, it offers a very clear demonstration of Carey's method of economic argumentation, distinguished by usage of history and statistics in sharp contradistinction to the emerging classical economics. Finally, *The New Olive Branch*, written as Carey was becoming most engaged with Adam Smith and classical economics, provides one of Carey's clearest discussions of why he rejected Smith and advocates of laissez-faire. Examining *The New Olive Branch* allows modern readers to understand better why Carey and others of his generation were unconvinced by Smith. This reissue also contains relevant sections from Carey's *Addresses of the Philadelphia Society for the Promotion of National Industry* (1822) that further elaborate Carey's rejection of Smith. These essays were published by the Philadelphia Society and by private individuals who distributed more than 2000 copies, free of charge, to the public in an effort to convince influential readers to support tariff legislation.[17] While those portions that are republished here offer important insight into Carey's thinking, the collection as a whole is far less accessible than *The New Olive Branch*; this is due to poor organization and the inclusion of very long excerpts from other sources – as well as some of the society's memorials and other items of little interest to modern readers. As Carey himself writes in the preface to his *Essays on Political Economy*, which includes these essays, "Many of the facts and arguments are repeated twice and thrice, and some few even four times."[18]

The New Olive Branch could be considered Carey's only original extended publication on political economy. Most of his other economic publications were series of essays written sporadically over long periods of time. Often written over pseudonyms such as Neckar, Colbert and Hamilton that reflected Carey's mercantilist orientation, they were produced to address specific, ephemeral problems rather than to elaborate a comprehensive vision. When Carey collected them into larger volumes they lacked a sense of continuity and drive, although some individual examples, particularly those in *Essays on Political Economy*, clearly elaborated aspects of his thought. By contrast, *The New Olive Branch*, like the political *Olive Branch*, is relatively clearly organized along chronological lines spanning the period from the American Revolution to 1820.

Like most of Carey's work, each chapter of *The New Olive Branch* includes a significant amount of material not written by Carey – usually statistical reports or public papers that he has pasted into the middle of a chapter to support or amplify his argument. Carey's use of these materials is important, and will be discussed below, but the effect of reading chapters organized in this way can be very alienating to modern readers. Nevertheless, *The New Olive Branch* represents Carey's least intrusive use of such sources. Edward Carter has calculated that nearly a third of the first edition of the political *Olive Branch* consists of such materials, and the much-expanded tenth edition contains 10 chapters that consist solely of such documents.[19] The *Address of the Philadelphia Society for the Promotion of Industry*, from which some of the essays in this Anthem reissue are drawn, includes a 31-page chapter consisting almost solely of extracts from Alexander Hamilton's *Report on Manufactures*. Compared to this, *The New Olive Branch* is a model of brevity.

Aside from improving readability, the chronological organization of *The New Olive Branch* also reflected Carey's historical approach to economics. For Carey, history played two roles. First, because Carey believed policy was the crucial determinant in economic progress, historical context was necessary to show the evolution and logic of economic policy over time. In the case of *The New Olive Branch*, Carey's particular concern was the development and implementation of tariff policy from the time of independence until 1820. He attempted to prove a number of historical propositions: that US tariff policy "from the commencement of its career, has been radically wrong," that it "sacrificed a large portion of the national industry," and that it tended "to render us tributary to other nations" (52). Thus, historical analysis was necessary to prove historical assertions. But Carey also viewed history as fertile ground for examples and counter examples to support his general economic assertions. In *The New Olive Branch*, to cite just two of many, many examples, he looks at the drop in land prices in the vicinity of Pittsburgh between 1813 and 1820 to illustrate the connection between manufacturing and agriculture (135) and the decline in employment in Pittsburgh during the same period to show the impact of foreign imports (105). Ranging further afield, he devotes a long section of the *Addresses of the Philadelphia Society for the Promotion of Industry* to a discussion of Frederick the Great's protective policies in the 1780s and their positive economic effects as a counter example to the allegedly damaging US policies of the same period.[20]

Even more than history, Carey's method stressed statistics. As Carey stated at the start of his introduction, "The grand object of such books is to convey information." He certainly takes that dictum to heart in *The New Olive Branch*. Every chapter and nearly every page contains extracts from some type of document or statistical table. Chapter nine, which discusses industry in Pittsburgh and Philadelphia, and has already been noted above, offers a good example. Carey begins with one of the book's crucial arguments: that government inaction and ineptitude after the War of 1812 caused the United States to lose the economic momentum it had gained when English imports were excluded from American ports during the war and the years leading up to it. Carey asserts that the economic distress caused by these policies was even worse than usually imagined. The second third of the chapter uses a variety of sources to document the decline, beginning with a page or so of extracts from "an investigation ordered during the last autumn by a town meeting of the citizens of Philadelphia" giving some unemployment statistics. From these figures, Carey calculates a loss of wages of $7,100,804. Next he moves on to a similar report about Pittsburgh, finding there an additional loss of $1,785,833 in wages. He then argues that "it will not be an unreasonable calculation" to suppose that nationally the loss was six times that of the Pennsylvania cities, but "to avoid cavil" he calculates it at $35.5 million, or three times the Pennsylvania losses. Although noting it would be "insanity to be debating about the cause of this distress," Carey nevertheless concludes it was due to legislators' neglect of protecting industry.

Next, he abstracts from a number of public documents, "which prove the distress of the country are more intense and extensive than had been previously conceived" (106) and that the "embarrassment" became "universal," beginning with Pennsylvania state senate and house reports on debt actions and imprisonments. Finally, using statistics from Tench Coxe's 1810 federal report on manufactures as a base line, he tries to calculate how rapidly American manufacturing would have progressed had it received proper tariff protection. Using statistics showing that cotton manufacture increased ninefold from 1810 to 1815, he conservatively estimates, in the absence of hard data, that other branches must have at least doubled during this period of accidental wartime protection to a total of $350 million. Finally, he infers "they would, under an efficient protection by the government, have increased from 1815 to 1820, fifty percent and of course would now be above 500,000,000 dollars" (107).

This chapter also illustrates some of the difficulties in reading Carey today. First, wading through all of these extracts can be quite trying for the modern reader, who is used to more authorial analysis and less accustomed to making sense of statistical information by his- or herself. For those who make the effort, Carey's method may seem suspect and perhaps pseudoscientific by today's standards. Assuming that a decline in wages proves the hazard of not protecting industry violates notions of cause and effect. The fact that two well-documented economic trends occur simultaneously hardly proves that they are causally connected – although, in Carey's defense, this is still a common error made by media analysts today. More troublingly, Carey's many guesstimates – for example, arbitrarily assuming, based on data for one leading sector, that industry on the whole had at least doubled between

1810 and 1815 and would have risen another 50 percent over the next five years with proper protection – do not come close to modern notions of statistical rigor. In essence, the apparent precision of the statistical data masks the real imprecision of these calculations.

Carey and the Statistical School

Despite his imprecision, Carey's use of statistics was in many ways quite modern and certainly on the cutting edge of early nineteenth-century political economy. At this time, the definition of statistics was both narrower and more capacious than it is today. On the one hand, statistics were not limited to mere numbers but might include so-called factual issues such as the memorials that Carey quoted. On the other hand, they generally referred only to facts about human conditions (modern-day social science) rather than to the natural or biological sciences. Statistics of this sort had been very difficult to come by before the nineteenth century, when there was far less predilection to count and when those statistics that did exist were often the property of the crown. The new United Sates, by implementing a decennial census and allowing the free flow of statistical information, made possible a new emphasis on the public circulation of such statistical material.

Carey was part of a circle of American authors who publicized and utilized such material. At least half of the 46 footnotes in *The New Olive Branch* refer to members of this group.[21] Adam Seybert, by far the most frequently footnoted author in *The New Olive Branch* (15 of 46 footnotes), was a Philadelphia congressman and manufacturing promoter who worked with Carey on the *Addresses of the Philadelphia Society for the Promotion of National Industry*.[22] In his *Statistical Annals*, Seybert placed himself within a circle of statisticians including Tench Coxe, whom Carey also cited, as well as Samuel Blodgett and Timothy Pitkin, whom Carey mentioned in the text of *The New Olive Branch*. Both Pitkin and Seybert were patronized by the federal government, which authorized a subscription of 500 copies of the *Statistical Annals*. Like Carey, Seybert stressed the importance of factual information over opinion. Seybert wrote that he "never did intend to load his work with mere opinions, speculations and estimates; and he will be satisfied, if his labours contribute to diffuse correct information concerning his native country." Admitting that his style might be "too sententious," Seybert contended that "his great object was *accurate* information for the people, who, in our country constitute the mainsprings of action, and direct the policy of the nation."[23]

Carey also cited Alexander Hamilton's *Report on Manufactures* three times. While Carey does not seem to have been personally acquainted with Hamilton, the first treasury secretary, he was an enormous admirer of him and his report. He reprinted portions of the report in *The American Museum* in 1792, excerpted most of it in *Essays on Political Economy* and later edited a reissue of it. In the reissue, Carey praised Hamilton's familiarity with the "details" of American manufacturing, before mentioning his "[sound] and lucid system." Hamilton's report, he wrote, "may be justly considered as one of the most splendid practical documents ever produced by the human mind."[21] Carey was most likely impressed by Hamilton's detailed description of the then current state of American manufacturing and the probable effect of protection on products ranging from iron to cotton, paper, books, refined sugar and many others. Like Seybert, Hamilton appeared to focus on factual details rather than on speculation or theoretical systems.

Carey maintained various connections to other members of this circle. As has already been noted, he was well acquainted with his fellow Philadelphian Tench Coxe, who was Hamilton's assistant and the uncredited author of portions of Hamilton's report. Coxe, who wrote the government sponsored 1810 census of manufactures, as well as many other promanufacturing books and pamphlets, was cited several times in *The New Olive Branch*.[25] Carey also occasionally corresponded with Jeremy Belknap, whose statistically oriented history of New Hampshire is cited in *The New Olive Branch*, and he published an economically oriented essay by Hugh Williamson, a Philadelphia born North Carolinian, in *The American Museum*.

Most members of this statistical school, like Carey, also rejected much of what is now considered the orthodoxy of classical economics. While seemingly forward looking and modern in their embrace of a social scientific approach, today, they, paradoxically, may appear backward looking in clinging to old mercantilistic doctrines of government regulation. However, for Carey and others, commitment to a statistical method naturally led to a rejection of what they viewed as Smith's and his followers' false conclusions. For Carey, Smith was a "theorist" unconcerned with what would now be termed hard data. "To a theorist," Carey wrote, "'facts are stubborn things,' not unlike those formidable obstructions in the Mississippi, which, in the elegant diction of the navigators of that immense river, are called *snags* and *sawyers*." With Adam Smith, Jean-Baptiste Say and David Ricardo in mind, Carey concludes that "in some of the grand systems of political economy that have acquired a great celebrity, you may travel through fifty or a hundred pages together of most harmonious prose, all derived from a luxuriant imagination, without your career being arrested by a single fact" (33).

Theoretical political economy was not only inaccurate, for Carey it could also be dangerous. "A theory, how plausible soever, and however propped up by a bead-roll of great names, ought to be regarded with suspicion if unsupported by fact – and, *a fortiori*, if contrary to established fact, ought to be unhesitatingly rejected," he wrote. The devastating economic effects of free trade on the United States, Spain and Portugal were, Carey argued, demonstrable examples of the wrongness of Smith's theories that were overlooked by proponents of classical economics. The distress of these countries "holds out an awful beacon against the adoption of theories, which, however splendid and captivating on paper, are fraught with ruin when carried into practice."[26]

Carey's charge that Smith ignored facts may at first seem rather odd. After all, an early review of *The Wealth of Nations* noted its "multitude of promiscuous facts," and readers today continue to marvel at the author's mastery of a wide range of arcana ranging from the intricacies of pin making to Roman monetary policy.[27] But Smith used facts differently than Carey and the statistical school. While interested in and knowledgeable about the minutiae of economic activity, Smith attempted to transcend historical trends to reach an abstract level of universal truth that could explain economic activity outside of the limitations of space and time. In this regard, *The Wealth of Nations* was an exercise in deductive logic attempting to show how the general pattern of economic activity fit into general laws that, in turn, could simplify understanding of economic behavior. In doing so, he very much echoed Enlightenment philosophers like John Locke, who attempted to derive universal laws of political behavior that transcended particular communities. This, no doubt, is why Carey viewed Smith as a speculative philosopher and an abstract theorist. Carey and the statistical school, by contrast, despite (or because of) their interest in historical statistics, were very much bound to the particularities of time and place. Rather than resembling the work of Enlightenment philosophers, their work is more similar to that of administrative officials such as Germany's cameralists, who sought a clearer understanding of the extent and nature of economic activity within the state in order to insure greater prosperity for all through proper economic regulation and taxation.[28] Hence, Carey, unlike Smith, has little interest in transcending historical realities to attain universal laws. Rather, he and his statistically minded brethren wanted to portray the economy in all its complexity.

Like the German cameralists, many of the American statisticians, such as Hamilton, Coxe and Seybert, were connected to the state. Their statistics, derived in part from the state apparatus of the census, were intended to promote better state regulation of the economy. Carey certainly feared that Smith's laissez-faire system endangered not only the ability of the state to regulate the economy, but the very national wealth it was supposed to maximize. "Abstract principles of political economy," he argued, with Smith in mind, appeared logical on paper, but when "brought into practice" they could be very inadequate and would be "defeated by unanticipated combinations, which give results never calculated; and re-actions are produced, that work effects never suspected."[29] In modern language, they were subject to the law of unintended consequences.

Carey and Adam Smith

Despite his lifelong engagement in political economy, Carey claimed not to have read Adam Smith before 1819.[30] While perhaps disingenuous, this claim was not entirely impossible. Scholars interested in Smith's reception in the United States have convincingly argued that the founding generation was familiar with *The Wealth of Nations* within a few years of its publication, well before most of their European counterparts.[31] Yet the question of how influential the work was in the United States remains vexed. John Adams, and others, first proposed a new "Model Treaty" that would allow "a free trade […] with all nations" in June of 1776, before they could have read *The Wealth of Nations*. English colonists were on the edge of revolt against the mercantilist system; the founding generation hardly needed a Scottish economist to prompt their denunciations of British trade restriction, and some had independently formulated ideas similar to Smith's well before 1776. Furthermore, the founders may also have been aware of earlier conceptions of free trade: as freedom from outright trade prohibitions and monopolies rather than from regulations such as tariffs.[32]

Whether or not they could be considered disciples of Smith, the founders were hardly the sort of strict laissez-faire advocates that Smith's nineteenth-century followers would become. Enthralled as they were by the liberating notions of free trade unrestricted by British prohibitions, there is little evidence that once they gained power the founders gave much consideration to the other side of Smith's doctrine – the imperative that they, as the government of a new nation, employ a hands-off policy on trade coming into the United States. Instead, following the Revolution they quickly moved to implement protective measures that clearly violated theories of free trade as understood today. As Carey points out, the very first Congress enacted a tariff, albeit one that was not particularly restrictive. James Madison, one of the earliest proponents of Smith's ideas, was also one of the chief movers behind this legislation.[33] When the founders went back to their state legislatures, many of them also established state tariffs, some of which, like Pennsylvania's, were considerably more restrictive than the federal tariff.[34] Some of the authors of these laws may have viewed them as necessary in a world where England's powerful navy continued to hamper American ships despite the new nation's belief in free trade, while others, drawing from older definitions of free trade, may have seen no contradiction between open markets and tariff protection.

By the 1790s, however, as free trade was becoming more universally associated with modern notions of laissez-faire, tariffs of any sort were becoming less ideologically defensible. As Smith's book came to be viewed "as a giant machine assembled to drive home the doctrine of free trade," it became particularly useful to opponents of the Scottish corn laws, which were aimed at raising the tariff on imported foreign grain.[35] By the late 1810s, the growing popularity and influence of Smith's work as a symbol of laissez-faire by those who opposed regulation of imports led Carey to worry that Smith's, Say's and Ricardo's dangerous generalities could become the new nation's guiding principles. In the South, the work of John Taylor of Caroline, heavily influenced by classical economics, was gaining much influence, particularly among those who opposed tariffs. By the close of the 1820s, Carey wrote that 2,000 copies of *The Wealth of Nations* and 2,750 copies of Say's *Political Economy* had been published in the United States and that Say's book, in particular, had sold very quickly. By contrast, he noted that Daniel Raymond's protectionist *Political Economy*, "a work far superior" to both Say and Smith, had only been printed in two small editions totaling 1,250 copies, about a third of which had been "sacrificed at auction" while the rest sold very slowly.[36] Clearly Carey's concern about the ascendancy of classical economics was an important factor pushing him to study Smith more closely.

Carey's new interest in *The Wealth of Nations* is evident in both *The New Olive Branch* and the *Addresses of the Philadelphia Society for the Promotion of Industry*. The best evidence of Carey's engagement with classical economics comes in the *Addresses*, but even there Carey gives little indication of having read anything other than Smith's crucial chapter, "Of Restraints upon the Importation from Foreign Countries of Such Goods as can be Produced at Home," in Book IV of *The Wealth of Nations*. In the *Addresses* Carey offers two criticisms of this chapter, with mixed results. First, he takes issue with Smith's famous dictum that, "If a foreign country can supply us with a commodity cheaper than we ourselves can make it, better buy it of them with some part of the produce of our own industry, employed in a way in which we have some advantage."[37] While opening new free markets for American shipping could hardly raise controversy, as Smith's own formulation suggests, opening the American market to imports could create disruptions and distress (even if temporary) for American producers. Clearly this was an important concern for Carey as a proponent of American manufacturing.

Oddly, Carey proposes to demonstrate the shortcomings of this argument with an agricultural example: cotton. He speculates that newly independent Latin American countries might soon be able to sell cotton in the US at 10 cents less per pound than southern planters. In that case, he asks, "ought we for the sake of saving a few cents per pound, to destroy the prospects, and ruin the estates of nearly 800,000 inhabitants of the southern states?" Carey probably chose this counterfactual example to make the point that free trade could hurt farmers as well as manufacturers, particularly at a time when cotton prices were slipping. However, considering that the vast majority of US cotton was already exported, southern planters were far less concerned about potential competition in the domestic market than they were about selling cotton in industrialized Britain. The price of cotton in the US would matter much more to the textile manufacturers that Carey represented, who would depend largely on southern planters for raw cotton. Furthermore, Smith states quite clearly that the expense of importing bulky raw materials acts as a sort of natural protection to domestic crops, as opposed to the relative inexpensiveness of shipping manufacturers, which are far more valuable on a per pound basis. Carey conveniently ignores this aspect of Smith's argument.[38]

Carey's second criticism of Smith, the devastating effect of free trade on labor, is more trenchant. In particular, Carey took offense at Smith's assertion that, when a nation "restore[s]" free trade and thereby destroys some manufactures protected by tariffs, "there are other collateral manufactures of so similar a nature, that a workman can easily transfer his industry from one of them to another."[39] Here, as elsewhere, Carey portrays Smith as a speculative philosopher out of touch with earthy realities and, "like many other theorists, [...] deluded by his own system." In reality, most, if not all, industries lack "collateral manufacturers," Carey argues. Even when some branches may be similar, such as cotton and woolen weaving, if all participants in one branch were thrown out of work, they would naturally find the other branch "full and overflowing" and be unable to find employment. Furthermore, if free trade were instituted, "the flood of importation [...] would bear down in one common ruin, all those manufactures, of which the articles fell within his description of being 'purchased cheaper elsewhere.'" In that case, there would be few or no remaining branches for the masses of unemployed workers to flee to. Unemployment would, therefore, be another example of "the masses of misery which Dr. Smith's system would produce."[40] This labor critique of Smith also effectively demonstrates the difference in perspective between Smith's universalizing approach and Carey's concern with historical and statistical detail. While Smith's focus on the system as a whole causes him to give short shrift to the plight of individual cotton workers, Carey's focus on the picayune details of the economy, particularly of manufacturing, brings such employment statistics to the fore.

Here, too, Carey's criticism runs into certain contradictions. While Smith wants to protect industrial capitalists by insuring that the movement to free trade "should never be introduced suddenly, but slowly, gradually, and after a very long warning," he neglects to suggest similar protections for laborers. [41]

In this regard Carey's concerns may seem to the modern reader to be a bottom up critique of capitalism. However, Carey was certainly not anticapitalist; he wrote his essays for the Society for the Promotion of National Industry, a group composed of wealthy industrialists. Additionally, much of *The New Olive Branch* is very sympathetic towards capitalists.[42] Despite associating with the rich, Carey's focus on labor may have come naturally to him due to his artisan roots. However, there may also have been an element of propaganda. Much as he used his cotton examples to try to convince southern planters that free trade could be detrimental to their interests, he may have hoped to convince laborers that Smith's doctrines were harmful to them. Carey's goal in writing his addresses, as he himself confirmed in his autobiography, was to promote the protection of manufacturers. American manufacturers, at a time when large-scale manufacturing was just being introduced in the US, needed little convincing that tariff protection would help them. Carey's larger task was to convince others, such as farmers and laborers, that doctrines of free trade, particularly when applied to protective tariffs, might be harmful to them.

But Carey's biggest point, and the core argument of *The New Olive Branch*, was that free trade had demonstrably failed in practice. Near the start of the book, Carey observes, "at the close of the revolutionary war, the trade of America was free and unrestrained in the fullest sense of the word, according to the theory of Adam Smith, Say, Ricardo, the Edinburgh Reviewers, and the authors of the Encyclopedia." Carey here refers to the contemporary criticism of the Confederation Congress that it was so weak it could not regulate trade even when regulations were necessary or desirable.[43] The subsequent depression that the new nation entered into, despite opening its markets to all, should disprove any abstract philosophical theories of the value of free trade once and for all, Carey argues. "If enthusiasts did not too generally scorn to trammel themselves by attention to facts, which are so very troublesome, and refuse to be dove tailed into their specious theories," he continues, "this case would settle the question of unrestrained commerce for ever – and prove that the system ought to be postponed till the millennium when it is possible it may stand a chance of promoting the welfare of mankind" (33). This argument is typical Carey: exaggerated, simplified, scornful of general theories and apparently commonsensical. Indeed, practically all of *The New Olive Branch* makes essentially the same point: relatively free and open markets have not added to the wealth of the new nation. Despite, or perhaps because of, its simplicity and lack of nuance, this becomes possibly his most powerful argument and one of the most sustained early attacks on free market theory in American literature.

Structure and Argument of *The New Olive Branch*

The New Olive Branch is very much a product of its time. Carey wrote it during one of the worst economic pullbacks the new nation had experienced. For readers in the 1820s, its most obvious utility would have been in explaining the causes of the Panic of 1819 and ensuing depression, to examine its effects, and to suggest ways of avoiding similar catastrophes in the future. For modern readers, Carey's approach may seem idiosyncratic. Throughout, he focuses on government policy rather than larger market forces. Governments, he writes, "are instituted for the protection, support, and benefit of the governed," by which he means, primarily, their property. Therefore, "government, by whatever name it may be called, is only estimable in proportion as it guards those sacred deposits" (18). Therefore, when an economic disaster on the magnitude of the Panic of 1819 occurs, "there must be something radically wrong in the people, or in the form of government, or radically vicious and pernicious in its legislation" (19). Carey clearly favors the last possibility and devotes most of his book to ideas for correcting such "pernicious legislation."

The assumption that legislation is the primary determinant of economic well-being or economic distress is quite different from that of modern classical-economics based thought. Modern analysis of the Panic of 1819 and of economic downturns generally focuses on prices, supply and demand, and market disruptions far more than on government policy. When classical economists concern themselves with government action, they usually are interested in instances of over-regulation or negative unintended consequences. For example, in considering the Panic of 1819, modern economists view faulty government monetary policy as a major causative factor. To paraphrase Ronald Reagan, they generally see legislation as a problem rather than as a solution For Carey, government was everything – both the problem and the solution. In *The New Olive Branch*, drawing from a long line of mercantilist and neomercantilist thinkers preceding Smith, Carey views the Panic of 1819 primarily as the result of poor legislation and inactivity on the part of Congress. He argues that the solution for the downturn must also come from Congressional action, specifically an expeditious and effective tariff to protect manufacturers.

Carey's argument can be divided into three parts. The first (chapters i–vi) examines the historic roots of the new nation's economy, paying particular attention to its tariffs. A second group of chapters (vii–x) builds on Carey's historical analysis to offer a deeper picture of the causes and effects of the Panic of 1819. Finally, the last section (chapters xi–xix) examines the three sectors of the economy in an effort to demonstrate how protective legislation would harmonize seemingly disparate economic interests.

The first section begins with an example of Carey's use of history as analogy. In this case, he parallels the economic history of the United States at the close of the American Revolution to that at the close of the War of 1812. After the Revolution, due to the lack of tariff protection, "the trade of America was free and unrestrained in the fullest sense of the word" (32). Consequently, imports flooded into the new nation from throughout Europe, creating for merchants "an El Dorado, where everything was to be converted into gold [...] " (34). But, Carey adds, "these glorious times soon came to a close, like those of 1815" (34). The causes of the downturn of the 1780s were twofold, according to his analysis. First, the lack of protection allowed for a glut of imports, which drove down the prices of domestic goods, and "accordingly domestic manufactures were arrested in their career." Readers would understand the parallels to the post–War of 1812 situation, as during the Revolutionary War, much as in the War of 1812, disruptions in the Atlantic trade and the need for manufactured goods prompted government and private individuals to promote manufacturing ventures – only to see them fail when the coming peace allowed Atlantic trade to resume. Secondly, "the payment for the foreign rubbish exhausted the country of nearly the whole of its specie" (35). In a classic balance of trade argument, Carey is complaining that all this importation created a negative balance of trade, draining America of its cash and, therefore, creating a cash shortage and, ultimately, a credit crunch; hard money became increasingly scarce, interest rates soared and creditors called in loans. This aspect of Carey's analysis was very much in line with contemporaneous views of the post-Revolutionary era and has been echoed by nearly all modern economic historians as well.[44]

Where Carey veered away from many of his contemporaries and most subsequent analysis was in his focus on tariff policies as he discussed the first 20 years of US economic history. Carey, long a Federalist supporter of the Constitution, argued that the new frame of government "operated like magic," clearing up most of the new nation's remaining economic problems. But the new legislators were a different story. Influenced by merchants and farmers, blinded by classical economics and the need for revenue, perhaps even influenced by foreign agents, Americans opposed protective tariffs. Under the sway of those antitariff prejudices and sectional jealousies, Congress passed only mild tariffs, designed to be high enough to raise revenues for the federal government but too low to dissuade foreign imports effectively enough to assist domestic manufacturing. It was only during the War of 1812 and the years immediately preceding it that wartime disruptions created a sort of natural tariff that protected American manufacturing until the war's end.

The biggest problem for Carey's analysis is that the United States remained quite prosperous in the 20 or so years of the mild-tariff regime. Carey addresses this problem when he observes in chapter V of *The New Olive Branch* that "a variety of circumstances [...] combined to rescue the United States from the ruinous consequences that would otherwise have naturally flowed from the impolicy of the tariffs of 1789, 1792, and 1804 [...] " (77). The most important factor was the great profits made by American merchants able to take advantage of their status as neutral carriers during the Anglo-French wars of 1794–1815. This reliance on neutral trade, however, according to Carey, "rested the prosperity of the nation on the sandy foundation of the wars, desolation, and misery of our fellow men." Furthermore, "as it was not probable that they would continue to cut each other's throats to promote our welfare, a close of this dazzling scene was to be expected, for which sound policy required provision to be made" (78). The problem, in Carey's opinion, was that Congress never seriously considered such provisions.

Unlike his analysis of the post-Revolutionary depression, Carey's discussion of the Panic of 1819 in the middle section of *The New Olive Branch* was not in line with most of his contemporaries nor with the accounts of modern writers. Once again, Carey believed government's failure to protect manufactures and the ensuing influx of foreign goods after the end of the natural tariff created by the war led to the panic and subsequent depression. By contrast, most historians downplay the importance of the post–War of 1812 glut of foreign manufactures. While all acknowledge the devastation wrought on the manufacturing sector by the resumption of imports after the war, these problems had been in effect for four years before 1819, making them unlikely triggers for the Panic. Rather, economic historians tend to point to the banking crisis that ensued when a credit bubble, inflated by a western land boom and rising export prices, burst.[45] Carey was well aware that many of his contemporaries made similar arguments. In his discussion of the parallel post-Revolutionary depression, he argued that the lack of banks then undercut arguments about their role in 1819. "Those of our citizens, who ascribe the existing [1820] calamities to the baleful career of the banks, are advised to consider this parallel case, wherein banks had no agency" (38).

Instead, in his analysis of the Panic of 1819, Carey focuses on how government policies failed manufactures. During the war, he asserts, "there was a sort of implied engagement on the part of the government, that having been found so useful in time of need, [manufactures] would not be allowed to be crushed, afterwards" (95). As usual, his focus is on policy rather than market activity, and he devotes an entire chapter (VIII) to Congress's unresponsiveness to the pleas of manufactures for protection. He contrasts this situation to the supposed responsiveness of the Russian government. Returning his focus to Congress, he writes, "Let us turn from this delightful picture of fostering and tender care, under a despotism, to the wretched, depressed, and vilified American capitalist, under a government which in its principles is really and truly the best that ever existed" (108). The American situation turns out to be far bleaker than in Russia, as the American capitalist seeking protection is "charged with extortion" by American farmers, eventually goes bankrupt and "dies of a broken heart" while his family and employees also suffer ruin (109). Carey also provides an excellent statistical analysis of the brutal effects of the depression on manufacturing workers (chapter IX).

Carey went to great lengths to exonerate the banks from his contemporaries' charges that they caused the Panic of 1819. Partly, he did so because he always supported banking as a means to provide capital to mechanics and manufacturers. But, more importantly, he must have feared that blaming the banks undercut his argument that lack of tariff protection led to the Panic. Carey argued that in 1819 banks simply did not possess sufficient capital for their collapse to cause the depression. Other analysts, he argued, had overestimated banking resources by mistaking authorized capital (i.e. the maximum allowed by the state) with actual capital on hand. In Pennsylvania, a state often cited for its banking excesses, Carey calculates that banks had only $7.4 million in *actual* capital assets as opposed to $16.1 million in *authorized* capital. Considering that Pennsylvania had perhaps $45 million in manufacturing capital in 1814 and averaged about $7 million annually in exports in the years before the Panic, Carey doubts bank collapses "could have produced such ruinous conditions" (138). Instead, he argues, the loss of manufacturing due to Congress's failure to pass protective tariffs had so weakened the state's economy, that the relatively trivial loss of banking capital created unnecessary problems.[16] "[Had] the industry of the state been protected," he writes, "and trade flourished, the great mass of [banks] would have gone on prosperously, and the whole would not have produced one tenth part of the injury that has resulted from those that have been ill-managed" (139).

The final chapters of *The New Olive Branch* examine the various sectors of the economy, their relationship to each other and to protective tariffs. Following the accepted contemporary wisdom, Carey understands the economy to be divided into three sectors: agriculture, commerce and manufacturing. *The New Olive Branch* is predicated on the notion that these economic interests do not necessarily conflict but in fact should work together in harmony. Carey emphasizes this notion beginning with the book's title page. In linking his book to the political *Olive Branch*, which had demonstrated the possibility of "mutual forgiveness and harmony" between seemingly irreconcilable political parties, he attempted to suggest the possibility for harmony among the three seemingly opposed economic interests. The book's subtitle reflects this "attempt to establish an identity of interest between agriculture, manufactures and commerce." In the early national United States, economic and political interests were closely aligned. Then, and now, observers sensed that Federalists were more congenial toward commerce and manufactures, while Democratic-Republicans were more closely aligned with agriculture. Carey deliberately includes promanufacturing quotes from both Thomas Jefferson, the Democratic-Republican leader most associated with agrarianism, and Federalist treasury secretary Alexander Hamilton to show that the two parties may in fact have shared more economic ground than is usually assumed.

Carey first addresses agriculture, which was far and away the largest of the three sectors in terms of both productivity and employment. The nation's many farmers, Carey notes, frequently accused even the new nation's modest tariffs of "taxing the many for the benefit of the few" (142), i.e., taking from farmers and giving to manufacturers. He argues that this common view was in fact a canard that "excited a deadly hostility in the minds of one portion of our citizens against another" (146). Carey notes that despite farmers' hostility to tariffs, agriculture itself was heavily protected. He finds that in 1818, Americans paid about $4.5 million in agricultural imposts, primarily on spirits and sugar. While that figure was still dwarfed by the $11 million paid on manufacturing duties, Carey argues that because most farmers were frugal and self-sufficient, they consumed fewer than half of all imported goods. Therefore, most of the duties would likely have been paid by urbanites. Overall, he calculates that the burden of tariffs was extremely light, averaging about $1.50 for each white American.

Furthermore, Carey argues, the establishment of more manufactures could only benefit farmers. Extrapolating from English and French statistical studies, he estimates that each American consumed 16 bushels of grain annually. He calculates that the 1.5 million Americans involved in manufacturing must have consumed at least 18 million bushels of domestic grain each year, bringing roughly $22.5 million to American farmers. Adding in estimates for other goods, he calculates that manufacturers spent $138 million annually on farm products. Additionally, because many manufactured products make use of agricultural materials such as cotton, wool, hemp and hides, manufacturers contributed still more to agriculture – perhaps, Carey estimates, as much as $29 million, bringing the total contribution to agriculture by manufacturers to $167 million. Through a series of further calculations, he finds that the manufacturing sector actually spent $100 million more on agricultural products than farmers spent on manufactures. He further notes that in manufacturing regions such as the Delaware and Brandywine valleys, the price of farm land doubled or tripled due to the rise of factories, thereby further benefiting farmers by making their land more valuable.

Carey is a bit more hostile toward commerce. While he does not doubt that commerce can be beneficial, "that it may be, and is occasionally, very injurious, is equally clear" (186). Commerce is "eminently pernicious" when a nation trades "raw materials which would find employment for its own people" for luxuries or unnecessary imports. Carey here assumes a labor theory of value for commerce. Trade that would not harm the nation's laborers is acceptable, but exporting items such as wool or cotton made by foreign laborers would be detrimental, because it would deprive domestic textile manufacturers of work. He writes that it would be "absurd" and "cruel" to unemployed citizens who could manufacture textiles "to export such quantities of raw cotton, and receive cambrics and muslins in return, as it would be for England to export her wool and import her woolen manufactures" (187).

As with agriculture, he also argues that commerce has continually benefited from government protection. For example, the first Congress passed duties on tea that gave American ships a monopoly on the China trade. "Thus, the foreign ship owner was at once shut out of our ports, beyond the power of competition, for the benefit of the American merchant; whereas the foreign manufacturer was invited in by a low duty: and the possibility of competition on the part of the American manufacturer wholly precluded!" (214). What is more, physically protecting American shipping is very expensive. Calculating the costs of operating a navy in order to protect American shipping, he finds that "for every dollar of the present gain of the merchants by commerce the nation at large pays nearly a dollar of tax entailed on it by that commerce!" (205).

Finally, Carey enlarges on his earlier argument: that protecting manufacturing would actually benefit commerce by giving the less successful merchants a different avenue for their capital. "The chief source of the misfortunes of our merchants," he writes, "has been the extravagant number of them" (206). If thousands of young Americans had been able to turn to manufacturing, rather than mercantile pursuits, then the numerous and damaging mercantile bankruptcies would have been minimized and, perhaps, the Panic of 1819 and ensuing depression averted. "Inordinate competition" among merchants, Carey writes, has also forced merchants "to buy our staples dear and sell them cheap," and, conversely, to enhance the price of incoming cargoes at the expense of American consumers (page).

For Carey, the real problem with encouraging foreign commerce at the expense of manufacturing is that it is detrimental to the harmony of economic interests that would arise if the domestic market were encouraged. He often contrasts American policy to that of England, where protection "secures them the *unlimited range of the domestic market*" and allows manufacturers to become so prosperous that they can even dominate poorly protected foreign markets like that of the United States [231??]. Addressing the perceived lack of skilled labor in the United States, Carey strongly urges the admission of skilled immigrants, who would help to beef up the manufacturing sector while consuming agricultural products for themselves and their factories. At the same time, overseas merchants would reorient themselves toward domestic commerce. Thus, with manufacturing properly protected, and adequate labor, merchants and farmers would also profit. With competing interests harmonized, the domestic market would create domestic happiness.

Carey and the Continuing Fight for Protection

Carey's influence on the tariff went far beyond *The New Olive Branch* and his essays. By his own reckoning, he wrote "at least a dozen memorials, and twenty-one circular letters" on the subject of protecting manufactures during the 1820s, and he filled an entire letter book with 412 letters on the issue during 1819–20. He traveled throughout the northeastern United States attempting to set up new promanufacturing societies in 1825, and he was the lead publicist for the Philadelphia protectionist movement from 1819 to 1828.[17] While his efforts were often unsuccessful and his publications not always well read, his name and arguments, especially those set forth in *The New Olive Branch*, came to be closely identified with the important protectionist movement of the 1820s.

Shortly after publication of *The New Olive Branch*, Congress began to deliberate the so-called Baldwin Tariff. Named for Henry Baldwin, a Pittsburgh congressman and chairman of the House Committee on Manufactures, the Baldwin Tariff would have offered substantial protection to manufactures. It seems likely that developing support for the measure was on Carey's mind when he wrote *The New Olive Branch*. Baldwin's lengthy report on the measure was, according to Carey, "one of the most powerful state papers that have appeared in this country."[18] Carey's admiration was not surprising, as the report, written in early 1821, shared the statistical style of Carey's writing and echoed many of the specific arguments developed in *The New Olive Branch*. Like Carey, Baldwin stressed the essential harmony of economic sectors, or, in his more elegant conception, the union of national interests. He also, like Carey, emphasized the mutual dependence of agriculture and manufacturing, noting that manufacturers eat agricultural products and use them as raw materials and that factories cause the value of farmland to rise. He also noted that tariffs had historically assisted farmers and merchants and should, therefore, also be used to help manufacturers. Much as Carey had, he called for the development of the domestic market, noting that, "as the importations of foreign manufactures might become lessened, it cannot be doubted that the increased internal communication would balance the losses to commerce."[49] Baldwin hardly parroted Carey, however. In fact, he was a much better writer, and one of his central and more powerful contentions, that, in the long run, protection would actually create more competition and thereby lower consumer prices, was one that Carey completely overlooked. Nevertheless, it cannot be doubted that, as a Pennsylvania protectionist, Baldwin was well aware of Carey's work and that the similarity of many of their arguments was no coincidence. Unfortunately, for both Baldwin and Carey, the Baldwin tariff was narrowly defeated in the Senate.

Carey's arguments remained influential throughout the tariff battles of the 1820s. Unfortunately for Carey, his personal influence was sometimes negative. Despite Carey's association with industrial capitalists, many of the public appear to have viewed him as a sort of protosocialist trying to give government control of the economy. In 1821, an influential Washington newspaper derided a "Careyan scheme of government" in which all property would be ceded to the government and placed under a board of trustees, styled the "Patrons of Industry," which would "guarantee to the people of the United States that thenceforth neither the capital nor labor of this nation should remain for a moment idle." Under this scheme, the government could manage Americans' property "according to its own fancy" and "shift capitalists and laborers from one employment to another." According to Carey, this sort of hostility damaged his bookselling business, particularly with his large southern customer base. "The hostility was carried so far," he wrote, "that persons who had subscribed for my editions of the Bible, refused to receive them when they found my name in the title page." This notoriety may also explain why the industrialists leading the Philadelphia protectionist movement began distancing themselves from Carey by the late 1820s.[50] For a while they replaced Carey with a new economic theorist: a young German named Friedrich List who arrived in the United States in 1825. List had read some of Carey's work in Germany and became still more familiar with it in the United States. His book *The National System of Political Economy* (1841), which continues to be one of the world's most important and influential protectionist texts, has many similarities to the work of Carey and other American protectionists, both in argument and in its use of historical data.[51]

Despite his fall from favor with Philadelphia industrialists, Carey continued to be an important national figure during the tariff wars of the late 1820s. He served as a delegate at the Harrisburg Convention of 1827, where delegates from 13 states laid the groundwork for the protective "Tariff of Abominations" of 1828. Although written by Hezekiah Niles of Baltimore, recognized along with Carey as one of the two most important national proponents of protectionism, the Address of the Harrisburg Convention reflected many of the arguments of *The New Olive Branch* and Carey's other work. It explicitly rejected Adam Smith and "other European writers on political economy" and included a number of the usual statistics, including a table of American exports and detailed statistical appendices. Niles provided a history of American tariffs from 1789 until 1827 that hit most of the same points made by Carey – including swipes at Lord Chatham for decreeing that "America should not be allowed to manufacture a hob nail" and an approving mention of Thomas Jefferson's promanufacturing letter to Benjamin Austin, which Niles reprinted in full in an appendix. Niles also stressed the harmony of interests. He noted that the convention delegates were "chiefly agriculturists" and that the convention was charged with considering "the great united and allied interests of agriculture and manufactures" and to establish the "protection of American farmers, manufacturers and merchants." The proposed tariff would achieve this goal by developing a "community of interest" between southern farmers (especially cotton planters), northern manufacturers (especially of textiles) and merchants who would handle the exchanges between the two in a protected home market.[52]

The antebellum protectionist movement would reach its peak with the 1828 tariff for which the Harrisburg delegates lobbied. Carey was credited with the success of the tariff in celebrations in Kentucky, Ohio and throughout Pennsylvania. Celebrants at a Philadelphia dinner offered him the following toast: "Although the friends of Jackson have burnt his effigy, his works have survived the conflagration, and will transmit his name to posterity as that of a public benefactor."[53] Carey's ideas would form the nucleus of the emerging Whig Party's so-called American System platform, which pushed for the development of the domestic market with protectionist tariffs for industry, a national bank to promote credit, and a national transportation system to facilitate exchanges between the sections. Henry Clay, the Whig leader, was well acquainted with Carey and his son, Henry, and well aware of his work from his time as Speaker of the House during the tariff battles of the 1820s. Clay quoted one of Carey's essays in an important 1824 speech, and Carey actively supported Clay's 1832 presidential campaign. The two were once burned together in effigy in South Carolina.[54]

While tariff supporters would have their share of success over the course of the nineteenth century, Carey's call for harmony was rarely heeded. Rather than tying the sections together, the tariff movement often provoked sectional conflict, culminating in South Carolina's 1832 effort to nullify the so-called Tariff of Abominations. The more laissez-faire Jacksonian Democrats mostly won the day in that conflict. However, protectionist arguments would continue to be influential, particularly within the Republican Party, and protective tariffs would reemerge as a central component of American economic policy after the Civil War. One of the leading political economists whose work supported that revival would be Mathew Carey's son, Henry C. Carey. Father and son, together were arguably the most important theorists of American protectionism for most of the nineteenth century.

Despite their influence and occasional tariff successes over that century, Mathew Carey, Henry Carey and their fellow protectionists ended up on the losing side of history. Viewed as illiberal by the late nineteenth century, in the early twenty-first century the neoliberal economic consensus has pushed protectionism to the margins of American economic discourse. It is widely eschewed in the academic world, where neoclassical economic ideas continue to rule the day. Furthermore, protectionism no longer makes sense as a pragmatic argument in a highly developed postindustrial nation like the United States. Underdeveloped nations, some in similar positions to the postcolonial early national United States, do from time to time take protectionist positions despite strong opposition from the world community and, particularly, the economic establishment of the IMF and World Bank. Certainly, Carey's arguments, as well as his failures, have continuing relevance to those nations.

Those in the better-developed nations ignore Carey and nineteenth-century protectionism at the risk of failing to understand that the current consensus was not foreordained, nor will it be permanent. In fact, the early twenty-first century bears many similarities to Carey's world. The so-called first-world countries are today grappling with a postindustrial economic paradigm after nearly a century of manufacturing dominance, just as early national United States was leaving the old agricultural economy to enter the new industrial paradigm. Also, as in Carey's world, the United States Congress today appears to be paralyzed with uncertainty over how to address the nation's changing economic fortunes. Economics has never been a purely academic endeavor. Popular writers like Carey have long played an important role in helping the public grapple with economic change. Focusing only on academic economists or only on those who chose the winning side gives us a dangerously lopsided and incomplete view of economic history and the history of economics. *The New Olive Branch* provides a good starting point for anyone who wants a more comprehensive view.

Notes

1 For a good, succinct biography see: James N. Green, *Mathew Carey: Publisher and Patriot*. (Philadelphia: The Library Company of Philadelphia, 1985).

2 An important exception, and perhaps harbinger of a changing tide, was the Ireland, America and the Worlds of Mathew Carey conference in Philadelphia, which featured two panels on economic matters, as well as panels on Carey as Irish Catholic and printer/bookseller.

See: "Ireland, America and the Worlds of Mathew Carey Philadelphia, 27–29 October 2011," accessed 23 June 2014, http://www.librarycompany.org/careyconference/papers.htm. Several of the essays have been published in *Early American Studies* 11 (3) (2013).

3 The Library of Congress holds a 1968 reprint of *Essays on Political Economy*, a 1972 reprint of *Essays on Banking* and a 1974 reprint of *Addresses of the Philadelphia Society for the Promotion of National Industry*.

4 Kenneth W. Rowe, *Mathew Carey: A Study in American Economic Development* (Baltimore: The Johns Hopkins Press, 1933); Paul K. Conkin, *Prophets of Prosperity: America's First Political Economists* (Bloomington: Indiana University Press, 1980), 177–78.

5 Lawrence A. Peskin, *Manufacturing Revolution: The Intellectual Origins of Early American Industry* (Baltimore: Johns Hopkins University Press, 2003), chap. 9.

6 Rowe, *Mathew Carey: A Study in American Economic Development*, 123–37.

7 *The Volunteer's Journal*, March 1, 1764; Joseph Massie, "Observations on the New Cyder Tax XXIII," reprinted in *Public Advertiser*, January 27, 1764; Peskin, *Manufacturing Revolution*, 20–21; Sophus A. Reinert, *Translating Empire: Emulation and the Origins of Political Economy* (Cambridge: Harvard University Press, 2011), 117–20; Rowe, *Mathew Carey: A study in American Economic Development*, 12–13, 16.

8 *The Volunteer's Journal*, January 12, 1784.

9 *The Volunteer's Journal*, May 12, 1784.

10 *The Volunteer's Journal*, February 9, 1784, April 5, 1784; Rowe, *Mathew Carey: A Study in American Economic Development*, 13–15.

11 Rowe, *Mathew Carey: A Study in American Economic Development*, 38; Mathew Carey, *Information to Europeans who are Disposed to Migrate to the United States: In a Letter from a Citizen of Pennsylvania to His Friend in Great Britain* (Philadelphia: Carey, Stewart and Co., 1790), 7; Mathew Carey to Rev. James Carey, September 12, 1791, (Philadelphia: Historical Society of Pennsylvania, 2008), Lea and Febiger Collection, Letterbook 1, August 12, 1788 – November 10, 1794.

12 James N. Green, *Mathew Carey: Publisher and Patriot* 6–8; Carey to Daniel Christoph Ebeling, March 20 [1793], Mathew Carey Letterbook 3; Carey to Coxe, October 1, 1788, *ibid.*, Letterbook 1, Lea and Febiger Collection, Historical Society of Pennsylvania. Carey, somewhat disingenuously, later denied that he ever wanted Coxe to be a partner.

13 Mathew Carey, *Address to the Printers and Booksellers Throughout the United States* (Philadelphia: Mathew Carey, 1801); Mathew Carey, *Letters to Dr. Adam Seybert: Representative in Congress for the City of Philadelphia, on the Subject of the Renewal of the Charter of the Bank of the United States* (Philadelphia: Mathew Carey, 1811), 20. For more on Carey's probanking views, see: Mathew Carey, *Desultory Reflections Upon the Ruinous Consequences of a Non-Renewal of the Charter of the Bank of the United States*, (Philadelphia: Fry and Kammerer, 1810); Rowe, *Mathew Carey: A Study in American Economic Development*, 59–62.

14 Edward C. Carter II, "Mathew Carey and 'The Olive Branch,' 1814–1818." *The Pennsylvania Magazine of History and Biography* 89 (1965): 399–415.

15 Mathew Carey, *The Olive Branch*, 10th ed. (Philadelphia: Mathew Carey, 1818), 43.

16 Mathew Carey, *Autobiographical Sketches. In a series of Letters Addressed to a Friend* (Philadelphia: John Clarke, 1829), (E. L. Schwaab, 1942), 72–73.

17 Carey, *Autobiographical Sketches*, 52–53.

18 Mathew Carey, *Essays on Political Economy* (Philadelphia: H. C. Carey & I. Lea, 1822), vii.

19 Carter, "Mathew Carey and 'The Olive Branch,' 1814–1818." 405.

20 Carey, *Essays on Political Economy*, 57–61.

21 As defined by authors mentioned in: Patricia Cline Cohen, "Statistics and the State," *The William and Mary Quarterly* 38, no. 1 (1981): 35–55.

22 Peskin, *Manufacturing Revolution*, 152–54.

23 Martin Ohman, "Calculating Prosperity in the Early American Republic: The Authority of Quantitative Data and Protectionist Political Economy." Paper presented at Ireland, America, and the Worlds of Mathew Carey conference, Philadelphia, PA, October 2011, 13; Adam Seybert, *Statistical Annals* (Philadelphia: Thomas Dobson & Son, 1818), v–vii.

24 Alexander Hamilton, *Report on the Subject of Manufactures*, ed. Mathew Carey (Philadelphia: William Brown, 1827). While Carey is not credited on the title page, the prefaces (written by Carey) make clear that he is the editor.

25 Jacob E. Cooke, 'Tench Coxe, Alexander Hamilton, and the Encouragement of American Manufactures,' *The William and Mary Quarterly* 32, no. 3 (1975): 369–92.

26 Carey, *Essays on Political Economy*, 15, 19.

27 Richard F. Teichgraeber III, "'Less Abused than I Had reason to Expect': The Reception of *The Wealth of Nations* in Britain, 1776–90," *The Historical Journal* 30 (1987): 345.

28 On cameralism, see: Keith Tribe, *Strategies of Economic Order: German Economic Discourse, 1750–1950* (Cambridge: Cambridge University Press, 2007); Keith Tribe, "Cameralism and the Science of Government," *The Journal of Modern History* 56 (1984): 263–84; David F. Lindenfeld, *The Political Imagination: The German Sciences of State in the Nineteenth Century* (Chicago and London: University of Chicago Press, 1997): 16–17; Albion W. Small, *The Cameralists: The Pioneers of German Social Policy* (Chicago: University of Chicago Press, 1909). Reprint, Kitchener: Batoche Books, 2001. Citations refer to Batoche Books edition.

29 Mathew Carey, *Addresses of the Philadelphia Society for the Promotion of National Industry* (Philadelphia: M. Carey & Son, 1819), 171.

30 Carey, *Autobiographical Sketches*, 48.

31 Daniel Walker Howe, "Why the Scottish Enlightenment Was Useful to the Framers of the American Constitution," *Comparative Studies in Society and History* 31 (1989): 572, 587; Samuel Fleishacker, "Adam Smith's Reception among the American Founders, 1776–1790," *William and Mary Quarterly* 59 (2002): 897–914.

32 Cathy Matson and Peter Onuf, *A Union of Interests: Political and Economic Thought in Revolutionary America* (Lawrence: University Press of Kansas, 1990), 21–26, 34; Cathy Matson, *Merchants and Empire: Trading in Colonial New York* (Baltimore: Johns Hopkins University Press, 1998); Douglas A. Irwin, *Against the Tide: An Intellectual History of Free Trade* (Princeton University Press, 1996), 45–63.

33 Drew R. McCoy, "Republicanism and American Foreign Policy: James Madison and the Political Economy of Commercial Discrimination, 1789 to 1794," *The William and Mary Quarterly* 31, no. 4 (1974): 633–46.

34 Peskin, *Manufacturing Revolution*, 89–91; Matson and Onuf, *A Union of Interests: Political and Economic Thought in Revolutionary America*, 42–47.

35 Teichgraeber, "'Less Abused than I Had Reason to Expect': The Reception of *The Wealth of Nations* in Britain, 1776–1790," 351; Emma Rothschild, *Economic Sentiments: Adam Smith, Condorcet, and the Enlightenment* (Cambridge, MA: Harvard University Press, 2001), 52–71.

36 Carey, *Autobiographical Sketches*, ix.

37 Adam Smith, *The Wealth of Nations* (New York: The Modern Library, 1937), 424.

38 Smith, *The Wealth of Nations*, 426, ff.

39 Ibid., 437. Teichgraeber, "'Less Abused than I Had Reason to Expect': The Reception of *The Wealth of Nations* in Britain, 1776–1790," 352 demonstrates that this was also the passage that offended Scottish proponents of the corn laws of the 1790s.

40 Carey, *Addresses of the Philadelphia Society for the Promotion of National Industry*, 21, 28–29.

41 Smith, *The Wealth of Nations*, 438.

42 Carey may in fact have been one of the earliest writers to describe industrialists as "capitalists."

43 Of course, American trade could hardly be entirely free so long as Britain's restrictions continued to apply. But as Carey later implies, it is foolhardy to think the United States had any control over those restrictions.

44 For classic studies of this period see Curtis P. Nettels, *The Emergence of a National Economy 1775–1815* (New York: Holt, Rinehart and Winston, 1962) and Douglas C. North, *The Economic Growth of the United States, 1790–1860* (Englewood Cliffs, NJ: Prentice-Hall, 1961). Recently: Terry Bouton, 'Moneyless in Pennsylvania: Privatization and the Depression of the 1780s', *The Economy of Early America*, ed. Cathy Matson (University Park: Pennsylvania State University Press, 2006), 218–262 focuses more on the role of banking.

45 North, *The Economic Growth of the United* States, 177–188; Murray N. Rothbard, *The Panic of 1819: Reactions and Policies* (New York: Columbia University Press, 1962), 1–23; Daniel S. Dupre, 'The Panic of 1819 and the Political Economy of Sectionalism', in *The Economy of Early America*, ed. Cathy Matson (University Park: Pennsylvania State University Press, 2007) 263–93.

46 More recently, in 'Pennsylvania Banks and the Panic of 1819: A Reinterpretation', *Journal of the Early Republic* 9 (Autumn 1989): 335–58, while not exonerating the banks, Robert Blackson has argued that their role may have been overemphasized.

47 Carey, *Autobiographical Sketches*, 118–19, 154, v.

48 Daniel Peart, "'Looking Beyond Parties and Elections: The Making of United States Tariff Policy during the Early 1820s, '" *Journal of the Early Republic* 33 (Spring 2013): 87–108; Carey, *Autobiographical Sketches*, 87.

49 United States Congress, *American State Papers: Documents, Legislative and Executive of the Congress of the United States* (Washington: Gales and Seaton, 1834), 616.

50 Rothbard, *The Panic of 1819: Reactions and Policies*, 175; Carey, *Autobiographical Sketches*, 47, 127–35.

51 Rowe, *Mathew Carey: A study in American Economic Development*, 116–18; William Notz, 'Frederick List in America', *The American Economic Review* 16 (June 1926) 249–65. List and Carey shared so many similar influences, including German cameralists and Alexander Hamilton (whose work Carey helped bring to Germany), that it is difficult to say who influenced whom.

52 Harrisburg Convention, *[Proceedings of the] General Convention, of Agriculturalists and Manufacturers, and others Friendly to the Encouragement and Support of the Domestic Industry of the United States* (Baltimore, 1827), 11–22, https://archive.org/stream/proceedingsofthe00harruoft#page/n3/mode/2up.

53 Rowe, *Mathew Carey: A study in American Economic Development*, 120–21.

54 Rowe, *Mathew Carey: A study in American Economic Development*, 103, 111–12.

LIST OF WORKS

Creating a complete bibliography of all of Carey's economic works is probably impossible and more overwhelming than useful to the reader. Much of his writing appeared either in newspapers or in short broadsides. A list of these items would certainly include hundreds of titles. Additionally, many of his works were reprinted multiple times, occasionally with different titles. Such are the hazards of tracking down the work of a man who owns a printing press. Rather than including every item ever penned by Carey, this list attempts to present only Carey's major works, primarily books or pamphlets of more than twenty pages. Broadsides and small pamphlets are almost entirely absent from the list. So are serials, including Carey's newspapers and magazines such as *The American Museum*. Additionally, Carey wrote many occasional pamphlets and newspaper essays under the pseudonyms of Hamilton and Colbert, some of which were collected into larger series. These are also absent for the most part from this list.

Anyone looking for a list of these smaller, less important publications should first consult the electronic catalogue of the Library Company of Philadelphia and then the list at the end of Rowe, *Mathew Carey: A Study in Economic Development*. The list below was based primarily (although not exclusively) on the catalog of the Library Company of Philadelphia.

A Calm Address to the People of the Eastern States, on the Subject of the Representation of Slaves; the Representation in the Senate; and the Hostility to Commerce Ascribed to the Southern States. Philadelphia: M. Carey, 1814.

A Defence of Direct Taxes and of Protective Duties, for the Encouragement of Manufactures. Philadelphia: U. Hunt, 1822.

A Citizen of Philadelphia [pseud.]. *A Plea for the Poor: An Enquiry how Far the Charges Against Them of Improvidence, Idleness, and Dissipation, are Founded in Truth.* Philadelphia: n.p., 1836.

A View of the Ruinous Consequences of a Dependence on Foreign Markets for the Sale of the Great Staples of This Nation, Flour, Cotton, and Tobacco: Addressed to the Congress of the United States: Read Before, and Ordered to be Printed by, the Board of Manufactures of the Pennsylvania Society for the Promotion of American Manufactures. Philadelphia: M. Carey & Son, 1820.

A Pennsylvanian [pseud.]. *A Warning Voice to the Cotton and Tobacco Planters, Farmers, and Merchants of the United States: On the Pernicious Consequences to Their Respective Interests of the Existing Policy of the Country*. Philadelphia: H. C. Carey & I. Lea, 1824.

Address Delivered Before the Philadelphia Society for Promoting Agriculture. Philadelphia: J. R. A. Skerrett, 1824.

Address Delivered Before the Philadelphia Society for Promoting Agriculture: At Its Meeting on the Twentieth of July, 1824. Philadelphia: Mifflin and Parry, 1827.

Address of the Philadelphia Society for the Promotion of National Industry to the Citizens of the United States. No. IX. Philadelphia: n.p., 1819.

Address to the Farmers of the United States, on the Ruinous Consequences to their Vital Interests, of the Existing Policy of this Country. Philadelphia: M. Carey & Son, 1821.

Address to the Wealthy of the Land: Ladies as well as Gentlemen, on the Character, Conduct, Situation, and Prospects, of Those Whose Sole Dependence for Subsistence, is on the Labour of their Hands. Philadelphia: W. F. Geddes, 1831.

An Appeal to Common Sense and Common Justice: or, Irrefragable Facts Opposed to Plausible Theories: Intended to Prove the Extreme Injustice, as well as the Utter Impolicy, of the Existing Tariff. Philadelphia: H. C. Carey & I. Lea, 1822.

A Pennsylvanian [pseud.]. *An Examination of the Report of a Committee of the Citizens of Boston and its Vicinity, Opposed to a Further Increase of Duties on Importation*. Philadelphia: J. Maxwell, 1828.

Autobiographical Sketches. Philadelphia: John Clarke, 1829.

Brief View of the System of Internal Improvement of the State of Pennsylvania. Philadelphia: Lydia R. Bailey, 1831.

Charter of the Pennsylvania Bank: To the Citizens of Pennsylvania at Large, but More Particularly Those of the City of Philadelphia. Philadelphia: n.p., 1829.

A Citizen of Philadelphia [pseud.]. *Common Sense Addresses, to the Citizens of the Southern States*. Philadelphia: Clark & Raser, 1829.

Cursory Reflexions on the System of Taxation, Established in the City of Philadelphia: With a Brief Sketch of Its Unequal and Unjust Operation. Philadelphia: M. Carey, 1806.

A Citizen of Philadelphia [pseud.]. *Cursory Views of the Liberal and Restrictive Systems of Political Economy: and of Their Effects in Great Britain, France, Russia, Prussia, Holland, and the United States*. Philadelphia: J. R. A. Skerrett, 1826.

Hon. George M'Duffie. *Defence of a Liberal Construction of the Powers of Congress, as Regards Internal Improvement, etc.: With a Complete Refutation of the Ultra Doctrines Respecting Consolidation and State Sovereignty*, ed. Mathew Carey. Philadelphia: Clark & Raser, 1832.

A Pennsylvanian [pseud.]. *Desultory Facts, and Observations, Illustrative of the Past and Present Situation and Future Prospects of the United States: Embracing a View of the Causes of the Late Bankruptcies in Boston. To which is Annexed, a Sketch of the Restrictive Systems of the Principal Nations of Christendom*. Philadelphia: H. C. Carey & I. Lea, 1822.

Desultory Reflections upon the Ruinous Consequences of a Non-Renewal of the Charter of the Bank of the United States. Philadelphia: Fry and Kammerer, 1810.

A Citizen of Philadelphia [pseud.]. *Essay on Free Trade: From Blackwood's Magazine, of May, 1825. To Which Are Prefixed a Preface and a Few Explanatory Notes*. Philadelphia: J. R. A. Skerrett, 1826.

Essay on Railroads. Philadelphia: n.p., 1830.

Essays on Banking. Philadelphia: M. Carey, 1816.

Essays on political economy; or, The Most Certain Means of Promoting the Wealth, Power, Resources, and Happiness of Nations: Applied Particularly to the United States. Philadelphia: H. C. Carey & I. Lea, 1822.

Essays on the Protecting System. Philadelphia: Mifflin and Parry, 1830.

Essays on the Public Charities of Philadelphia. Philadelphia: J. Clarke, 1829.

A Citizen of Philadelphia [pseud.]. *Essays Tending to Prove the Ruinous Effects of the Policy of the United States, on the Three Classes, Farmers, Planters, and Merchants: Addressed to Edward Livingston, Esq.* Philadelphia: J. R. A. Skerrett, 1826.

A Pennsylvanian [pseud.]. *Examination of a Tract on the Alteration of the Tariff, Written by Thomas Cooper, M.D.* Philadelphia: H. C. Carey & I. Lea, 1824.

Examination of the Pretensions of New England to Commercial Pre-Eminence. Philadelphia: M. Carey, 1814.

A Citizen of Philadelphia [pseud.]. *Letters on the Condition of the Poor: Addressed to Alexander Henry, Esq.* Philadelphia: Haswell & Barrington, 1835.

Letters to Messrs. Abbot Laurence, Patrick Jackson, and Jonas B. Brown, Boston – : Messrs. P. H. Schenck and Erastus Elsworth, New York – Messrs. Samuel Richards and Mark Richards, Philadelphia – Messrs. John M'Kim and H. W. Evans, Baltimore – and Mr E. I. Dupont, Wilmington. Philadelphia: n.p., 1832.

Letters to the Directors of the Banks of Philadelphia. Philadelphia: M. Carey, 1816.

"Look Before You Leap": Addresses to the Citizens of the Southern States. Philadelphia: Haswell & Barrington, 1835.

Miscellaneous Essays. Philadelphia: Carey & Hart, 1830.

Narrative of the Proceedings of Edward Gray, Samuel F. Bradford, and Robert Taylor: Previous and Subsequent to the Bankruptcy of C. & A. Conrad & Co. Philadelphia: M. Carey, 1813.

National Interests & Domestic Manufactures: Address of the Philadelphia Society for the Promotion of Domestic Industry, to the Citizens of the United States. Boston: William W. Clapp, 1819.

Nine Letters to Dr. Adam Seybert. Philadelphia: M. Carey, 1810.

Colbert [pseud.]. *Outline of a System of National Currency: And Substitute for a Bank of the United States.* New York: William Pearson, 1834. [Note: Rowe does not believe this should be attributed to Carey. See Rowe, 134.]

Pamphlets and Papers. 7 Volumes. Philadelphia: J. R. A. Skerrett, 1826.

Cassandra [pseud.]. *Prospects on the Banks of the Rubicon.* Philadelphia: n.p., 1814.

Prospects on the Rubicon. Part II. Philadelphia: Clark & Raser, 1832.

Reflections on the Consequences of the Refusal of the Banks to Receive in Deposit Southern and Western Bank Notes. Philadelphia: M. Carey, 1815.

Reflections on the Present System of Banking, in the City of Philadelphia: With a Plan to Revive Confidence, Trade, and Commerce, and to Facilitate the Resumption of Specie Payments. Philadelphia: M. Carey, 1817.

Alexander Hamilton. *Report of the Secretary of the Treasury, on the Subject of Manufactures, Made the Fifth of December, 1791,* ed. Mathew Carey. Philadelphia: J. R. A. Skerrett, 1824.

Sketches Towards a History of the Present Session of Congress. Philadelphia: M. Carey & Son, 1820.

Societies For Promoting Manual Labour in Literary Institutions. Philadelphia: Clark and Raser, 1833.

Strictures on Mr. Cambreling's work, entitled, "An Examination of the new tariff." Philadelphia: n.p., 1821.

Hambden [pseud.]. *Strictures on Mr. Lee's Exposition of Evidence on the Sugar Duty, in Behalf of the Committee Appointed by the Free-Trade Convention.* Philadelphia?: n.p., 1832.

A Pennsylvanian [pseud.]. *The Crisis: A Solemn Appeal to the President, the Senate and House of Representatives, and the Citizens of the United States, on the Destructive Tendency of the Present Policy of this Country, on its Agriculture, Manufactures, Commerce, and Finances.* Philadelphia: H. C. Carey & I. Lea, 1823.

The New Olive Branch: or, An Attempt to Establish an Identity of Interest Between Agriculture, Manufactures, and Commerce. Philadelphia: M. Carey & Son, 1820.

The Tocsin: A Solemn Warning Against the Dangerous Doctrine of Nullification. Philadelphia: W. F. Geddes, 1832.

Thirteen Essays on the Policy of Manufacturing in This Country. Philadelphia: Clark & Raser, 1830.

Three Letters on the Present Calamitous State of Affairs: Addressed to J. M. Garnett, Esq., President of the Fredericsburg Agricultural Society. Philadelphia: M. Carey & Son, 1820.

A Pennsylvanian [pseud.]. *Twenty-one Golden Rules to Depress Agriculture, Impede the Progress of Manufactures, Paralize Commerce, Impair National Resources, Produce a Constant Fluctuation in the Value of Every Species of Property, and Blight and Blast the Bounties of Nature, How Bounteously Soever Lavished on a Country*. Philadelphia: H. C. Carey & I. Lea, 1824.

Vindication of the Small Farmers, the Peasantry, and the Labourers of Ireland. Philadelphia: n.p., 1836.

NOTE ON THE TEXT

This edition of *The New Olive Branch* is based on a scan of the 1820 edition that has been copyedited closely to make sure that there were no scanning errors. Carey's spelling, which is typical of the less standardized spelling of the early nineteenth century, has been mostly left as is, only using *sic* to indicate errors that would have been apparent in the nineteenth century. All footnotes are Carey's original notes. Endnotes provide editorial assistance to modern readers. Where Carey included very long verbatim passages from other sources or where he provided long and only marginally relevant materials, these items have been moved into appendices to make the text more readable for modern readers. Where material has been removed, the text is broken with a row of asterisks. Page numbers have been updated to refer to the pages of this edition. This edition of *The New Olive Branch* also includes the preface and first two essays of Carey's *Addresses of the Philadelphia Society for the Promotion of National Industry to the Citizens of the United States*. These items have been scanned from Carey's *Essays on Political Economy* (Carey and Lea 1822) and have been edited in the same way as *The New Olive Branch*.

THE

NEW OLIVE BRANCH:

OR,

AN ATTEMPT TO ESTABLISH AN IDENTITY OF INTEREST

BETWEEN

AGRICULTURE, MANUFACTURES, AND COMMERCE;

AND TO PROVE,

THAT A LARGE PORTION OF THE MANUFACTURING INDUSTRY OF THIS
NATION HAS BEEN SACRIFICED TO COMMERCE; AND THAT
COMMERCE HAS SUFFERED BY THIS POLICY NEARLY
AS MUCH AS MANUFACTURES.

BY M. CAREY,

AUTHOR OF POLITICAL OLIVE BRANCH, VINDICIÆ HIBERNICÆ, &c. &c.

*" But few examples have occurred of distress so general and so severe as that
" which has been exhibited in the United States."*—Report of the Secretary of
the Treasury.

*" If any thing can prevent the consummation of public ruin, it can only
" be new councils; a sincere change, from a sincere conviction of past errors."*
Chatham.

*" Men will sooner live prosperously under the worst government, than starve
" under the best."*—Postlethwait's Dictionary.

" A merchant may have a distinct interest from that of his country. He
" may thrive by a trade that will prove her ruin."—*British Merchant.*

" Manufactures are now as necessary to our independence as to our com-
" fort."—*Jefferson.*

" It is the interest of the community, with a view to eventual and per-
" manent economy, *to encourage the growth of manufactures.*"—Hamilton.

PHILADELPHIA:

M. CAREY & SON.

1820.

The New Olive Branch (1820)[1]

Mathew Carey

AN EXEMPLAR OF FREE AND EQUAL GOVERNMENT.

"Allegiance is due only to protection." —Bishop of Derry.[2]

AGRICULTURE.

Our farmers and planters have, from the organization of the government, enjoyed 99/100ths of the domestic market; and, until lately, have had excellent foreign markets.

Protecting duties.

	Per cent.
Cheese	90
Coals	38 ½
Spirits	70 to 80
Manufactured tobacco	100
Snuff	90
Cotton	30
Tobacco in the leaf	15
Potatoes	15
Rice	15
Wheat	15
Beans	15
Oats	15
Pitch	15
Tar	15
Turpentine	15
Beef	15
Pork	15
Hams	15

MANUFACTURES.

Our manufacturers are supplanted in the domestic market by France, England, Ireland, Scotland, Italy, Russia, Sweden, the East Indies, &c.

And are almost altogether shut out of all the foreign markets.

Protecting duties.

	Per cent.
Watches	7 ½
Silks	15
Clocks	15
Linens	15
Worsted shoes	15
Woollens	25
Cottons	25

Expenses for the protection of Manufactures.

Bounties	$ 0000
Premiums	0000
Loans	0000
Immunities	0000
	=====
Total expense for protecting manufactures for 30 years	$ 0000

COMMERCE.

Our merchants have enjoyed the whole of the coasting trade for 30 years.

Their shipping has carried on 86 per cent of the foreign trade for the same space of time.

Past expenses for the protection of Commerce.

Foreign intercourse for 20 years, from 1796 to 1815	$ 9,615,140
Naval department	52,065,691
Barbary Powers	2,349,568
War debt	78,579,022
Total for 20 years	$ 142,609,421
Average per ann. from 1796 to 1815	$ 7,130,471

Present expenses for Commerce.

Interest on $ 78,579,022, debt contracted during the last war	$ 4,714,741
Secretary's estimate for navy, 1820	3,527,640
Actual annual disbursement for commerce	$ 8,242,381
Average annual export, from 1796 to 1819	$39,816,088

Thus the actual disbursements are above

NATIONAL INDUSTRY

"In all its shapes and forms."

PROTECTED.	UNPROTECTED.
19. Cordial attachment to a good government.	31. Disaffection to a government regardless of the sufferings of its citizens.
18. New towns springing up.	30. Monied men engrossing the estates of the distressed.
17. General prosperity.	29. Legal suspension of the collection of debts.
16. Property rising in value.	28. General distress.
15. Debts easily collected.	27. Failure of revenue.
14. Capital, talent, and industry, sure of success.	26. Property depreciating daily.
13. Revenue increasing.	25. Houses falling to decay.
12. Credit preserved at home and abroad.	24. Rents reducing.
11. Numerous houses building.	23. Sheriffs' sales.
	22. Banks stopping payment.
10. Great accession of immigrants and capital.	21. Credit impaired at home and abroad.
9. Bankruptcies rare.	20. Staples sinking in price.
8. Poor rates diminishing.	19. Capital, talents and industry, without employment.
7. Population rapidly increasing.	18. Emigrations in quest of an asylum abroad.
6. Early and numerous marriages.	17. Immigration discountenanced.
5. Every person able and willing to work employed.	16. Population sluggish.
4. Industry protected.	15. Marriages rare.
3. Moderate importations.	14. Merchants and traders following in their train.
2. Protecting duties.	13. Manufacturers bankrupt.
1. Prohibitions of what can be made at home.	12. Manufacturing establishments in ruins.
	11. Soup houses.
	10. Increase of idleness, pauperism and guilt.
	9. Poor rates augmented.
	8. Workmen discharged.
	7. Decay of national industry.
	6. Remittances of government and bank stock.
	5. Drain of specie.
	4. Great bargains of cheap foreign goods.
	3. Immense importations.
	2. Light duties on manufactures.
	1. Heavy duties on teas, wines, coffee, spirits, &c.

CONTENTS

INTRODUCTION

This work may be considered as a second edition, much enlarged and improved, of the Three Letters to Mr. Garnett, recently published; as it contains nearly the whole of the matter of those letters. It is nevertheless presented to the public in a state that requires apology for its imperfections. This apology rests upon the circumstances which have given rise to it, and the situation of the country. Books, written as this has been, on the spur of the occasion, to shed light on passing subjects of policy, on which the decision may be precipitated previous to their appearance, (if not hurried through the press,) cannot, without injustice, be tried by the rigorous rules of general criticism. This would be almost as unfair as to scan a house erected in haste for a new settler in the wilderness, by the rules laid down by Palladio—or to criticise the dress of a lady whom circumstances have forced to appear before the eye in entire dishabille, as rigorously as if she had made her entrée into a ball room on a gala evening.

The grand object of such books is to convey information. Ornaments of composition are but secondary considerations. Whatever effect they are likely to produce, depends on the time of their appearance. The object may be wholly defeated by the delay of a week, perhaps of a day. I therefore trust, that the pretensions of the New Olive Branch, as a literary composition, being humble, and its author only claiming the merit of sincere devotion to the best interests of his country, its imperfections will be regarded with a liberal spirit of indulgence.

It has been written with a thorough conviction, that there is a complete identity of interest between agriculture, manufactures and commerce; that when any one of them suffers material injury, the others largely partake of it; and that a great proportion of the distress of this country has arisen from the erroneous views of our statesmen on the subject of manufactures, which have been cramped and stunted, and finally in part annihilated in the most important branches, for want of that fostering care bestowed on them in England for ages, and recently in France in the most exemplary manner, and with the most beneficial effect.

I have, therefore, endeavoured to prove—

1. That the policy pursued by this nation in its tariff, from the commencement of its career, has been radically wrong.
2. That this tariff has sacrificed a large portion of the national industry; to the incalculable injury of the United States, and to the immense advantage of the manufacturing nations of Europe.
3. That its tendency has been to render us tributary to those nations— converting a large portion of our population into hucksters and retailers of their productions, instead of producers for our own consumption; and rendering the great mass of the remainder consumers of those productions—thus prodigally lavishing our wealth to support foreign manufacturers and foreign governments—and impoverishing the nation to an alarming degree.

    This system has had the obvious and pernicious effect of narrowing the field for the exercise of native industry and talent—and consequently of crouding immoderately those professions that were open to the national enterprize. From this source has arisen the great number of merchants, so far beyond what was required by the commerce of the country.
4. I have hence deduced the ruin of so large a proportion of that class. It was a necessary consequence of the over-driven spirit of competition. This may be exemplified in every department of human industry. In a town which would support two storekeepers genteelly, three would barely make a living, and four be ruined. And finally—
5. I have endeavoured to shew, that a due degree of protection to manufactures would have been highly serviceable to agriculture and commerce.

These views of our affairs are presented to the public with a sincere belief of their soundness. But, like other theorists, I may have deluded myself. However, whether right or wrong, the discussion cannot fail to prove useful— as it will shed light on the most important subject that can occupy the public attention—the means of promoting individual happiness, and national "wealth, power, and resources"[3]—of removing the present intolerable evils, of which the secretary of the treasury, in his report of the 21st ultimo, has justly declared, that "*few instances have occurred, of distress so general, and so severe, as that which has been exhibited in the United States.*" This important subject is worthy of the undivided attention of every man interested for the public welfare.

If my views be incorrect, I shall rejoice to have the errors pointed out, and shall cheerfully recant them. Any suggestions on the subject will be received with thankfulness, and attended to. But if the ground I have taken be correct, I hope and trust the investigation may lead to a different course of policy, calculated to enable us to realize the blessings promised to us by our constitution and our natural advantages, which at present so provokingly elude our grasp.

M. C.
Philadelphia, March 17th, 1820

CHAPTER I

Preliminary observations. State of the nation. Whence it arises. Short-sighted policy. Decline of commerce inevitable. Substitutes ought to have been provided for the superfluous mercantile capital, talent and industry.

It is impossible for any one who can say with Terence[1]—"I am a man—interested in whatever concerns my fellow men"—to take a calm and dispassionate view of the existing state of affairs, in this heaven-favoured land, without feeling deep distress, and a melancholy conviction, that we have made a most lamentable waste of the immense advantages, moral, physical, and political, we enjoy—advantages rarely equalled, scarcely ever exceeded; and that our erroneous policy has, in five years, produced more havoc of national wealth, power, and resources, and more individual distress, than, *in a period of profound peace,*[*] has taken place in the same space of time, within two hundred years, in any nation of Europe, except Portugal.

That governments are instituted for the protection, support, and benefit of the governed, is a maxim as old as the dawn of liberty in the world. The administrators are the mere agents of their constituents, hired to perform certain duties, for which they are here paid liberal salaries.

The grand objects of their care are—the security of person—security of property acquired, and in the acquisition of property—with the right of worshipping God as each man's conscience dictates. And government, by whatever name it may be called, is only estimable in proportion as it guards those sacred deposits. Our dear-bought experience proves, that the happiness of individuals and the prosperity of nations are by no means proportioned to the excellence of their forms of government. Were that the case, we should rank among the happiest of nations, ancient or modern: whereas, unfortunately, at present we occupy a low grade.

It is a mealancholy [sic] feature in human affairs, that no institutions, however perfect—no administration, however upright or wise—can guard

---

[*] Other nations usually and naturally recover in peace from the injuries inflicted by war. We rose in war—and alas! are sinking in peace!!! What an awful view!

the whole of a nation against distress and embarrassment. Accidents, not to be foreseen, or, if foreseen, not to be guarded against—imprudence, extravagance, and various other causes, will frequently, in the most prosperous communities, produce a large portion of distress. This state of things is no impeachment to the goodness of the form of government, or the wisdom of its administrators.

But when large bodies of people, whole sections of a nation, are involved in distress and embarrassment—when capital, talents, industry, and ingenuity afford to their possessors no security of prosperity—when productive industry is laid prostrate—when the most useful establishments, the pride, the glory, the main spring of the wealth, power, and resources of nations, are allowed to fall to ruins, without an effort to save them on the part of the legislative power—when the constituents, writhing in distress and misery, call in vain on their representatives for relief, which is within their power to afford—there must be something radically wrong in the people, or in the form of government, or radically vicious and pernicious in its legislation.[5]

The policy of a free government, good or bad, emanates from the legislative body, which has the destinies of the nation in its hands. The executive officers in such nations, who are generally stiled the administration, have little power to avert the evils of a vicious, or to prevent the beneficent consequences of a wise legislation. This is peculiarly the case in our country.

Preparatory to stating the plan I propose to pursue in this pamphlet, it is proper to exhibit a view of the actual situation of the country, to justify the strong ground I mean to take. And believing the sketch given in the second Address of the Philadelphia Society for the promotion of National Industry to be correct, and its brevity being suited to the limits I am obliged to observe, I annex it.[6]

---

1. Our profitable commerce is nearly annihilated.
2. Our shipping reduced in value one-half.
3. Of our merchants a considerable portion bankrupt, and many tottering on the verge of bankruptcy. The commercial capital of the country reduced, it is believed, seventy millions of dollars.
4. Our manufacturing establishments in a great measure suspended, and numbers of them falling to decay.
5. Many of their proprietors ruined.
6. Thousands of citizens unemployed throughout the United States.
7. Our circulating medium drawn away to the East Indies and to Europe, to pay for articles which we could ourselves furnish, or which we do not want.

8. A heavy annual tax incurred to Europe in the interest payable on probably 20 to 25,000,000 of dollars of government and bank stock, likewise remitted in payment.
9. Real estate every where fallen thirty, forty, or fifty per cent.
10. Our great staples, cotton, flour, tobacco, &c. reduced in price from thirty to forty per cent.
11. Our merino sheep, for want of protecting the woollen manufacture, in a great measure destroyed, and those that remain not worth ten per cent. of their cost.
12. Large families of children become a burden to their parents, who are unable to devise suitable means of employment for them.
13. Numbers of our citizens, possessed of valuable talents, and disposed to be useful, but unable to find employment, are migrating to Cuba, where, under a despotic government, among a population principally of slaves, and subject to the horrors of the inquisition, they seek an asylum from the distress they suffer here!
14. Hundreds of useful artisans and mechanics, who, allured by our form of government, migrated to our shores, have returned to their native countries, or gone to Nova Scotia or Canada, broken hearted and with exhausted funds.
15. Men of capital are unable to find any profitable employment for it in regular business.
16. Citizens who own real estate to a great amount—have large debts due them—and immense stocks of goods, cannot mortgage their real estate, dispose of their stocks but at extravagant sacrifices, nor collect their debts.
17. Citizens possessed of great wealth, have it in their power to increase it immoderately, by purchasing the property of the distressed, sold at ruinous sacrifices by sheriffs, marshals, and otherwise—thus destroying the equality of our citizens, and aggrandizing the rich at the expense of the middle class of society.
18. The interest of money extravagantly usurious.
19. Distress and misery, to an extent not to be conceived but by those who have an opportunity of beholding them, spreading among the labouring class in our towns and cities.
20. Bankruptcy and poverty producing an alarming increase of demoralization and crime.
21. The attachment to our government liable to be impaired in the minds of those who are ruined by the policy it has pursued.
22. After having prostrated our national manufactures, lest we should injure the revenue, the revenue itself fails, and we are likely to be obliged to recur to loans or direct taxes to meet the exigencies of the government.

23. Numbers of banks in different parts of the union, deprived of their specie by the extravagant drains for Europe and the East Indies, obliged to stop payment.
24. Legislatures driven by the prevalence of distress, to the frightful measure of suspending the collection of debts.

―――――

That such an awful state of things could not exist in a time of profound peace, without some great natural calamity—some radical defects in the people—great vice in the form of government—or an unsound system of policy, will not be controverted.

Our distresses do not arise from any natural calamity. None has befallen us.

Nor from the people. They are shrewd, intelligent, industrious, active, and enterprizing to a high degree. A wise legislator or statesman could not desire sounder materials to form the structure of a happy and prosperous society, and render his name immortal.

Nor from the form of government. That, like every work of man, it has defects, must be conceded. But that it is the best the world ever witnessed, is susceptible of full proof on fair comparison with any that at present exist—or that ever existed.

They are therefore chargeable to our policy, which, I repeat, emanates from our general legislature, to whom, if our evils are not irremediable, we must apply for relief.

This declaration, as to the source of our distresses, requires qualification, so far as regards the diminution of our commerce, and the depreciation of the prices of our staples generally, which congress could not have prevented.

Cotton is an exception. For the ruinous reduction that has taken place in that article, they are answerable to their country. They might have readily made a domestic market, which would have preserved the price from any material depreciation, and saved the cotton planters above 7,000,000 of dollars, and the merchants who purchased before the reduction, nearly 4,000,000.

Had our statesmen considered the subject profoundly, as their duty demanded, they might have readily foreseen that the new state of affairs throughout the world required a total change of policy.[7] As we could no longer hope to be the carriers for Europe; and as the immense armies disbanded by the different belligerants, would be devoted partly to the labours of the field, and partly to work-shops and manufactories, whereby not only the markets for our staples, bread-stuffs particularly, would be diminished, but the quantity of manufactures there would be greatly increased; it required but little sagacity to see that a large portion of the talents, the capital, and the industry of our merchants, would be bereft of their usual employment, and that every motive of policy and regard for the public and private welfare required that *some other channel should be opened to give them activity*. But these were views beyond the grasp of most of our statesmen; and far from holding out any new inducements to enter on manufacturing pursuits, which would have absorbed all the superfluous mercantile capital, they unwisely diminished those that existed, by repealing the double duties in June, 1816, whereby the revenue lost millions of dollars, and the manufacturing industry of the country received a mortal wound.

It required but slender consideration to have foreseen, at an early period, the goal to which the policy we pursued after the late war,[8] tended. The domestic exports of the country, the grand legitimate fund for the payment of our imports, for twenty years, from 1796 to 1815, inclusive, amounted to only 698,676,879 dollars, or an average of nearly 35,000,000. Whereas our imports in the year 1815, exclusive of re-exportations, amounted to above 118,000,000. Lives there a man who could for a moment doubt where such a course of proceeding would land us? or, that our exports, which, under the immense advantages we enjoyed during the French Revolution, only rose to the above average, would never, in a time of peace, enable us to pay for such extravagant importations? It was impossible to take a most superficial view of the subject, without being satisfied that we were as completely in the high road to destruction as a young man who has attained to the possession of a large estate, and who expends more than double his income.

A wonderful feature in the affair is, that the net impost which accrued in 1815, was 36,306,022 dollars, being one million more than the preceding average of our exports for twenty years!!

Independent, therefore, of all concern for our manufacturers, and indeed, were there not a single manufacturer in the country, some decisive efforts ought to have been made to diminish our imports, in order to arrest the career of national impoverishment. But the flourishing state of the revenue, which with too many of our statesmen, absorbed all other considerations, appeared to promise a new fiscal millennium. And hence the fatal repeal of the internal duties, which was carried by the overwhelming majority, in the house of representatives, of 161 to 5, in December, 1817—than which a more wild and injudicious measure could hardly have been devised. We have lived to see its folly, and to deplore its consequences.

What would be thought of the skill of a physician, who, while bleeding his patient to a state of inanition, was congratulating himself on the quantity and excellence of the blood pouring out of his veins!—such is the case precisely of those statesmen, who form their ideas of national prosperity from the great extent of the customs, more frequently a sign of decay, as it has proved with us. What a sound lesson Ustariz,[9] a Spanish author, gives on this subject!—how deserving of attention! but how little attended to!

"It aggravates the calamity of our country that the customs have improved and yielded more by the increase of imports; since it is so unfortunate a circumstance for us, that *in order to advance them a million of dollars, estimating one duty with another at the rate of eight per cent., after an allowance for frauds and indulgences, there must be drawn out of the kingdom twelve millions of dollars.*"*

It cannot be too deeply lamented, that in placing before congress the calamitous situation of our manufactures and manufacturers, (which, by the way, is but very lightly touched on) both the president and the secretary of the treasury,[10] the former in his message, and the latter in his annual report, in recommending attention to the relief of this suffering class of citizens, express some hesitation on the subject, and speak hypothetically, particularly the secretary.

The president states:—

"It is deemed of importance to encourage our domestic manufactures. In what manner the evils which have been adverted to may be remedied, and how it may be practicable in other respects, to afford them further encouragement, *paying due regard to the other great interests of the nation,* is submitted to the wisdom of congress."

The observation of the secretary is—

"*It is believed* that the present is a favourable moment for affording efficient protection to that increasing and important interest, *if* it can be done *consistently with the general interest of the nation.*"

Good heavens! what an appalling *if!* Was there ever such an unlucky word introduced into a public document! "*If* it can be done consistently with the general interest of the nation!" As if a statesman could for an instant doubt whether protecting and fostering the national industry—reducing our imports or expenses, within our exports or income—and arresting the progress of distress and decay, could, in any possible case, be otherwise than "*consistent with the general interest of the nation.*" As if it could be a matter of doubt, whether the contingency of a farmer or planter paying twenty, thirty, or forty dollars more per annum, (supposing that to be the case, which I shall prove to be as destitute of foundation, as the sublime theory that this earth rests upon a tortoise) is to be

---

*   Ustariz on the theory and practice of commerce and maritime affairs, vol. I. p. 6.

put into competition with the bankruptcy of our manufacturing capitalists—
the beggary of our working people—and the impoverishment of the nation!

Intending to investigate the rise and progress of the calamities of this country,
I shall divide the subject under the following heads:—

1. Present calamitous state of affairs. Causes.
2. State of the nation from the peace of Paris till the year 1789.
3. Adoption of the federal constitution. Consequences of that measure. Tariff of 1789. Fatal errors. Mr. Hamilton's Report.
4. Tariff of 1804.
5. Declaration of war. Disgraceful situation of the country.
6. State of the nation at the close of the war.
7. Mr. Dallas's[11] tariff.
8. Ruin of the manufacturers and decay of their establishments.
9. Dilatory mode of proceeding in congress.
10. Destruction of industry in Pennsylvania.
11. Erroneous causes assigned for the existing distress.
12. The complaint of taxing the many for the benefit of the few.
13. Immense advantages enjoyed by the farmers and planters for thirty years.
14. Fallacy of the clamours on the ground of extortion.
15. Advantages to agriculture from manufacturing establishmens [sic].
16. General reflexions on commerce. View of that of the United States.
17. Fostering care of commerce by congress.
18. Contrast between the conduct of the British government and that of the United States.
19. Advantages that might have arisen from the proper encouragement of manufactures, by the accession of immigrants.

Some of my friends have endeavoured to dissuade me from using the
freedom of style, which prevails in this work. They declare it imprudent,
as likely to irritate congress, and prevent their attending to the applications
of the manufacturers. I have duly weighed this very prudent advice, and
cannot persuade myself to adopt it. The manufacturers require no favours.
They only seek justice. Believing the system pursued radically vicious and
pernicious, it is the right and the duty of every man who suffers by it, to enter
his protest against the ruinous course pursued—to trace it to its causes—and

to display its consequences. I have used the language of a freeman. If the conduct I denounce, betrays a manifest departure from duty, can there be any impropriety in marking the departure? In countries less free than the United States, far greater severity is used in discussing the conduct of government. Why then should it be criminal or improper here? If any of my statements be incorrect, or my inductions illogical, I shall freely retract and apologize for them. But till then, I throw myself on the good sense of the community, and dare the consequences.

CHAPTER II

Sketch of the state of the nation from the peace of Paris till the organization of the present federal government. Analogy with our present state. Unlimited freedom of commerce fairly tested.

At the close of the Revolutionary War, the trade of America was free and unrestrained in the fullest sense of the word, according to the theory of Adam Smith, Say,[12] Ricardo,[13] the Edinburgh Reviewers,[14] and the authors of the Encyclopædia.[15] Her ports were open, with scarcely any duties, to the vessels and merchandize of all other nations.

The rate of duties in Pennsylvania, was only two and a half per cent. Even these were nugatory: because there was a free port established at Burlington, by the state of New Jersey, where goods intended for Philadelphia were entered, and conveyed over to this city clandestinely. The same fraudulent scenes were acted in other states, and thus trade was, as I have stated, wholly free.

If enthusiasts did not too generally scorn to trammel themselves by attention to facts, which are so very troublesome; and refuse to be dove-tailed into their specious theories, this case would settle the question of unrestrained commerce for ever—and prove, that the system ought to be postponed till the millennium, when it is possible it may stand a chance of promoting the welfare of mankind. But till then, woe to the nation that adopts it. Her destruction is sealed.

To a theorist "facts are stubborn things," not unlike those formidable obstructions in the Mississippi, which, in the elegant diction of the navigators of that immense river, are called *snags* and *sawyers*. When their barks come in contact with them, a wreck ensues. They therefore take all imaginable care to avoid them. Thus it is with the true theorist. He carefully avoids all the facts that endanger his system, how strong or convincing soever they may be. This saves an immensity of trouble. Hence in some of the grand systems of political economy, which have acquired great celebrity, you may travel through fifty or a hundred pages together, of most harmonious prose, all derived from a luxuriant imagination, without your career being arrested by a single fact. But on a little reflection or examination, you may as readily find a single fact, recorded elsewhere in ten lines, which demolishes the whole.

From almost every nation in Europe, large shipments were made to this country—many of them of the most ludicrous kind, which implied an utter ignorance of the wants, the situation and the resources of the United States. Among the rest, the recesses of Monmouth street, in London, and Plunket Street, in Dublin, the receptacles of the cast-off clothes of the two metropolises, were emptied of a portion of their contents; for it was supposed that the war had rendered the nation destitute of every thing, even of covering. Happy was the man who could send "*a venture,*" as it was called, to this country, which the misguided Europeans supposed an El Dorado, where every thing was to be converted into gold with a cent. per cent. profit at least. Goods often lay on the wharves for many days for want of store room. House rent rose to double and treble the former rates. The importers and con signees at first sold at great advances—and believed they were rapidly indemnifying themselves for the deprivations and sufferings of the war.

But these glorious times soon came to a close, like those of 1815. From "day dreams" and delusive scenes of boundless wealth, the citizens awoke to pinching misery and distress. The nation had no mines to pay her debts. And industry, the only legitimate and permanent source of individual happiness, and national wealth, power, and resources, was destroyed, as it has recently been by the influx, and finally by the depreciation of the price, of the imported articles: for the quantity on hands being equal to the consumption of two or three years, of course the great mass of goods fell below cost—often to half and one-third. All our citizens were at once converted into disciples of Adam Smith. They purchased every species of goods "cheaper than they could be manufactured at home."[16] Accordingly domestic manufactures were arrested in their career. The weaver, the shoemaker, the hatter, the saddler, the sugar baker, the brewer, the rope maker, the paper maker, &c. were reduced to bankruptcy. Their establishments were suspended. Their workmen were consigned to idleness and beggary. The payment for the foreign rubbish exhausted the country of nearly the whole of its specie, immense quantities of which had been introduced to pay the French armies, and likewise from the Spanish colonies. Two-thirds probably of the specie then in the country were composed of French crowns.

However calamitous the present state of affairs, we have not yet sunk to so low an ebb, as at that period. I have in 1786 seen sixteen houses to let in two squares, of about 800 feet, in one of the best sites for business in Philadelphia. Real property could hardly find a market. The number of persons reduced to distress, and forced to sell their merchandize, was so great, and those who had money to invest, were so very few, that the sacrifices were immense. Debtors were ruined, without paying a fourth of the demands of their creditors. There were most unprecedented transfers of property. Men worth large estates, who had unfortunately entered into business, were in a year or two totally ruined—

and those who had a command of ready money, quadrupled or quintupled their estates in an equally short space. Confidence was so wholly destroyed, that interest rose to two, two and a half, and three per cent. per month. And bonds, and judgments, and mortgages were sold at a discount of twenty, thirty, forty, and fifty per cent. In a word, few countries have experienced a more awful state of distress and wretchedness.

While our citizens were writhing under these evils, destitute of a circulating medium, industry universally paralized, thousands every where deprived of the means of supporting their families, bankruptcy daily swallowing up in its vortex our merchants, tradesmen, manufacturers, and artisans—it is not wonderful that recourse was had to various indefensible means to palliate the evils. The real source, that is, the want of an adequate tariff to protect national industry by high duties and prohibitions, was not explored—and even if it had been, there existed no authority competent to apply a remedy.[17]

Among the expedients employed, emissions of paper money, legal tenders, appraisement acts, and suspensions of the operation of courts of justice in regard to the collection of debts, were the most prominent. These were but miserable palliatives of a disorder arising solely, I repeat, from the destruction of the national industry, and which nothing but its resuscitation could remove.

In Massachusetts, the sufferings rose higher than in any other part of the United States. Riotous collections of people assembled in various parts at the periods for convening the courts of common pleas, to prevent their proceedings, and actually in every instance but one, according to Judge Marshal, carried their purposes into execution.[18] In fact, so severe was the distress, and so numerous were the debtors, that they had a majority in the legislature more than once. The evil under the existing form of government was incurable. It ended in an open insurrection, under Shays, a revolutionary officer, which was crushed by the energy of governor Bowdoin[19] and his council—and the decision of generals Lincoln and Sheppard.

Some idea may be entertained of the state of public affairs, quite as deplorable as those of individuals, from the circumstance that governor Bowdoin having raised four thousand militia against the insurgents, there was not money enough in the treasury to support that small army for one week; and they could not have been marched but for the patriotism of a number of public-spirited individuals, who subscribed the sum necessary for the purpose.

The insurrection produced a salutary effect, by spreading a conviction of the utter inefficacy of the existing form of government, and of the imperious necessity of adopting a new one. The difficulty under which the federal constitution laboured in its progress, notwithstanding the impetus it received from this alarming event, shews that it would have probably failed of success, had not the public distress arrived at its highest pitch.

Those of our citizens, who ascribe the existing calamities to the baleful career of the banks, are advised to consider this parallel case, wherein banks had no agency. When the war closed, there was but one bank in the United States, that of North America, located in the city of Philadelphia, with a capital of 400,000 dollars. And in 1785, when distress and misery pervaded the state, many of the citizens, in casting round to discover the source, believed, or affected to believe, that they sprang from the operation of this institution. Accordingly petitions were presented to the legislature to repeal its charter. Counsel were heard at the bar of the house for and against the bank—the late respected Judge Wilson in defence, and Jonathan Dickinson Sargeant, father of the present member of congress from Philadelphia, in opposition. The state, let it be observed, was then divided into two parties, very violently embittered against each other. The repeal was quite a party question, and decided by party views. The majority in the legislature were hostile to the institution, and repealed the charter, which measure they regarded as a sovereign remedy for all the existing evils. Had the repeal been effectual, it would have multiplied instead of diminishing them. But having a charter from congress, the bank set the legislature at defiance, and pursued "the even tenor of its way," unruffled by "the peltings of the pitiless storm."

It may gratify curiosity to see the view given of the tremendous influence which was conjured up for this institution, in order to alarm the citizens, and justify the repeal.

The committee to whom the petitions were referred, in their report stated—

"That foreigners will doubtless be more and more induced to become stockholders, until the time may arrive when *this enormous engine of power may become subject to foreign influence.* This country may be agitated with the politics of European courts; and *the good people of America reduced once more into a state of subordination and dependence upon some one or other of the European powers!*"*

On the 17th of Feb. in the year 1784, the Massachusetts Bank was incorporated, with power to hold in real estate 50,000*l.* and to raise a capital stock of 500,000*l.* The subscription did not, I have reason to believe, exceed at that time 400,000 dollars.

In the same year, the state of New York incorporated the bank of that name, with the extent of whose capital I am unacquainted.

These were the only banks in existence in the United States, previous to the adoption of the federal constitution. And as distress and embarrassment equally pervaded those states where there were none, it is absurd to ascribe the evil to those institutions where they existed.[20]

*   *   *   *   *

---

*   Journal of the house of representatives, March 28 1785.

This distressing state of things accounts for a fact which has always excited deep regret, and which, I believe, has never been traced to its source. I mean the depreciation of the public securities, which the holders were obliged to part with at ten, twelve and fifteen cents in the dollar, whereby a large portion of the warmest friends of the revolution, who had risked their lives and embarked their entire property in its support, were wholly ruined, and many of its deadly enemies most immoderately enriched. [21] Never was Virgil's celebrated line more applicable—

Sic vos—non vobis, mellificatis, apes. [22]

The reader is requested to bear these pictures of distress in mind, during the perusal of the chapter in which I propose to investigate the causes assigned for the evils under which the community labours at present. They shed strong light on the subject.

Well as I am aware of the pertinacious adherence of mankind to theory, and the difficulty of breaking the intellectual chains by which it holds the mind, I cannot refrain from again urging the strong case of this country at that period on the most serious consideration of the disciples of Adam Smith, Say, Ricardo, and the other political economists of that school. It ought to dispel for ever the mists, on the subject of unrestrained commerce, which that abstruse work, the Wealth of Nations, has spread abroad. Here the system had fair scope for operation. The ports of this country, I repeat, were open to the commerce of the whole world, with an impost so light as not even to meet the wants of the treasury. The consequences followed, which have never failed to follow such a state of things. Our markets were glutted. Prices fell. Competition on the part of our manufacturers was at an end. They were beggared and bankrupted. The merchants, whose importations had ruined them, were themselves involved in the calamity. And the farmers who had felicitated themselves on the grand advantage of "buying foreign merchandize cheap," sunk likewise into the vortex of general destruction.

Would to heaven that the precious and invaluable lessons these facts afford may not in future be thrown away on our statesmen and the nation at large! Had they been duly attended to, at the close of the late war,[23] the United States, instead of the afflicting scenes they now exhibit, would present a picture of prosperity, public and private, which would have realized the fondest anticipations of the philosophers of both hemispheres—anticipations which have been most lamentably disappointed—and *"like the baseless fabric of a vision,"* scarcely *"left a trace behind."*[24]

CHAPTER III

Adoption of the federal constitution. Its happy effects. Utter impolicy of the tariff. Manufactures and manufacturers not protected. Hamilton's celebrated report. Glaring inconsistency. Excise system. Its unproductiveness.

The adoption of the federal constitution operated like magic; produced a total change in the state of affairs; and actually removed no small portion of the public suffering, by the confidence it inspired, even before the measures of the government could be carried into effect.[25]

The United States began their career in 1789 with advantages never exceeded, rarely equalled. The early administrators of the government had a high degree of responsibility. They were laying the foundations of an empire which may be the most extensive and powerful the world ever knew, and whose destinies they held in their hands.

The tariff was fraught with errors of the most grievous kind.[26] Disregarding the examples and the systems of the wisest nations of Europe, it was calculated to sacrifice the resources of the country for the benefit of foreign manufacturing nations. And indeed had it been framed by an agent of any of those nations, it could not have answered the purpose better. It afforded them nearly all the benefits usually derived from colonies, without the expense of their support. It deprived our manufacturing citizens of all the advantages of reciprocity in their intercourse with the rest of the world.

The era is not long passed over, when any man who dared to arraign the conduct of the early congresses under the federal constitution, and accuse them of having established tariffs which sacrificed the dearest interests of their country, and clipped its wings in its flight towards the high destinies to which its extent, its government, the energies of the people, and the great variety of other advantages which it possessed, bid it aspire, would be regarded with jealousy, and covered with obloquy. The voice of reason, of truth, and of history, would have been smothered amidst the loud clamours of prejudice and party. But I trust the fatal results of the system have prepared the public mind to hear with patience, and judge with candour, the facts on which I ground these opinions, and the inductions I draw from them.

To those who consider the mode in which the members of congress are elected—the various quarters from which they come—the different degrees of illumination that prevail in the districts they respectively represent—how many neglect to prepare themselves fully for the stations they occupy—it will not appear wonderful that the views of a portion of them are contracted, and do not embrace on a broad and comprehensive scale, the interests of the nation as one grand whole.

The want of adequate protection to the productive industry of the manufacturers, conspicuous in the first and the succeeding tariffs, may be accounted for from the concurrence in one object, of four descriptions of citizens, whose particular views, however, were entirely different.

I. The most influential members of the mercantile class have appeared at all times jealous of the manufacturers, and been disposed to regard adequate protection to them as injurious to the prosperity of commerce. Hence they have too generally and too successfully opposed prohibitions and prohibitory duties as limiting their importations of bale goods. Although there are many gentlemen of this class whose views are expanded and liberal, there is a large proportion whose opposition remains unabated.

II. The agriculturists too have been equally jealous of the manufacturers— opposed the imposition of duties adequate to the protection of their fellow citizens—and not allowed a single article to be prohibited. They dreaded an extravagant rise of price as a necessary result of securing the home market to our own citizens. It does not appear to have ever entered into their calculations, that, in a country like the United States, where monopolies are excluded, and where industry and enterprize so generally prevail, and are so wholly uncontrolled, the competition would, to use the words of Alexander Hamilton, assuredly *"bring prices to their proper level."*

III. The third description comprised the disciples of Adam Smith, who contended that trade ought to be allowed to regulate itself—that commerce should be left unrestrained—that all nations ought to buy wherever they could procure articles cheapest, &c. &c.

IV. The fourth class considered themselves, and were regarded by others, as of a higher order. The whole of their political economy was, however, confined within very narrow limits. It never travelled beyond the collection of revenue. The ways and means were their alpha and omega, their sine qua non. Provided the treasury was overflowing, they had neither eyes, nor ears, nor tongue for any other object. The spread of bankruptcy throughout our cities—the decay of splendid manufacturing establishments—the distress of thousands of useful men—the wailings of helpless women and children—never excited any alarm. The importation of foreign goods, to the amount of 60,000,000 dollars, which exhausted the country of its specie, produced almost universal distress and devoted thousands of workmen to idleness, and part of them to beggary, was a subject of rejoicing—for it brought 15,000,000 dollars into the treasury! This was the salve for every sore—the panacea, which, like the waters of the Jordan, cleansed off all the ulcers and foulnesses of the body politic.

This statement may appear too severe. But I beg the reader will not decide on the correctness or incorrectness of it, till he has read the chapter on the contumelious and unfeeling neglect of the pathetic applications of the manufacturers to congress for relief in 1816, 1817, and 1818.

The views of these four descriptions of citizens were aided by the extensive prevalence of a host of prejudices, which were sedulously inculcated by foreign agents, whose wealth and prosperity depended on keeping this market open to their fabrics, and repressing the growth of our manufactures.

1. The idea of the immense superiority of agricultural pursuits and agriculturists over manufactures and manufacturers, was almost universally prevalent. It had been fondly cherished by Great Britain and her friends here during the colonial state of the country, and long afterwards: and no small portion of the citizens of the United States were unable to divest their minds of the colonial trammels, when the country assumed its independent rank among nations.
2. The same keen sensibility on the subject of smuggling was manifested, as we have so often witnessed more recently. This was assigned as a reason for admitting three-fourths of all the manufactured merchandize under a duty of five per cent.!!
3. The miserable outcry on the subject of *"taxing the many for the benefit of the few,"* which is still used as a sort of war whoop against the manufacturers, was then in full force.
4. The back lands, it was asserted, ought to be cultivated before the labour of our citizens was diverted off to manufactures.
5. The high price of labour in this country was by many regarded as an insuperable bar, and a proof that "we were not yet ripe for manufactures."
6. The demoralization asserted to be inseparable from manufacturing establishments, was among the prominent objections.

———————

There is a magic in great names which renders their errors highly pernicious. That Mr. Jefferson[27] is a truly great man, is now, I believe, universally admitted, since the baleful passions, excited by party, have subsided, and the atrocious calumnies with which, in the days of faction and delusion, he was overwhelmed, have sunk into deserved oblivion. But that he has had no small degree of instrumentality in giving currency to the system we have pursued, it would be vain to deny. He has drawn a contrast between manufactures and agriculture, so immensely advantageous to the latter, as to have fostered the old, and excited new prejudices against the former, many of which still maintain their sway. Mr. Jefferson was born, brought up and lived in a slave-holding state, a large portion of the industry of which is devoted to the culture of tobacco, one of the most pernicious kinds of employment in the world. It more completely exhausts the soil, and debases and wears out the wretched labourer, than any other species of cultivation. How, under such circumstances, he could have drawn such a captivating picture of the labours of the field, it is difficult to say. His Arcadia must have been sought, not in Virginia or Maryland, but in the tales of Chaucer or Sir Philip Sydney.

This is not a place to enter into a comparison of these occupations, otherwise the boasted superiority might be found not to rest on so stable a basis as is generally supposed.

Mr. Jefferson lately retracted his opinions on those subjects. In a letter to B. Austin,[28] Esq. of Boston, he distinctly states:—

"*To be independent for the comforts of life, we must fabricate them ourselves. We must now place the manufacturer by the side of the agriculturist.*"

"Experience has taught me, that *manufactures are now as necessary to our independence, as to our comfort.*"

In order to justify the character I have given of the tariff of 1789, I annex a description of two tariffs, one calculated to protect and promote individual industry and national prosperity, and the other to destroy both.

FEATURES

A sound tariff	*A pernicious tariff*
1. Renders revenue subservient to the promotion of individual industry and national prosperity.	1. Regards revenue as the grand object of solicitude.
2. Prohibits such articles as can be fully supplied at home on reasonable terms.	2. Prohibits no article whatever, however competent the country may be to supply itself.
3. Imposes heavy duties on articles interfering with the rising manufactures of the country.	3. Imposes such low duties on manufactures, as, while they serve the purposes of revenue, cannot promote national industry, or prevent or materially check importation.
4. Admits articles that do not interfere with the manufactures of the nation on light duties.	4. Raises as large a portion of the revenue as possible on articles not interfering with the manufactures of the nation.

CONSEQUENCES

A sound tariff	*A pernicious tariff*
Secures employment to industry, capital, talent, and enterprize.	Deprives a large portion of the industry, capital, talent, and enterprize of the citizens of employment.
Preserves the circulating medium, and daily adds to the wealth, power, and resources of the nation.	Drains away the circulating medium, and exhausts the national resources.
Extends prosperity and happiness in every direction.	Spreads misery and distress through the country, as we find by dear bought experience.

If the tariff in question be tried by this standard, which I trust will be found correct, and by its results, I shall be exonerated from censure. It was extremely simple. It enumerated about thirty manufactured articles, subject to seven and a half and ten per cent. duty—Coaches, chaises, &c. to fifteen—and about eight or ten to specific duties. All the remainder were thrown together, as non-enumerated, and *subject to five per cent.!!* Its protection of agriculture is reserved as the subject of another chapter.

*　　*　　*　　*　　*

In order to form a correct estimate of the effect of those duties as protection, it is necessary to take a view of the situation of this country and of those with which our citizens were to compete—which were principally, Great Britain, France, Germany, and the East Indies.

The United States had recently emerged from a desolating war of seven years duration, and a peace of six years had been as destructive to their resources. Their manufacturers were possessed of slender capitals, and as slender credit. Workmen were inexperienced—and wages high. All the expenses, moreover, of incipient undertakings were to be encountered. The chief counterbalance for all these disadvantages, was the freight and commission on the rival articles.

Great Britain possessed every possible advantage in the conflict. Her manufacturers had the secure possession of their domestic market—and had only to send their surplus productions to this country—their machinery was excellent—they had drawbacks, in general equal to, and often greater than, the expenses of transportation—skilful workmen—and wages comparatively low. Her merchants were possessed of immense capitals, and gave most liberal credits.

The cheapness of living and labour in France, Germany, and more particularly in the East Indies, afforded the people of those countries advantages over our manufacturers, only inferior to those enjoyed by Great Britain.

Under these circumstances, I trust it will be admitted by every man of candour that it would be a mere mockery and insult to common sense, to pretend that five per cent., which, as appears above, was the duty on seven-eighths of all the manufactured articles imported into this country, was imposed with a view to protection. Revenue alone was the object.

Having to struggle with such a lamentably impolitic system, it is wonderful that our manufactures made any progress. It reflects great credit on our citizens, that they were able to emerge from such an overwhelming mass of difficulties, as they had to encounter.

While the grand leading manufactures of cotton, wool, iron, steel, lead, flax, and pottery; were thus subject to only five per cent. duty, lest smuggling should be encouraged, it may afford some gratification to curiosity to exhibit a statement of the very high duties on tea, coffee, rum, &c. which were wholly unrestrained by any fear of smuggling.

	1789.	*Price.*	*Duty.*	*Per cent.*
Souchong,	per lb.	39	10	25
Hyson	do.	49	20	40
Bohea	do.	15	6	40
Madeira,	per gallon	100	18	18
Jamaica rum,	do.	40	10	25
Coffee,	per lb.	12 ½	2 ½	20
Sugar,	do.	5	1 ½	30
Salt,	per bushel	12	6	50

Thus a yard of broad cloth or muslin, value four dollars, paid no more duty than a pound of hyson tea, value 49 cents!

The amount of goods subject to ad valorem duties, imported in 1789, 1790, and 1791, was as follows—

Per cent.	*1789*	*1790*	*1791*
5	$ 7,136,578	$ 14,605,713	$ 11,036,477
7 ½	520,182	1,067,143	7,708,337
10	305,248	699,149	1,114,463
12 ½	5		314,206
15	2,700	4,876	5,654
	$ 7,969,731	$ 16,376,881	$ 19,179,137[*]

The duties on the above were about 2,600,000 dollars: and the whole amount of the impost for those three years, was 6,494,225 dollars.[†]

---

[*]   Seybert, 158.

[†]   Idem, 395.

The residue, about 3,800,000, was collected principally from teas, wines, sugar, salt, spirits, spices, and coffee! This completely justifies the character of the tariff, that as large a portion as possible of the impost was levied on articles not interfering with national industry; and that the duties on manufactured merchandize were as light as the exigencies of the government would admit.

The manufacturers at this period, as they have done so often since, besought the protection and threw themselves on the liberality of congress; but they experienced the same degree of slight as they have done in 1816–17

* * * * *

It would require a long chapter to develope [*sic*] the utter impolicy of this tariff, and its inauspicious effects on the industry and happiness of a large portion of our citizens, and on the national prosperity. My limits forbid me to display the whole of its deformity. I annex one further view of it:

In 1793, the amount of merchandize imported
at 7 ½ and 8 per cent., was about $ 15,328,000[*]
On which the net duty was about $ 1,151,000
This included all articles of clothing, whether cotton, woollen,
or silk, (except India goods, subject to twelve and a half per cent.)
The net duty on coffee for the same year was $ 1,226,724[†]
Or nearly ten per cent more than on the whole
of the clothing of the nation!
Let us examine how this might have been arranged for
the promotion of the prosperity of the country.
Suppose that the duty on coffee had been reduced so
as to raise only $ 700,000
And that the duty on cotton and woollen goods had been
raised to 20 per cent., which might have reduced the
importation to $8,500,000, and produced 1,700,000
$ 2,400,000
which is beyond the aggregate of the duties stated.

Or, suppose that the duty on coffee had remained unaltered, and on cottons and woollens been increased to 25 per cent.—and that the importations had been diminished to 5,000,000 of dollars, the revenue would have been unimpaired.

---

* Seybert, 158.
† Idem, 438.

What an immense difference! In one case nearly 7,000,000, and in the other 10,000,000 of dollars saved to the country! Three or four hundred thousand people rendered happy! A market for the farmers for probably 3,000,000 lbs. of wool! and for the planters for 4,000,000 lbs. of cotton!

But it is a humiliating truth, that very few of our statesmen have ever predicated their measures on national views. They are almost all sectional. They do not fall within Rousseau's description:—

"*It belongs to the real statesman to elevate his views in the imposition of taxes, above the mere object of finance, and to transform them into useful regulations.*"

It is a melancholy operation for a real friend to the honour, power, resources, and happiness of the United States, to compare the tariff of 1789, and the principles on which it is predicated, with the preamble to a law of the state of Pennsylvania, passed anno 1785, four years before. The sound policy, the fostering care of its citizens, and of the resources of the state displayed in the latter, form a strong and decisive contrast with the utter impolicy of the tariff.

* * * * *

In the year 1790. Alexander Hamilton, who saw the errors of the tariff of the preceding year, presented congress with his celebrated Report on Manufactures, the most perfect and luminous work ever published on the subject. It embraces all the great principles of the science of political economy, respecting that portion of the national industry applied to manufactures, and is admirably calculated to advance the happiness of the people, and the wealth, power, and resources of nations. It more richly deserves the title of "The Wealth of Nations," than the celebrated work that bears the name.[29]

This Report swept away, by the strongest arguments, all the plausible objections on which the paralizing influence of the tariff rested for support. The lucid reasoning, as level to the most common capacity, as to the most profound statesman, is not enveloped in those abstractions and metaphysical subtleties which abound in most of the books on this subject, and which, like the airy spectres of the dreamer, elude the grasp of the mind.

I annex a few of those grand and sublime truths, with which this work abounds, and which bear the strongest testimony against, and condemnation of, the course which this country has pursued.

"The substitution of foreign for domestic manufactures, *is a transfer to foreign nations of the advantages of machinery in the modes in which it is capable of being employed with most utility and to the greatest extent.*"*

---

*   Hamilton's Works, Vol. I.

How many millions of the wealth of this country have been thus "transferred to foreign nations" during the thirty years of our career! How much of this wealth was used to scourge us at Washington, on the frontiers of Canada, and in the Chesapeake![30] What a lamentable use we have made of the advantages which heaven has lavished on us!

"The establishment of manufactures is calculated not only to increase the general stock of useful and productive labour, but even *to improve the state of agriculture in particular*."*

What a lesson is here for the farmers and planters, who have been unhappily excited to view with jealousy and hostility those citizens who contribute so largely to their prosperity!

"It is the interest of the community, *with a view to eventual and permanent economy*, to encourage the growth of manufactures. In a national view, a temporary enhancement of price must always be well compensated by a permanent reduction of it."*

"The trade of a country, which is both manufacturing and agricultural, will be *more lucrative and prosperous than that of a country which is merely agricultural*."*

"The *uniform appearance of an abundance of specie, as the concomitant of a flourishing state of manufactures*, and of the reverse where they do not prevail, afford a strong presumption of their favourable operation upon the wealth of a country."*

"*Not only the wealth, but the independence and security of a country, appear to be materially connected with the prosperity of manufactures*. Every nation, with a view to these great objects, ought to endeavour to possess within itself all the essentials of national supply. These comprise the means of subsistence, habitation, clothing, and defence."*

"Considering a monopoly of the domestic market to its own manufactures as the reigning policy of manufacturing nations, *a similar policy on the part of the United States*, in every proper instance, is dictated, it might almost be said *by the principles of distributive justice—certainly by the duty of securing to their own citizens a reciprocity of advantages*."*

Mr. Hamilton, however, displayed an extreme degree of inconsistency. Notwithstanding the conclusive and irresistible arguments of his report, in favour of a decided protection of manufactures, and notwithstanding the failure of many promising efforts at their establishment, in consequence of the deluge of goods poured into the market, instead of recommending an adequate enhancement of duties to supply some deficiency of revenue in 1790, he submitted a plan for an excise on spirituous liquors, which was one of the most universally odious and unpopular measures that could be devised.

---

*   Hamilton's Works, Vol. I

It excited the western insurrection; thereby tarnished the character of the country; and jeopardized the government in its infancy.

However strong the arguments may be in favour of an excise on spirits, in a moral point of view, it was under existing circumstances extremely impolitic. For the paltry amount raised from it for a considerable time after its adoption, it was not worth while to incur the disaffection of the citizens. The receipts for the first four years were—

In 1792	$ 208,942
1793	337,705
1794	274,689
1795	337,755
Four years	$ 1,158,491[*]
Average	$ 289,622

What a miserable sum as a set off against the oppression and vexation of an excise—and the insurrection it excited! How incalculably sounder policy it would have been, to have increased the duties on manufactured articles, which would not only have answered the purpose of meeting the additional demands of the treasury, and given a spring to the industry of our citizens; but made an important addition to the wealth, power and resources of the nation!

The importations in 1792, subject to five and seven and a half per cent. duty—

Amounted to	$16,221,000[†]
1793, at 7 ½ and 8	14,966,000
1794, at 7 ½ and 10	17,700,000
1795, at 10	16,447,000
Four years,	$ 65,334,000
Two per cent. on this sum would have been	$ 1,306,620
Annual average	$ 326,655

more than the net revenue arising from the excise, and with scarcely a dollar additional expense in the collection.

---

[*]   Seybert, 477.
[†]   Idem, 159.

CHAPTER IV

Memorials to congress. Deceptious report. List of exports. Tariff of 1804. Wonderful omission. Immense importations of cotton and woollen goods. Exportations of cotton.

In the years 1802, 3, and 4, memorials were presented to congress from almost every description of manufacturers, praying for further protection. In the two first years they were treated with utter slight, and nothing was done whatever.

In 1804, the committee on commerce and manufactures made a very superficial report, from which I submit the following extract as a specimen of the sagacity of its authors.

"*There may be some danger in refusing to admit the manufactures of foreign countries; for by the adoption of such a measure, we should have no market abroad, and industry would lose one of its chief incentives at home.*"

This paragraph is superlatively absurd, and indeed more than absurd. It is wicked. In order to defeat the object of the memorialists, it assumes for them requisitions which they did not contemplate, and which of course their memorials did not warrant. No sound man in the United States ever contemplated the total "*exclusion of foreign manufactures.*" It was merely requested that the memorialists should not themselves be "*excluded*" from the domestic market by foreign rivals—and that the industry of our citizens should be so far patronized, that they might be enabled to supply a portion of the thirty millions of dollars, principally of clothing, imported that year.

But admitting for a moment, for the sake of argument, that foreign manufactures had been excluded, who could persuade himself, that we should therefore "have no market abroad for our produce?" War at that time raged in almost every part of Europe, and the West Indies: and those who purchased our produce, had at least as powerful reasons to purchase as we had to sell. The inhabitants of an island in danger of starvation would suffer more from being deprived of supplies, than the producers by the privation of a market.

To evince the futility of the ground assumed in the report, I annex a list of some of the great leading articles exported in that year:—

Flour	barrels	810,000
Indian corn	bushels	1,944,873
Beef	barrels	134,896
Indian meal	barrels	111,327
Hams	pounds	1,904,284
Butter	pounds	2,476,550
Cheese	pounds	1,299,872
Lard	pounds	2,565,719
Candles	pounds	2,239,356
Cotton	pounds	35,034,175
Tar	barrels	58,181
Turpentine	barrels	77,827
Staves and heading	feet	34,614,000
Boards, plank and scantling	feet	76,000,000*

These, gentle reader, are the kinds of produce, which the framers of this very profound report were fearful would not find a market, if "foreign merchandize was excluded." Such are the displays of wisdom and political economy made to the legislature of "the most enlightened nation in the world."

This subject deserves to be further analyzed. To reduce it to plain English, it means, that, if the United States laid heavy or prohibitory duties on silks, sattins, shawls, &c. or prohibited East India cotton goods, &c. the people of the West Indies would refuse to purchase our lumber—the Manchester manufacturers our cotton—and the governments of Spain and Portugal, our flour, Indian meal, &c. &c. Such profound views of political economy cannot fail to excite a high degree of respect and admiration.

In the year 1804, the demands of the treasury had greatly increased by an augmentation of expenditure, and by the $ 15,000,000 of debt funded for the purchase of Louisiana. This required an increase of duties. But the same impolicy and neglect of affording adequate protection to the productive industry of the country that prevailed in the former tariffs, appear in that of this year.

The old system was continued, of raising as large a portion as possible of the impost on articles not interfering with our manufactures, and laying duties comparatively light on manufactures. Accordingly the duties on teas, wines, coffee, sugar, &c. were raised without fear of smuggling.

---

* Seybert, 110.

	1804.	*Price.* Cents.	*Duty.* Cents.	*Per cent.*
Bohea tea	per lb.	14	12	85
Souchong	do.	41	18	44
Hyson	do.	56	32	57
Hyson skin	do.	24	20	83
Imperial	do.	75	32	40
Lisbon wine	per gallon	80	30	37 ½
London market Madeira	do.	160	58	36
Coffee	per lb.	15	5	33

While these articles were dutied thus high, cotton and woollen goods, which formed the great mass of the clothing of the country, were subject to only fifteen per cent., which, in the improved state of the machinery of Great Britain, and, so far as respects cotton, the low price of labour in the East Indies, was so wholly inadequate for protection, that very few attempts were made to establish them on an extensive scale, and thus the nation was drained of immense sums, for articles of which it could have supplied a superabundance.

It is a remarkable and most extraordinary fact, that *cotton goods were never mentioned in the tariff, before* 1804—*nor woollen goods before* 1816, when the government had been in operation 27 years! They were passed over, and fell within the class of non-enumerated articles. It is impossible to reflect on this fact, without astonishment, and a conviction that there never was adequate attention bestowed on the concoction of the tariff, which, while it was silent respecting those important articles, descended to the enumeration of artificial flowers, cosmetics, bricks and tiles, dentifrice, dates, dolls, essences, fans, fringes, glue, tassels and trimmings, limes and lemons, mittens, gloves, powders, pastes, washes, tinctures, plums, prunes, toys, wafers, &c. &c.

* * * * *

Although we supplied Great Britain with more than a third of the cotton she used, so little protection was afforded to the manufacture of the article here, that in the year 1805, our consumption was only 1000 bags; whereas, had the fostering care of the government been extended to it, we might have used 100,000. And this all-important manufacture, for which this country is so peculiarly fitted by its capacity of producing the raw material to any extent; its boundless water powers, its admirable machinery, and the skill of its citizens, never took root here until the non-intercourse and other restrictive measures, affording our citizens a fair change in their own market, they were encouraged to turn their attention, and devote their talents and capital to this grand object. In five years, that is, in 1810, merely through this encouragement, the consumption increased ten-fold, to 10,000 bales, or 3,000,000 lbs. In five more, in consequence of the war, it rose to 90,000 bales, or 27,000,000 lbs. This affords a clear and decisive proof that nothing but a sound policy was necessary to have brought it early to perfect maturity.

There is not perhaps in history a greater instance of utter impolicy and disregard of the maxims of all profound statesmen, or of the solid and substantial interests of a nation, than this most lamentable fact exhibits. An inexhaustible source of national wealth, power, and resources, and of individual happiness, was bestowed on us by heaven, and prodigally lavished away, in favour of foreign nations who made use of the wealth thus absurdly bestowed, to jeopardize our independence;—under the absurd idea that as we had so many millions of acres of back lands uncultivated, we ought not to encourage manufactures!! Ineffable delusion! As if the thousands of men brought up to cotton weaving, who, under proper encouragement, would have migrated to this country, could be immediately transformed into back country farmers, and induced to encounter all the horrors of clearing the wilderness! This would be on a level with some of the Metamorphoses of Ovid. And as if the vast numbers of old men, of women, and children, who might be most advantageously employed for themselves and for the nation, in this branch, were in any degree calculated for a country life, even under its most inviting form!

CHAPTER V

Various causes which prevented the ruinous operation of the early tariffs. Declaration of war. Blankets for Indians. Disgraceful situation of the United States. Governor Gerry. Sufferings of the army. Rapid progress of national industry.

A variety of circumstances, which ought to have been noted in page 52, combined to rescue the United States from the ruinous consequences that would otherwise have naturally flowed from the impolicy of the tariffs of 1789, 1792, and 1804; of which, as I have already stated, the obvious tendency was to afford the manufacturing nations of Europe, nearly all the advantages they could have derived from this country in its colonial state.

The provision in 1790, for funding the debt of the United States, threw into circulation an immense capital, which gave life and activity to business. The establishment, about the same time, of the Bank of the United States, afforded additional facilities to trade and commerce. And the wars of the French revolution opened a market for the productions of our agriculture, in many instances at most exorbitant prices; for instance, occasionally from fifteen to twenty dollars per barrel for flour in the West Indies, Spain, and Portugal, and other articles in proportion. We were thus enabled to pay for the extravagant quantities of manufactures which we consumed, and with which we could and ought to have supplied ourselves.

The dreadful scenes in St. Domingo brought immense wealth into this country with the emigrants who purchased safety by flight from their paternal estates and their native land.

For a considerable time, moreover, we were almost the sole carriers of the colonial produce of the enemies of Great Britain; as her fleets were in full possession of the seas, and there was no safety for the vessels of those powers in hostility with her.

But it was obvious that this system rested the prosperity of the nation on the sandy foundation of the wars, desolation, and misery of our fellow men. And as it was not probable that they would continue to cut each other's throats to promote our welfare, a close of this dazzling scene was to be expected, for which sound policy required provision to be made. But this duty was totally neglected. We proceeded as if this state of affairs were to last for ever. At length we were abruptly cut off from the markets of Europe, and then a new order of things arose, to dispel the prevalent delusion.

On the 18th of June, 1812, war was declared against Great Britain. This event placed the ruinous and deplorable policy of our government, on the subject of its manufactures, in a glaring point of light. With raw materials in abundance, skill, enterprize, industry, water power, and capital to the utmost extent, to secure a full supply for nearly all our wants, we had, in defiance of the soundest maxims of policy, absurdly *depended on foreign nations for a great variety of necessary articles, and even, Oh, shame! for our clothing, than which the mind of man can hardly conceive of more utter want of policy.*

In consequence of this miserable system, at the commencement of the war, the nation suffered the disgrace of a regular proposition being offered to congress by the secretary at war, *to suspend the non-importation act for the purpose of importing a supply of five or six thousand blankets for the Indians,* for whom the department had not been able to make provision! and who had of course become clamorous at the disappointment! This melancholy tale will hardly find credence. It is, nevertheless, sacredly true; and if dear-bought experience were of any avail in the regulation of the affairs of nations, this simple fact would be an invaluable lesson to our statesmen, to warn them against the rock of abandoning national industry. But, alas! to the incalculable injury of the nation, it was entirely disregarded in four short years, as will appear in the sequel.

The good old governor of Massachusetts, Elbridge Gerry, felt deep distress at the bitter draught of the dregs of the chalice of humiliation swallowed at this crisis by the government of the United States, and brought the affair before the legislature of that state.

*   *   *   *   *

What a melancholy difference between the two epochs, 1775, and 1812! Strength and vigour in youth—feebleness and decay in manhood! What lamentable havoc of national resources in the interim!

Mr. Gerry says, "*as a nation we are independent of every other.*" This is a most egregious error. "*As a nation*" extent of resources considered, there was not then, nor is there now, a more dependent people, perhaps, in the world. In our towns and cities, one-half of our population, males and females, are covered with the fabrics and in the fashions of foreign nations. He should have said, "*we may and ought to be independent.*" Two or three small words make an immense difference.

If any thing could add to the mortification and regret which this circumstance must excite, it is, that the quantity of wool sheared in 1810 was estimated at 13 or 14,000,000 lbs., and in 1812, at 20 or 22,000,000;* and that various promising attempts to establish the woollen manufacture, had been made at different periods, during the preceding years, which, for want of protection, had failed of success.

Next to the waste of the immense advantages we possess for the manufacture of cotton, is to be lamented the impolitic and irreparable destruction of the merino sheep, of which we had to the value of about one million of dollars, which government, by an increase of duty on woollens, might have easily preserved. The contrast between our abandonment of them, and the great pains taken, and expense incurred by different nations to possess themselves of this treasure, is strong and striking.

Hundreds of our ill-fated soldiers, it is said, perished for want of comfortable clothing in the early part of the war, when exposed to the inhospitable climate of Canada.†

The war found us destitute of the means of supplying ourselves, not merely with blankets for our soldiers, but a vast variety of other articles necessary for our ease and comfort, of which the prices were accordingly raised extravagantly by the importers. Our citizens, and among them numbers of our commercial men, entered on the business of manufactures with great energy and enterprize; invested in them many millions of capital; and having, during the thirty months which the war continued, the domestic market secured to them, they succeeded wonderfully.

Never was there a prouder display of the (I had almost said) omnipotence of industry, than was afforded on this occasion. It furnishes an eternal lesson to statesmen. Our citizens exhibited a spectacle perhaps without precedent. *Unaided by the expenditure of a single dollar by our government*, they attained in two or three years, a degree of maturity in manufactures, which required centuries in England, France, Prussia, &c., and cost their monarchs enormous sums in the shape of bounties, premiums, drawbacks, with the fostering aid of privileges and immunities bestowed on the undertakers. The supply became commensurate with the demand; and full confidence was entertained that the government and nation, to whose aid they came forward in time of need, would not abandon them to destruction, after the purposes of the moment were answered. Fatal delusion!

Our exports for 1813 and 1814, were only about 31,000,000 of dollars, or 15,500,000 per annum. Hostile fleets and armies desolated those parts of

---

*   Tench Coxe's Tables, preface, page xiii.
†   I have heard a story, for which, however, I do not vouch, that the capture of Amelia Island, by Governor Mitchell, was ordered by government with a view to provide blankets for our suffering soldiers.

the country to which they had access. Yet the nation made rapid strides in prosperity by the creative powers of industry. Every man was employed, and every man fully recompensed for his labours. It may, however, be supposed that the farmers suffered heavily by the exclusion of their productions from foreign markets. The fact is otherwise. I state the prices of three articles, flour, beef, and hemp, in the Philadelphia market, in proof of this assertion. Other articles commanded proportionable prices.

	Flour per barrel.	Beef per barrel.	Hemp per ton.
1813. Aug. 23	$ 8 25	$15 50	$210
Nov. 22	10 00	15 50	210
1814. Jan. 31	8 00	13 50	275
July 4*	6 86	17 00	250
Dec. 5	8 37	19 00	250

What a contrast at present! We have exported—

In 1816	$ 64,784,896
1817	68,338,069
1818	73,854,437
	$ 206,997,402
Average	$68,999,230

That is, above four hundred per cent. more than in 1813 and 1814—and a premature decay has nevertheless been rapidly gaining ground on the nation by the prostration of its industry! What an important volume of political economy! How much more instructive than Condorcet,[31] Smith, Say, Ricardo, and the whole school of economists of this class!

*   *   *   *   *

---

*   Specie payments were continued till August, 1814.

CHAPTER VI

State of the country at the close of the war. Pernicious consequences to the manufacturers. Mr. Dallas's tariff. Rates reduced ten, twenty, and thirty per cent.

The war was closed under the most favourable auspices.[32] The country was every where prosperous. Inestimable manufacturing establishments, in which probably 60,000,000 of dollars were invested, were spread over the face of the land, and were diffusing happiness among thousands of industrious people. No man, woman, or child, able and willing to work, was unemployed. With almost every possible variety of soil and climate—and likewise with the three greatest staples in the world—cotton, wool, and iron—the first to an extent commensurate with our utmost wants, and a capacity to produce the other two—a sound policy would have rendered us more independent probably of foreign supplies, for all the comforts of life, than any other nation whatever.

Peace, nevertheless, was fraught with destruction to the hopes and happiness of a considerable portion of the manufacturers. The double duties had been imposed with a limitation to one year after the close of the war. And a tariff as a substitute was prepared by the secretary of the treasury, with duties fixed at the minimum rates which he thought calculated to afford them protection. On many of them, these rates were insufficient. Yet had his tariff been adopted, it would probably have saved the country forty or fifty millions of dollars—and prevented a large portion of the deep distress that pervades the land, and which is driving legislative bodies to the desperate measure of suspending the course of justice.* But a deep-rooted jealousy of manufacturers was entertained by many of the members of congress, on the ground of imputed extortion during the war: and the old hacknied themes of "taxing the many for the benefit of the few"—the country not being ripe for manufactures—wages being too high—the immensity of our back lands, &c. &c. &c. were still regarded as unanswerable arguments. In consequence of the combined operation of these causes, the rates were reduced on most of

---

* Measures of this description are adopted, or under consideration by four or five states. Others will probably follow the example. It is contagious.

the leading articles ten, fifteen, and in some cases thirty per cent. Every per cent. reduced was regarded by many of the members as so much clear gain to the country. Some of them appeared to consider manufacturers as a sort of common enemy,* with whom no terms ought to be observed; and there was no small number who were disciples of Colonel Taylor,[33] of Caroline county, Va.† who holds the broad, unqualified doctrine that every dollar paid as duty or bounty to encourage manufactures, is a dollar robbed out of the pockets of the farmers and planters! Wonderful statesman! Profound policy! How all the Sullys, and Colberts, and Frederics of Europe must "hide their diminished heads" when their practice is put in contrast with this grand system of political economy![34]

To convey a correct idea of the spirit that prevailed in that congress towards their manufacturing fellow citizens, I annex a statement of various articles, with the duties as reported by Mr. Dallas,[35] and as finally adopted.[36]

*   *   *   *   *

The various reductions of two and three per cent. evince the huckstering spirit that prevailed, utterly unworthy of the legislature of a great nation. Mr. Dallas made a difference of five and one-third per cent. between the two great articles, cottons and woollens, rating the former at thirty-three and a third, and the latter at twenty-eight, in consequence of our possessing a boundless supply of the raw material of the former, whereas that of the

---

*   Ex-Governor Wright, of Maryland, was among the most violent of the members. His jealousy and hostility were without the least disguise, and were carried to an extent that is hardly credible. A motion for a reduction of the duty on cottons having failed, he attempted to have it re-considered—on the ground that some of the members who voted in the majority, were concerned in the cotton manufacture!

†   Colonel Taylor is, I believe, a tobacco planter—and has never, in any of his plausible works, raised his voice against the extravagant duties on snuff and manufactured tobacco. On this tender topic he is silent as the grave. Yet a chapter on it would have come from him with great propriety. It is a subject with which he ought to be thoroughly acquainted. I venture to hint that he might with great advantage read the instructive fable of the lawyer's goring bull, which, with a suitable commentary on snuff and tobacco duties, might be very well prefixed as part of the prologomena to some of the amusing chapters of his Arator. It may not be amiss likewise to whisper gently in his ear, that even tobacco in the leaf is subject to fifteen per cent., which is exactly the same duty as that imposed on silks, linens, clocks, brazing copper, gold leaf, hair powder, printed books, prints, slates, starch, stuff and worsted shoes, sealing wax, thread stockings, &c. &c. Who, then, can reflect without astonishment, that this gentleman and Mr. Garnett take a lead in the opposition to the protection of manufactures, although their own rude produce is protected by the same duty as the above finished manufactures! After this, we may well ask, with amazement, "*what next?*" Be it what it may, it cannot surprise us.

latter was rather limited. After an ardent struggle, the duties were reduced, and both rated alike at twenty-five per cent. All the southern members voted for the reduction, except five, Messrs. Jackson, Marsh, and Newton, from Virginia, and Messrs. Calhoun and Mayrant, from South Carolina, who enjoy the melancholy consolation of having endeavoured to stem the storm. The cotton planters who united in the vote for the reduction, have dearly expiated their error, in rendering their fortunes and the prosperity of their country dependent upon the contingencies of foreign markets, instead of securing a large and constantly increasing market at home. This ought to be eternally sounded in their ears. Rarely has there been much greater impolicy—and rarely has impolicy been more severely and justly punished. They fondly and absurdly thought that thirty cents per lb. for cotton would last for ever.

The committee of commerce and manufactures; many of the most enlightened members of congress; and the agents of the manufacturers, strongly remonstrated against the reduction of duty; and, as with a spirit of prophecy, predicted the fatal consequences, not merely to the manufacturers, but to the nation. But they might as well have attempted to arrest the cataracts of Niagara with a mound of sand. Prejudice was deep, inveterate, and unassailable. It has never in times past had eyes nor ears; and, notwithstanding the elevation of character, and the superior illumination to which we fondly lay claim, we are not likely to offer to the admiring world an exception to the general rule. Of this unpalatable position our brief history, alas! affords too many damning proofs.

CHAPTER VII

Ruin of the manufacturers, and decay of their establishments. Pathetic and eloquent appeals to congress. Their contumelious and unfeeling neglect. Memorials neither read nor reported on. Revolting contrast between the fostering care bestowed by the Russian government on their manufacturers, and the unheeded sufferings of that class of citizens in the United States.

From year to year since that time, ruin spread among the manufacturers. A large portion of them have been reduced to bankruptcy, from ease and affluence. Many are now on the brink of it. Most of them had entered into the business during the war, under an impression, as I have already stated, that there was a sort of implied engagement on the part of the government, that having been found so useful in time of need, they would not be allowed to be crushed, afterwards. To what extent there was any foundation for this idea, I am unable to decide. Suffice it to say, that all the calculations predicated on it were wholly and lamentably disappointed. The strong arm of government, which alone could save them from the overwhelming influx of foreign manufactures, by which they were destroyed, was not interposed in their behalf. Noble establishments, the pride and ornament of the country, which might have been rendered sources of incalculable public and private wealth, and which Edward III, Henry IV, Frederic the Great, and Catharine II, would have saved at the expense of millions, if necessary, are mouldering to ruins. And to crown the whole, millions of capital, which had every claim to the protection of government, has become a dead and heavy loss to the proprietors.

At every stage of this awful progress, the devoted sufferers not only appealed to the justice, but threw themselves on the mercy of their representatives. The utmost powers of eloquence were exhausted in those appeals, some of which may be ranked among the proudest monuments of human talents.

In the second session of the fourteenth congress, 1816–17, there were above forty memorials presented to the house of representatives from manufacturers in different parts of the United States, and some of them, particularly that from Pittsburg, fraught with tales of ruin and destruction, that would have softened the heart of a Herod. *Not one of them was ever read in the house!* The Pittsburg memorial was, it is true, printed for the use of the members.

*   *   *   *   *

No description of mine could do justice to the force of some of these memorials. I shall therefore present a few short specimens of the facts and reasonings they placed before the eyes of congress, to enable the reader to form a correct estimate of the extremely culpable neglect of the voice of their constituents, displayed by that body. The applications were as ineffectual as those of the congress of 1774, to the ministers of George III, and were treated with as little ceremony.

From the Philadelphia memorial.
"*We regard with the most serious concern the critical and dangerous situation in which our manufactures are placed by the recent extravagant importations of rival articles;* which, owing to the great surplus of them, and to the pressure for money, are in many cases sold at such reduced prices, as to render it impossible for our manufactures to compete with them. We believe that with the interests of the manufacturers are connected the best interests of the nation—and that if the manufactures of the country are deprived of that support from the legislature of the United States, to which we think they are fairly entitled, *the evil will be felt not by us merely, but by the whole nation; as it will produce the inevitable consequence of an unfavourable balance of trade, whereby our country will be impoverished, and rendered tributary to foreign powers, whose interests are in direct hostility with ours.*"

*   *   *   *   *

These memorials were all referred to the committee of commerce and manufactures, which was then, so far as regarded them, a committee of oblivion. After a lapse of two months, that is, about the middle of February, a bill for the relief of the iron masters was reported—read twice—and suffered to die a natural death; having never been called up for a third reading. All the other memorials passed wholly unnoticed—and were never even reported on by the committee! What renders this procedure the more revolting, is, that some of them were from large bodies of men of the first respectability. That from New York was signed by the governor of the state, and other eminent characters. And, moreover, many of the petitioners had agents at Washington to advocate their claims.

The senate displayed the same culpable disregard of the applications, the sufferings, and the distresses of their fellow citizens, engaged in manufactures, as the house of representatives. They afforded no relief—nor did they even once consider the applications of the petitioners. But they paid somewhat more regard to decorum. The petitioners and memorialists had in succession *leave granted them to withdraw their papers*, on the motion of a member of the committee of commerce and manufactures!!

The practice of congress, it appears, is to read the heads of petitions; and then, without further enquiry, to refer them to the committee to which the business properly appertains. It cannot fail to excite the astonishment of the citizens of the United States to learn, that when they have found it necessary to meet and address their representatives, elected to guard their interests, and paid liberally for their services, those representatives do not condescend even to hear or read what are their grievances, or the mode of redress proposed! This is really so very indecorous and so shameful as to be absolutely incredible, if the fact were not established on good authority. Many of the most despotic princes of the East usually read the petitions of the meanest of their subjects. But under the free government of the United States, the great cities of New York, Philadelphia, Baltimore, and Boston, may combine together to seek relief from intolerable grievances; respectfully address their representatives; and have their prayers not merely rejected, but not even heard! The annals of legislation may, I am persuaded, be ransacked in vain for a parallel to this outrageous conduct.

When we reflect on the waste of time in frothy speeches on points of little importance—or on points of great importance, after the subject has been completely exhausted—and compare it with that economy of time which forbids the spending ten or fifteen minutes in reading a petition from a great city, the capital of a state, with a population of above a million of people, we are lost in astonishment at the introduction of a practice which so egregiously violates every rule of duty, decency, and propriety.

In the ensuing session, 1817–18, the same pathetic appeals to the justice, the humanity, the generosity, the public spirit of congress were made, and with little more effect.

Two unimportant acts alone on the subject of manufactures were passed at this session. One increasing the duties on iron, and the other on copper, saddlery, harness, cut glass, tacks, brads, sprigs, and Russia sheetings. But on the great and important articles of cotton and woollen goods there was no increase of duty. The additional duties on iron have been ineffectual—as the manufacture is at present in a most prostrate state.

Allegiance and protection are reciprocal duties. To withhold the one forfeits the claim to the other. And it is due to justice to state, that the manufacturers of the United States, who, with their families and persons of every description depending on them, amount to 1,500,000 souls—with a capital of $150,000,000, and producing probably $350,000,000 per annum, have not had that protection from the government to which their numbers and their importance give them so fair a claim.

A large portion of mankind, probably, even in this country, three-fourths, have no property but in the labour of their hands. To so many of them as are divested of this by an erroneous policy, *one of the grand objects of government is destroyed*—And therefore, so far as property is concerned, their situation is no better than that of the subjects of despotism.

I go further: *The situation of the manufacturing capitalist in the United States is incomparably worse than that of the manufacturing subjects of the monarchs of Europe*, so far as regards the protection of property.

This strong expression will excite the surprize of some superficial readers. But it is a crisis that demands a bold expression of truth. And the assertion need not be retracted or qualified. Here is the proof. Let Mr. Garnett, or Mr. Pegram,[37] or any of the agricultural delegates refute it. Let us suppose a subject of Russia,* to invest a capital of one hundred thousand dollars in a manufacture of calicoes. He has no foreign competitor to dread. The fostering care of the government watches over him with the tenderness of a parent. He has loans if necessary. Bounties are also occasionally afforded. No combination of foreign rivals can operate his destruction. The domestic market is secured to him, with no other than the fair and legitimate competition of his fellow subjects, which always guards the rest of the nation against imposition. His plans arrive at maturity. He reaps the rich reward of his talents, his time, his industry, his capital. He gives support to hundreds, perhaps thousands, and is daily adding to the wealth, power, resources, and independence of the country which affords him full protection; and amply repays her kindness.

Let us turn from this delightful picture of fostering and tender care, under a despotism, to the wretched, depressed, and vilified American capitalist, under a government which in its principles is really and truly the best that ever existed. He invests one hundred thousand dollars in a similar establishment; engages hundreds of people in a useful and profitable manufacture; finally conquers all the various difficulties that new undertakings have to encounter; and brings his fabrics to market, in the hope of that reward to which industry, capital, and talent have so fair a claim. Alas! he has to meet not only the competition of his fellow citizens, but of all the manufacturing world. While he is excluded absolutely by prohibition, or virtually by prohibitory duties, from nearly all the markets in Europe, and indeed elsewhere, the East Indies,

---

* The reasoning applies equally to France, England, and Austria.

England, France, and Italy divide the home market with him, which is crowded with cargoes of similar articles, by the cupidity or the distresses, but as often by the stratagems, of foreign manufacturers, in order to overwhelm him, and secure the market ultimately to themselves. Their goods are sent to vendue, and sacrificed below prime cost in Europe. His cannot find a market, but at a sacrifice which ruins him. He implores relief from his unfeeling countrymen. But he implores in vain. Their hearts are steeled against his sufferings. They meet all his complaints, all his prayers, with trite common places about "taxing the many for the benefit of the few, free trade," &c. &c.—and he is charged with extortion by men who for thirty successive years received from him and his brethren extravagant prices for all their productions! He becomes bankrupt, and dies of a broken heart. His family, born to high expectations, are reduced to a state of dependence. His workmen are driven to idleness and want, and exposed to the lures of guilt. The state is deprived of a useful citizen, who might have added to her "*wealth, power, and resources.*"—His fate operates as a beacon to others, to beware of his career—And the wealth of the nation is exhausted to pay for foreign articles, substitutes for which he could have furnished of far better quality, and, though nominally dearer, in reality cheaper. This is the policy, and these are its consequences, advocated by the agriculturists of Virginia!! And this is the deleterious policy, fraught with destruction to the happiness of a large portion of its citizens, that is pursued by the United States of America.

Hundreds of capitalists throughout this country—thousands of workmen—millions of destroyed capital—and the general impoverishment of the nation, bear testimony to the correctness of this hideous portrait, so disgraceful to our country, such a libel on its mistaken policy.

To such a man what does it signify by what name you call the government? It is, you say, a republic. True. But, alas! he is ruined by its impolicy. The most despotic government in the world could do no more than ruin him. And some of them, it appears, would have protected him. Therefore, I repeat, so far as property is concerned, the difference is against the United States. In fact, the better the form of government, the more grievous his distress. Under a despotism "to suffer and submit" would be "his charter." But to be mocked and deluded with the promise of equal rights and equal protection under a free government, and unfeelingly consigned to destruction by his own fellow citizens, and representatives, by the men whom he has clothed with the power to destroy him—barbs the dart with tenfold keenness.

Having submitted this portrait to the citizens of the United States, I ask, whether there be a greater contrast between the conduct of a fond mother towards her only and darling child—and that of a rigorous step-mother, towards a stepchild, which interferes with her views towards her own offspring, than there is between the treatment of manufacturers in Russia and in the United States?

If these views be unpalatable, the fault is not mine. Let those answer for them, who have rendered their exposure necessary. Their truth can be judicially proved.

The situation of a very considerable portion of our citizens, is far worse than in the colonial state. They had then no competitors in the markets of their country but their fellow subjects of Great Britain. Now they have competitors from almost every part of Europe and from the East Indies. The case of the paper makers affords a striking illustration of this position. One-half of them in the middle states are ruined—not by the importation of British paper, of which little comes to this market—but by French and Italian, with which our markets were deluged for two or three years after the war.

CHAPTER VIII

Dilatory mode of proceeding in Congress. Lamentable waste of time. Statement of the progress of bills. Eighty two signed in one day! and four hundred and twenty in eleven! Unfeeling treatment of Gen. Stark. Culpable attention to punctilio. Rapid movement of compensation bill.

To every man interested in the honour and prosperity of the country, it is a subject of deep regret to reflect on the mode in which the public business is managed in and by congress. It is among the sources of the distress and embarrassment of our affairs, and requires an early and radical remedy. While in session, a considerable proportion of the members are employed in chatting—writing letters to their friends, or reading letters or newspapers. They pay little or no attention to the arguments of the speakers, except to those of a few of distinguished talents. To some of the orators, however, this is no great disappointment; as their speeches are too often made for the newspapers, and to display their talents to their constituents.

But the lamentable waste of time by the spirit of procrastination in the early part of the session, and by never-ending speechifying throughout its continuance, is the greatest evil, and is discreditable to congress and highly pernicious to the public service. There is in almost every session some subject of real or factitious importance, on which every member capable of speaking thinks himself bound to harangue, and to "keep the floor," for two, three, four, five or six hours. The merits of the speeches are generally measured by the length of time they occupy. They are all, to judge by the puffs in the newspapers, elegant, wonderful, powerful, admirable, excellent, inimitable.

In most cases, it will be found, as is perfectly natural, that the early speeches, on each side, particularly if by men of talents, exhaust the subject; and that those which follow them, do little more than retail the arguments previously advanced. It surely requires no small disregard of decorum for a member to occupy the time of a public body, to whose care are entrusted the concerns of a great nation, with such fatiguing repetitions.

The debate on the repeal of the compensation act[38] cost some weeks; that on the Seminole War,[39] fills six hundred octavo pages; which, if divested of the duplications, triplications, and quadruplications, the rhetorical flourishes, and extraneous matter, would be reduced to two hundred—perhaps to one hundred and fifty. The Missouri question[10] will probably fill from eight hundred to one thousand pages. Some of the prologues to these speeches are, as was humourously observed by a member long since, like "sale coats," calculated to suit almost any other subject equally well. And during this miserable waste of time, excitement of angry passions, and seditious threats of separation, there is a total suspension of the business of the nation, whose blood flows at every pore—whose revenues are failing—whose manufactures are paralized—of whose commerce one-half is annihilated—whose merchants and manufacturers are daily swallowing up in the vortex of bankruptcy—whose great staples have fallen in price at least thirty per cent.—and which exhibits in every direction most appalling scenes of calamity and distress!

Some idea may be formed of the mode in which the business of this nation is conducted by its legislature, from the following chronological statement of the periods at which the acts of successive sessions were approved by the presidents. Between their passage in the two houses and the dates of the presidents' signatures, there may be some few days difference, for which the reader will make allowance. But be that allowance what it may, it cannot remove the accusation of a most ruinous waste of time, and a most culpable and shameful procrastination of public business in congress.

*   *   *   *   *

This system of procrastination has been coeval with the government. I am informed by a gentleman of veracity, that General Washington, when an extraordinary number of acts were presented to him on the last day of a session, more than he could correctly decide upon, has expressed a strong and most marked disapprobation of so incorrect a procedure.

Analysis.

Sessions of congress		9
Duration		months 39 ½
Acts passed		988
Of which were signed in eleven days		<u>420</u>
	Viz.	
1812	July 6th	29
1813	March 3d	23
	August 3d	24
1814	April 18th	34
1815	March 3d	31

1816	April 26th, 27th and 29th	90
1817	March 3d	82
1818	April 20th	52
1819	March 3d	<u>55</u>
Acts signed in eleven days		<u>420</u>

Thus it appears that in *three years and three months* there were 568 acts signed—and in *eleven* days, as I have stated, 420!! Wonderful system of legislation!

No small share of the censure due to the procrastination of the public business, so visible in the above proceedings, justly attaches to the speaker for the time being. He ought to keep a docket of the business brought before the house, and urge committees to perform their duty. Certain days should be appointed to make reports, which ought then to be called for. If not ready, others should be fixed. And whenever the public business is unnecessarily or wantonly procrastinated, his duty requires the use of strong animadversion. This arrangement would be productive of the most salutary consequences. But for want of this or some other system, a very large portion of every session is literally thrown away. And so much of the business is crowded together at the close, that it is impossible to concoct it properly. Ever since the organization of the government, three-fourths of all the important acts have been passed within the last week or ten days of each session.

Is it then surprising that the national business is egregiously ill-managed? That the reiterated requests of so large portion of our citizens, for a bankrupt and other salutary acts, are of no avail?—How is it possible for the members—how is it possible for a president—to discharge their respective duties conscientiously, with such a system? Can any powers short of superhuman enable the latter to decide on the justice, the propriety, the constitutionality of twenty, thirty, forty, fifty, sixty, seventy, or eighty acts in one or two days? Is not this making a mere mockery of legislation?

Two, three, and sometimes four months are drawled away in the early part of the session—with three, four, six, eight, ten or twelve acts—and afterwards all the business is hurried through with indecent haste. In the one portion of the time, the progress resembles that of the snail or the sloth—in the other, that of the high mettled racer. In fact and in truth, if Congress desired to bring republican government into disgrace, to render it a bye-word and a reproach, it would not be very easy to devise a plan more admirably calculated for the purpose than a considerable part of their proceedings.

One ruinous consequence attending the system pursued, is, that at the close of every session, some of the most important bills are necessarily postponed.

It is frequently said in justification of the procrastination of congress, and the little business that is executed in the early part of the session, that the committees are employed in digesting and preparing their reports. It is obvious, that this must require time. But whoever considers the nature of a large portion of the business that is discussed in that body, will be convinced that it might be dispatched in a fifth part of the time it occupies.

Among the acts hurried through at the close of the session, there are frequently some, and among them private ones, which have "dragged their slow length along" for months before, and which might as readily be decided on in a week as in six months. I annex the dates of introduction and of signature of a few to exemplify this.

	Reported	Signed
Act to divide the state of Pennsylvania into districts,	1818. Feb. 4	April 20
Act for publication of laws,	Jan. 16	April 20
Act for relief of B. Birdsall,	Jan. 27	April 20
Act for incorporating Columbian Institute,	Feb. 3	April 20
Act for relief of Gen. Brown,	Feb. 9	April 18
Act for relief of T. & J. Clifford	Jan. 20	April 20

The bill for the relief of T. & J. Clifford, which was three months on its passage through the houses, contains about twenty lines, and was for the remission of duties paid on articles not subject to duty. Three days would have answered as well for the discussion as seven years. Such is the case with half the bills that are crowded together at the last day of the session.

It may not be uninteresting to make a few further extracts from the journals, shedding additional light on this important subject.

1819. April 18. "Engrossed bills of the following titles (*nine in number*) were severally read a third time and passed."

April 20. "Bills from the senate of the following titles (*ten in number*) were severally read a third time and passed."

Eodem Die. "A message from the senate that they have passed bills of this house of the following titles, to wit—(*eighteen in number.*)"

By a careful search through the journals of different sessions, we might find three or four hundred bills, thus bundled together, and hastily read off, ten or a dozen en suite.

The case of General Stark[11] deserves to be put on record, to corroborate some of the opinions offered in this chapter.

On the 6th of March, 1818, a petition was presented by this old veteran, representing his necessitous circumstances, and praying that the bounty of the national government might be extended to him, in the decline of life, in compensation of his faithful services in defence of his country. It was referred to a committee, who reported a bill on the 9th, which was read the first and second time on that day. *It then lay over untouched for above five weeks, till Saturday the 18th of April*, when it was passed and sent to the senate, where it was read and referred to the committee on pensions, who reported it on that day without amendments. It was read the third time on Monday the 20th, in committee of the whole, and agreed to *with amendments*. It being against a rule of the senate to pass a bill under those circumstances, on that same day, Mr. Fromentin[12] moved that the rule be dispensed with. *But this motion was unfeelingly rejected.* And as the session was closed that day, the bill of course was lost; and the venerable old hero, about ninety years of age, and bending over the grave, was disappointed at that time of receiving the pittance intended for him. The importance of his victory at Bennington, which led to those all-important events, the battle of Saratoga and the capture of General Burgoyne, which stand conspicuous among the proudest triumphs of the Revolutionary War, is so deeply impressed on the public mind, that every good man in the nation felt deep regret at this very ill-timed and ungracious punctilio.

The compensation bill, which was to render *members of congress salary officers, at the rate of* 1500 *dollars per annum*, passed by a former congress, forms a proper contrast to the bill in favour of General Stark.

It was read the first and second time in the house of representatives	March 6th, 1815.
Read a third time and passed	9th
Read first time in senate	11th
Second time	12th
Third time and passed	14th
Laid before the president	18th
Approved same day.	

What wonderful economy of time!

Thus a bill for their own benefit which introduced a novel principle into the country, in twelve days passed through all its stages from its inception to the presidential approbation!!

What a reproach to congress arises from a contrast of this case with that of the veteran Stark! How wonderfully their personal interest accelerated their movements!

The citizens of the United States, however, are answerable for a large portion of the derelictions of congress. Most of the members are ambitious of popularity; which forms one of the principal inducements to seek a seat in that body. And the utter inattention too generally displayed by the citizens to the conduct of their representatives, induces a degree of indifference towards the interests and wishes of the constituents. A more frequent call for the yeas and nays, by those members who are sincerely desirous of discharging their duty, and of having the public business punctually attended to, together with a publication of lists of votes on all important questions, previous to elections, would operate powerfully on the feelings of the members. If every member whose votes militated with the substantial interests of his country, were sure to be discarded, as he ought to be, on the day of election, the proceedings of congress would exhibit a very different appearance from what they do at present.

CHAPTER IX

Attempts to prove the state of affairs prosperous. Their fallacy established. Destruction of industry in Philadelphia and Pittsburg. Awful situation of Pennsylvania. 14,537 suits for debt, and 10,326 judgments confessed in the year 1819. Depreciation of real estate 115,544,629 dollars.

For a considerable time elaborate efforts were made to prove that the great mass of our citizens were highly prosperous. Even official messages, at no very distant day, announced this idea. But the veil that obscured the appalling vision of public distress is removed, and there is now no diversity of sentiment on the subject. Bankruptcy of banks—individual ruin—and sheriffs' sales to an extent never known before—the idleness of thousands of those who have no property but in the labour of their hands—resolutions of town meetings—memorials and petitions from almost every part of the middle and eastern states—messages of governors—deliberate instructions of the representative bodies in some of the states—*acts of legislatures, suspending the collection of debts*—and, to close the long train of calamity, the emigration of American citizens to a Spanish colony,[13] seeking an asylum from the misery they suffer in their own country—all distinctly proclaim a deplorable state of society, which fully evinces a radical unsoundness in our policy, loudly and imperiously demanding as radical a remedy. No temporizing expedients will suffice. Nothing short of a complete and permanent protection of the national industry, so as to enable us *to reduce our demands from Europe, within our means of payment,* will arrest us in the career of impoverishment—and enable us to regain the ground we have unhappily lost—and take that high and commanding stand among nations, which nature and nature's God, by the transcendent advantages bestowed on us, intended we should enjoy—advantages which for five years we have so prodigally squandered.

———————

Although the prevailing depression and distress are generally well known, yet few are fully acquainted with their extreme intensity. Indeed, it is at all times difficult and scarcely possible to realize, from general description, the extent of suffering which mankind endure—whether by war, famine, pestilence, or want of employment. In the last case, it would be necessary to traverse by-lanes and alleys—to ascend to garrets—or descend to cellars—to behold the afflicted father, after having pawned his clothes and furniture, destitute of money and credit to support his famishing wife and children—his proud spirit struggling between the heart-rending alternatives of allowing them to suffer under hunger and thirst, or else sinking to apply to the over-seers of the poor—to ask alms in the street—or to have recourse to soup-houses for relief.[*] These are afflicting realities, with which, I hope, for the honour of human nature, the presidents and delegates of agricultural societies, who enter the list to prevent the relief of their fellow citizens, and perpetuate their sufferings, are wholly unacquainted.

I cannot here enter into particulars of the awful scenes that overspread the face of the land, and shall confine myself to a slight sketch of the lamentable devastation of national prosperity and private happiness, experienced in Philadelphia and Pittsburg, which so many worthy, but mistaken men are labouring to perpetuate.

By an investigation ordered during last autumn by a town meeting of the citizens of Philadelphia, and conducted by gentlemen of respectability, it appears, so great was the decay of manufacturing industry, that in only thirty out of fifty-six branches of business there were actually 7728 persons less employed in 1819 than in 1816, whose wages amounted to $ 2,366,935. No returns were procured from twenty-six branches.

$$*\quad*\quad*\quad*\quad*$$

Assuming only half the number, in these twenty-six, that were in the other thirty, the aggregate would be 11,592—and, were only one woman or child dependent on each person, the whole, out of a population of about one hundred and twenty thousand,

Would amount to	persons	23,184
Whose wages would be		$ 3,550,402
And allowing the work to be double the wages,		
which is a moderate calculation, the value would be		$ 7,100,804
lost in a single city in one year!		

---

[*] Some idea may be formed of the state of our cities, from the circumstance, that in Baltimore, there are no less than twelve stations for distributing soup tickets. In Philadelphia, the distribution is very great, at the rate of a pint to each person.

Let us now survey Pittsburg, where we shall behold a similar scene of devastation. This city in 1815, contained about six thousand inhabitants. It then exhibited as exhilarating a scene of industry, prosperity and happiness, as any place in the world. Its immense local advantages, seated at the confluence of two noble rivers, forming the majestic Ohio; its boundless supplies of coal; and the very laudable enterprize of its inhabitants, had for a long time rendered it the emporium of the western world. But, alas! the immoderate influx of foreign manufactures poured in there shortly after the peace, produced a most calamitous reverse. The operations of the hammer, the hatchet, the shuttle, the spindle, the loom, ceased in a great degree. Noble establishments, which reflected honour on the nation, were closed; the proprietors ruined; the workmen discharged; a blight and a blast overspread the face of the city; and the circumjacent country, which had shared in its prosperity, now equally partook of its decline.

By a recent and minute investigation, conducted by citizens of high standing, the following appeared to be the—

Actual state of the city of Pittsburg.

Persons deprived of employment, or less employed in 1819 than in 1816	1288
Supposing only one woman or child depending on each of the above	1288
It would amount to	2576
The amount of work done in 1816 was	$ 2,617,833
In 1819	832,000
Loss to Pittsburg	1,785,833
Loss to Philadelphia, as before,	7,100,804
Annual loss in two cities in one state	$ 8,886,637

When the other cities and towns throughout the union, where similar devastation has occurred, are taken into view, it will not be an unreasonable calculation to presume it six-fold elsewhere: but to avoid cavil, I will only suppose it treble—

Which will amount to	$ 26,659,911
Philadelphia and Pittsburg	8,886,637
Total loss of industry	$ 35,546,548

By the wretched policy of fostering foreign manufactures and manufacturers, and foreign governments; buying cheap bargains abroad, and consigning our own citizens to bankruptcy and beggary!

With these overwhelming facts staring us in the face, is it not insanity to be debating about the causes of the existing distress? Who can entertain a doubt as to the grand and primary cause? Is it not as plain as "the hand writing on the wall?" Does it not clearly arise from the destruction of national industry? What! an annual loss in two cities, containing about 125,000 inhabitants, of nearly nine millions of dollars, and proportionable losses almost every where else! Such a course, steadily continued, would impoverish China more rapidly than she has accumulated her immense treasures. It is not therefore wonderful that it has, in a few years impoverished a nation whose sole patrimony was her industry.

Some public documents have recently appeared, which prove the distress of the country far more intense and extensive than had been previously conceived. A committee of the senate of Pennsylvania, appointed to enquire into the extent and causes of the general distress, addressed circulars to all the prothonotaries and sheriffs in the state, whence they collected the following awful facts:

The number of actions brought for debt in the year 1819, were	14,537
The number of judgments confessed	10,326
Exclusive of those before justices of the peace, about half the number:	
Imprisonments for debt in the city and county of Philadelphia	1,808
In Lancaster county	221
In Alleghany county	286

A report made to the house of representatives, by a committee appointed for the same purpose as that in the senate, appears to estimate the depreciation of the real estate in Pennsylvania at one-third of the value ascertained by the United States assessment in 1815, which was $ 316,633,889—of course the depreciation is $ 115,544,629.

A memorial referred to in another report, states—

"That embarrassment is universal; that the sordid and avaricious are acquiring the sacrificed property of the liberal and industrious; that so much property is exposed to sale under execution, that buyers cannot be had to pay more for it than the fees of office."

Would to God, that this affecting picture could be placed in large characters in Congress Hall, in the president's house, and in the offices of the secretaries of state and the treasury, that they might be led to take the necessary measures as early as possible to relieve such sufferings.

This, let it be observed, is far from the whole of the evil. The comparison is only a retrospective one—to shew the precipitous descent we have made from a towering height. Let us now see the point to which we might, and by a proper policy would, have arrived. In five years, from 1810 to 1815, as already stated, the manufacture of cotton increased from 10,000 to 90,000 bales, or 270,000,000 lbs. The other manufactures of the country increased very considerably, but not in the same proportion.

By the statements of the marshals, and the calculations of Mr. Coxe,[11] a gentleman perfectly competent to this service, it appears that the manufactures of the United States in 1810, amounted to 172,000,000 dollars.

Let us suppose that in place of a multiplication nine-fold, such as took place in the cotton branch between 1810 and 1815, the increase was only double, it follows, that in 1815, the whole of our manufactures must have amounted to nearly 350,000,000 dollars.

Inferring from past experience, they would, under an efficient protection by the government, have increased from 1815 to 1820, fifty per cent and of course would now be above 500,000,000 dollars.

It is impossible to pursue this train of reflexion, and compare what we might be, with what we are, without sensations of the keenest distress, and a clear conviction of the radical unsoundness of a policy, which has in a few years produced so much destruction of happiness and prosperity.

CHAPTER X

Since public attention has been drawn to explore the causes of the existing evils, some of our citizens have ascribed them to the abuses of banking, and others to "*the transition from a state of war to a state of peace*"—overlooking the real cause, the destruction of the national industry—and likewise overlooking the strong fact, that all nations have fallen to decay, in proportion as they abandoned, and have prospered in proportion as they protected, the industry of their people.

Let us briefly examine both of these alleged causes of distress.

It is impossible to defend the legislative bodies, who incorporated such hosts of banks at once. They are deserving of the most unqualified censure; and it is to be regretted that they cannot be rendered individually responsible for the consequences. But the mischief that has arisen from those banks, has been greatly overrated. I submit a few facts and reflexions on the subject.

With the state of Pennsylvania I am more familiar than with any of the others; and shall therefore found my reasoning on the system pursued here. It will apply, *mutatis mutandis*, to all those which have carried banking to excess.

In 1814, the legislature of this state incorporated forty-one banks, of which only thirty-seven went into operation—of these I present a view—

	Capital authorized.	*Capital paid in.*
Thirty-three country banks	$ 12,665,000	$ 5,294,238
Four city banks	3,500,000	2,134,000
	$ 16,165,000	$ 7,428,238

Two reports, recently made to the legislature of Pennsylvania, convey an idea that the capital of these banks was much greater than it really was.

"The people of Pennsylvania, during an expensive war, and in the midst of great embarrassments, established forty-one new banks, *with a capital of* 17,500,000 *dollars* —and authority to issue bank notes to double that amount."*

"A bill, authorizing the incorporation of forty-one banking institutions, *with capitals amounting to upwards of* 17,000,000 *dollars*, was passed by a large majority."†

Several of them had been in operation previous to the act of incorporation— particularly the Commercial Bank in Philadelphia, with a capital of 1,000,000 dollars, and others with probably capitals of $ 750,000: so that the addition then made to the banking capital of the state was only about 5,700,000 dollars. It is perfectly obvious, that in calculating the effects produced by these banks, we must have reference not to the capital *authorized*—but to that actually *paid in.*

Had every one of these banks been fraudulently conducted, and become bankrupt, would it account for the excessive distresses of the state? It would be idle to pretend it. The circumstance would have produced great temporary embarrassment—but our citizens would soon have recovered, had their industry been protected.

The population of the state is above 1,200,000. Its manufactures in 1810, as stated by Mr. Coxe,[15] were 32,000,000 of dollars—and had probably risen in 1814, to 45,000,000. Its domestic exports for the last three years, have been above 20,000,000, or nearly 7,000,000 per annum. Now, can it be believed that the specified increase of banking capital in a state with such great resources, could have produced such ruinous consequences? Surely not.

In cases of great calamities, arising from embargoes, blockades, unexpected war, or peace, New York and Philadelphia have each suffered nearly as much loss as the whole capital of all those banks, and speedily revived like the Phœnix from her ashes.

Let it be observed, that after deducting the capitals of—

The Bank of Lancaster‡	$ 600,000
Marietta	239,430
Pittsburg	316,585
Reading	299,440
Easton	211,830
	$ 1,667,285

The remaining country banks only average about 125,000 dollars each. Some of them operate in a space, of which the diameter is thirty, forty, or fifty miles.

---

*   Report to the house of representatives.
†   Report to the senate.
‡   Four of these towns are places of importance, and carry on trade very extensively.

Surely the doctor's apprentice, who, finding a saddle under his patient's bed, ascribed his illness to his having devoured a horse, was not much more ludicrously in error, than those who ascribe the whole or even the chief part of the sufferings of the state to this cause.

Let it be distinctly understood that I freely admit that some of those banks have done very great mischief, and that several have been improperly conducted. But had the industry of the state been protected, and trade flourished, the great mass of them would have gone on prosperously, and the whole would not have produced one-tenth part of the injury that has resulted from those that have been ill-managed.

Before I quit this subject, let me observe, that the greater portion by far of these banks have been, I believe, fairly and honourably conducted: and that little inconvenience was felt by or from any of them, from the time of resuming specie payments, till of late, when the unceasing drain of specie exhausted them of the pabulum on which banks are supported, and obliged them to diminish their issues, and to press on their debtors, of whom many were ruined. Notwithstanding all their efforts, several of the banks have been obliged to stop payment.

The idea that the public distresses have been a necessary consequence of "*the transition to a state of peace,*" is still more extravagant. To Great Britain the transition was truly formidable. She had by her orders in council, blockades, and fleets, engrossed the supply of a large portion of the continent of Europe, which, on the return of peace, relied on itself, and therefore deprived her of various profitable markets. But I ask any man of common sense, how this applies to our case? Were we, at the treaty of Ghent, excluded from any foreign markets which we enjoyed during our short war? Surely not. Far from having our markets circumscribed by "*the transition to a state of peace,*" they were greatly enlarged. In 1815, our exports were, as appears below, seven hundred per cent more than in 1814, and treble in the three entire years subsequent to the peace, what they were in the three preceding years.

Domestic Exports from the United States.

1812	$ 30,032,109	1815	$ 45,974,403
1813	25,008,152	1816	64,781,896
1814	6,782,272	1817	68,313,500
	61,822,533		179,069,799
Average	20,607,511	Average	59,689,933

That the "*transition,*" from an average export of $20,000,000, to nearly $60,000,000, can account for the lamentable and precipitous fall we have experienced, no person of candour will pretend. It would be equally wise to assert, that a man was ruined by raising his income from two thousand dollars to six thousand per annum. If, however, he renounced his industry, and, when he only trebled his income, increased his expenses six fold, then his ruin would be as easily accounted for, as the lamentable picture this country exhibits.

I was, however, in error. The "*transition*" did produce the effect. Should it be asked how? I reply—*The war protected the domestic industry of the nation.*—It throve and prospered under that safeguard, which the peace tore down *de fonds en comble*. And congress, whose imperious and paramount duty it was to step in, and replace the protection, failed of that duty. The consequences were foretold. The industry of the country was laid prostrate—its circulating medium drained away—its resources exhausted—and distress overspread the face of the land. But it is too farcical for argument to assert that a peace which trebled our exports, necessarily brought on a state of distress and impoverishment, which is chargeable wholly to our shortsighted policy.

CHAPTER XI

The everlasting complaint of "taxing the many for the benefit of the few." *Fallacy and injustice of it. Amount of impost for fourteen years. For the year* 1818. *Impost for the protection of agriculture in that year above* 4,500,000 *dollars.*

The changes[16] have been rung throughout the United States, since the commencement of the government, on the immensity of the favours conferred on the manufacturers, in point of protection—their insatiable temper—the impossibility of satisfying them—and the dreadful injustice of "taxing the many for the benefit of the few," which has been used as a sort of war whoop for exciting all the base passions of avarice and selfishness in battle array against those to whom the tax is supposed to be paid.

It rarely happens, in private life, that vociferous claims for gratitude can stand the test of enquiry. When weighed in the balance of justice and truth, they are uniformly found wanting. And as a public is an aggregation of individuals, acted upon by the same views, and liable to the same and greater errors, it would be extraordinary, if similar claims of collections of people were not found to rest on as sandy a foundation.

To investigate the correctness of this everlasting theme has become a duty. To place the subject on its true ground, will dispel a dense mist of error and delusion with which it is enveloped. If the debt can be paid, let it, in the name of heaven, be discharged, and let us commence *de novo*. If it be beyond the power of payment, let the delinquent parties take the benefit of the insolvent act, and exonerate themselves from a load, by which they are crushed as between "the upper and the nether millstone."

The expenses of our government require revenues, which have risen from 4,000,000 to 27,000,000 dollars per annum. Provision must be made for this sum in one or all of three modes—by excise—direct taxes—or customs. The first is universally abhorred here. The second are almost equally obnoxious. It therefore follows, that the impost is the next and grand resource. The sum required must be raised without regard to manufactures or manufacturers—and indeed if there were not a manufacturer in the country. It is out of the power of the government to raise the necessary revenue without laying considerable duties on manufactures—as all other articles, such as tea, sugar, wines, coffee, are dutied as high as they will bear. Therefore the manufacturers, who, let it be observed, *bear their own share of all these duties of every description*, are under no obligation of gratitude whatever for them.

But let us examine the subject more closely. Let us suppose that these duties had been laid solely to serve the manufacturers, without any regard to the emergencies of government—and that the proceeds had been reserved in the treasury. Let us see what would be the extent of the mighty boon.

The whole of this enormous and inextinguishable debt is comprised in the duties imposed on such foreign merchandize as would rival our own manufactures. The utmost cravings on the score of gratitude will not dare to charge to the account the duties on sugar, coffee, tea, wine, salt, &c.

The entire impost for fourteen years, from 1801 to 1814, inclusive, was $ 159,762,602[*]

On Spirits	$ 25,441,543	
Wines	7,646,476	
Sugar	19,455,110	
Salt	4,057,047	
Teas	8,565,874	
Coffee	10,777,113	
Molasses	4,980,650	
Sundry articles	7,470,317[a]	
		88,434,130[†]
Leaving a balance of		$ 71,328,472
[a]To which add half of the last item of sundries,		
as probably on manufactures		3,735,158
Total		$ 75,063,630

This is the whole amount levied on *manufactures* of every kind, for fourteen years, being about five millions and a half per annum!

The white population of that period averaged probably about 7,000,000. Of course the duties paid *on manufactures* amounted to about eighty cents per head! And this is the sum and substance of the "*taxes levied on the many by the few*" and the immense favours conferred on "the few" by "the many!" which have furnished matter for so many tedious speeches in congress, tiresome declarations at public meetings, and verbose newspaper essays and paragraphs without end or number; with which "the welkin has rung"—and which,

---

[*]   Seybert, 454.
[†]   Idem, 398 to 405.

I repeat, have called into activity all the base passions of our nature, and excited a deadly hostility in the minds of one portion of our citizens against another. The clamour would have been contemptible, had the whole sum been granted as an alms, or through generosity. But when it is considered that every dollar of this sum has been raised for the mere purpose of revenue, language cannot do justice to the feelings the affair is calculated to excite.

I shall now consider the subject at a more recent period.

The whole amount of duties ad valorem for 1818, was	$ 11,947,260
To which add for manufactures of lead, iron, and steel; glass bottles, copperas, allum, and other articles subject to specific duties	694,493
Total on manufactures	12,641,753
A large portion of those duties was levied on silks, high-priced cambrics and muslins, gauzes, fine linens, lace shawls, lace veils, pearls, embroidery, gold lace, &c. &c. which our citizens do not manufacture. These duties are by no means chargeable to the protection of manufactures—suppose	1,500,000
Balance of impost supposed for protection of manufactures	$ 11,141,753
Against this we must set off all the duties levied for the protection of agriculture, viz.	
On spirits, for the encouragement of the culture of grain, and the protection of the peach brandies, rye whiskey, &c. of the farmers	$ 2,646,186
Sugar	1,508,892
Cotton	126,542
Hemp	148,873
Indigo	19,049
Coals	46,091
Cheese	16,694
Impost for protection of agriculture	$ 4,572,327
Leaving a balance against the manufacturers of	$ 6,569,426

When we consider how frugal and economical the great body of our farmers are in the eastern, middle, and western states; how few of them, comparatively speaking, purchase imported articles, except groceries; and how expensively the inhabitants of our cities and towns live in general; it will appear more than probable, that of the goods on which the above duties are collected, not nearly one-half are consumed by farmers.

A view of the preceding tables and statements affords the following results—

1. That the whole amount of the duties levied on manufactured articles, of every description, for the year 1818, having been only about 12,600,000 dollars, and the population of the United States at present being about 10,000,000, of whom probably eight are white, the average is only about one dollar and a half for the white population.
2. That of this amount about one-eighth part is levied on articles not interfering with our manufactures.
3. That there are duties levied in favour of agriculture equal in amount to more than a third part of those levied on manufactures.
4. That when the latter duties are set off against those levied for the protection of manufactures, the remainder is about seventy-five cents for each free person in the United States.
5. That probably more than half of the goods on which those duties are levied, are consumed in towns and cities—and of course that the amount paid by the farmers and planters is not above sixty cents per head, notwithstanding the senseless and illiberal clamour excited on the subject.
6. That were all the duties on manufactured articles removed, the burdens of the community would not be diminished a single dollar; as there is no more revenue raised than the emergencies of the government require, and of course some other tax or duty must be devised.

CHAPTER XII

Immense advantages enjoyed by the farmers and planters for nearly thirty years, viz. a domestic monopoly—and excellent foreign markets. Exorbitant prices of the necessaries of life. Great extent of the domestic market. Internal trade of the United States.

For nearly thirty years, the farmers and planters of this country enjoyed a high degree of prosperity. They had almost universally excellent foreign markets for all their productions—and, from the commencement of the government, have had a monopoly of the domestic market, having had the exclusive supply of the manufacturers, who have not consumed of foreign vegetables, bread-stuffs, butcher's meat, fowls, fuel or any other of the productions of agriculture, to the amount of one per cent. per annum. It is, nevertheless, a fact, however incredible, that those citizens, enjoying this important domestic monopoly, and having laid very high duties on all the articles that interfere with their interests, as snuff, tobacco, cotton, hemp, cheese, coals, &c.; accuse their manufacturing fellow citizens as monopolists; who are not only shut out of nearly all the foreign markets in the world by prohibitions and prohibitory duties; but, even in their own markets are exposed to, and supplanted by, foreign adventurers of all countries!!! It is difficult to conceive of a more unjust charge, or one that comes with a worse grace from the accusers.

During this long period, the farmers sold in all cases at high, and in many at most exorbitant prices. To instance a few articles, in order to illustrate the remark: we paid them ten and twelve, and thirteen dollars a barrel for flour—twelve to eighteen cents per lb. for beef and pork—twelve to fourteen cents for tobacco—fifteen to thirty cents for cotton; and in the same proportion for all their other productions, though it is well known, they could have afforded them at half those prices, and made handsome profits. In one word, the history of the world affords few, if any instances, of such a long-continued scene of prosperity as they enjoyed.

The manufacturers cheerfully paid those prices. The cotton-weaver, the smith, the shoemaker, the carpenter, the labourer, who earned six, seven, or eight dollars per week, never lisped a word of complaint, when they paid twelve or thirteen dollars per barrel for flour, eight or ten cents per pound for mutton, &c. &c. Would to heaven they had experienced the same degree of liberality from their farming and planting fellow citizens! which, alas! they have not.

It remains to ascertain the effect of this monopoly in favour of their agricultural fellow citizens, which our manufacturers have for thirty years afforded them without the least murmur.

It is impossible to ascertain with precision the number of our citizens engaged in manufactures, with their families. The census is miserably defective in this respect. It does not furnish the population of the towns and cities, which would afford a tolerable criterion. We are therefore left to mere estimate.

The highest number that I have ever heard surmised, is two millions; the lowest, one. Truth, as is generally the case, may lie in the medium. I will therefore assume one million and a half.

As there may be some objections on the subject of the number thus assumed, I annex the ground on which it rests.

I suppose, as I have stated, the white population of the country to be about eight millions, and to be proportioned as follows—

10–16ths, agriculturists	5,000,000
3–16ths, artists, mechanics, manufacturers, &c.	1,500,000
3–16ths, professors of law and physic, gentlemen who live on their income, merchants, traders, seamen, &c.	<u>1,500,000</u>
	<u>8,000,000</u>

I believe I would not have been wide of the mark, in adding 500,000 to the second item, and deducting 250,000 from each of the others. But I prefer taking ground as little as possible liable to cavil.

Dirom,[47] an eminent English statistical writer, estimates the average annual consumption of grain in England, at two quarters, or sixteen bushels, for each person.* Colquhoun,[48] strange to tell, estimates it only at one quarter. I will assume the medium of twelve bushels. At this rate the consumption of the manufacturers would be about 18,000,000 of bushels per annum.

The average price of wheat in the United States during the wars of the French Revolution, was about one dollar and seventy-five cents per bushel. For the last two years, it has been about one dollar and twenty-five cents. At this rate the amount of grain would be 22,500,000 dollars.

---

* "The average prices of all these several kinds of grain being 20*s.* 6*d.*, the price of two quarters for the maintenance of each person in these years, only amounts to 41*s.*"— *Dirom on the corn laws and corn trade of Great Britain, Appendix, page* 51.

Dirom states the average daily consumption of flesh meat in Paris at about five ounces and three quarters for each person. An average for London he supposes* probably more than double that amount, or eleven and a half, which is about five pounds per week. As our citizens eat meat oftener, and our working people more generally, than those of most other nations, it will be fair to assume six pounds per week for each person, which is equal to about three hundred and twelve pounds and a half per annum. At eight cents per pound, a moderate average till lately, this amounts to twenty-five dollars per annum, or for the whole 37,500,000 dollars.

Allowing for milk, butter, eggs, vegetables, fruit, lard, fire-wood, coals, home-made spirits, &c. &c. one dollar per week, it amounts to 78, 000,000 of dollars.

Summary.

Grain	$ 22,500,000
Animal food	37,500,000
Milk, butter, fuel, &c. &c.	78,000,000
Consumption of the manufacturers	$ 138,000,000

Now, this is the market, for bare subsistence, of which the manufacturers furnish a monopoly to their agricultural fellow citizens, who have uniformly regarded them with jealousy and murmuring—often with decided hostility—and who have *always assumed, that duties imperiously required for the purposes of the treasury are favours conferred on manufacturers!*

That this calculation is not materially wrong, will appear from the following view—A quarter dollar per day, or a dollar and three quarters per week for the maintenance of each individual, which, as our citizens live, is moderate, would amount to ninety-one dollars per annum, or—

For one million five hundred thousand people	$ 136,500 000

Let me further observe, that this is a market which might have been immensely increased annually by emigration, had a sound policy held out any encouragement to invite the manufacturers of Europe.

It is not easy to calculate the extent of the market for raw materials which the manufacturers afford their agricultural fellow citizens, and which might have been doubled by a correct system. I will state what I suppose it must have been in 1815, previous to the prostration of manufactures.

---

* "The daily consumption of each individual in Paris, is pretty accurately ascertained, from the tax on cattle paid at the barriers, to be about five ounces and three quarters. In London it is probably more than double."—Idem, 248.

Cotton	$ 9,000,000
Wool*	10,000,000
Hemp	2,000,000
Hides, skins, furs, timber for houses and ship-building, barley, hops, oats, &c.	8,000,000
	29,000,000
Brought forward for sustenance	138,000,000
Total	$ 167,000,000

As the illiberal prejudices that prevail on this topic, tend to excite jealousies and disgusts, that may eventually prove dangerous to the harmony of the nation, too much pains cannot be taken to remove them. I shall therefore place the subject before the reader in a new and not less striking point of view.

I have shewn that the market afforded to their agricultural fellow citizens by the manufacturers, amounts per annum to $ 167,000,000.

It is proper to examine the extent of the market reciprocated to them.

It may be assumed that each white person in the union consumes in furniture and clothing, at the average rate of forty dollars per annum.

This, for the whole of the agriculturists, whom
I have estimated at 5,000,000, amounts to $ 200,000,000
And for the slaves, supposed to be 1,500,000,
at 15 dollars per head, to   22,500,000

Per contra   222,500,000

One-half the farmers throughout the union
make three-fourths of their own clothing,
which is equal to   75,000,000
The remaining half probably manufacture
about one-third of their clothing, equal to   33,000,000
The clothing for the slaves is principally of family
fabrics. This would warrant the deduction of the
whole 22,500, 000. But I suppose the planters
may purchase to the average amount of five dollars
for each slave, this is $ 7,500,000, which leaves
of family fabrics   15,000,000
Total amount of household fabrics consumed
by the agriculturists.   123,000,000

---

*   Mr. Coxe states an opinion in his tables, that the growth of wool in the United States in 1812, was from 20 to 22,000,000 lbs.

Leaving the amount of clothing and
    furniture purchased by them   99,500,000
Of this amount probably 10 per cent is
    of foreign manufacture   9,950,000
One-half of the manufacturers, say 750,000,
    live in country towns or in the country, and
    purchase probably one-half of their clothing
    from the farmers in the neighbourhood, say   15,000,000
                                            24,950,000

Balance, being the whole of the consumption
    of articles purchased of manufacturers
    by agriculturists $ 74,550,000

It thus appears, notwithstanding the clamour against the manufacturers, that they purchase of the agriculturists, nearly 100,000,000 dollars more than the latter purchase of them.

A contrast between the domestic exports and the internal trade of the nation cannot fail to be interesting, as it will enable us to ascertain whether they have borne in the minds of our citizens and statesmen the comparative rank to which they are entitled.

The domestic exports of the United States for
    twenty-four years, from 1796 to 1819, inclusive,
    have been $ 955,586,088
Average $ 39,816,088

I shall proceed on the assumptions on which I have already ventured; that the agriculturists embrace about 5,000,000 of our white population; that all the other classes who are consumers of the productions of the farmers and planters are 3,000,000; and that each of the latter consumes to the amount of one dollar and seventy-five cents per week in food and drink. Let us see the result—

3,000,000 of people at one dollar and seventy-five cents
    per week, equal to $ 5,250,000 per week, or per annum $ 273,000,000

Once more.

Our present population is about	white	8,000,000
	black	1,500,000
		9,500,000

The average expenditure of forty dollars per annum, already assumed, for 8,000,000 of white people,

Amounts to	$ 320,000,000
1,500,000 slaves, each 15 dollars	22,500,000
	345,500,000
Of which we import about	60,000,000
Leaving a balance furnished by our own industry, of	285,500,000
To which add the above sum for food and drink	273,000,000
It gives a total of	558,500,000
Raw materials as before	29,000,000
Annual internal trade of the U. States	$ 587,500,000

What exhilarating views! The domestic market for food and drink is nearly seven hundred—and the internal trade fifteen hundred per cent. more than the average of our exports! How infinitely more worthy of the attention of our citizens and to be protected by our statesmen than they have appeared! How transcendently superior to that foreign commerce, which has been fostered with so much care; has excited so many collisions with foreign powers; cost us so much for foreign embassies, navy, and war; and entailed on us so heavy a national debt.

———————————

Again.

Our farmers will be astonished to learn that the consumption of Philadelphia in food and drink, supposing the population 125,000 persons, is very nearly equal to the amount of all the *eatable* articles exported from this country to every quarter of the world.

125,000 persons, at one dollar and seventy-five
    cents per week, consume to the amount of
    218,500 dollars per week, or per annum   <u>$ 11,375,000</u>

Total exports from the United States for 1819, *of the following articles.*

			Custom-house valuation.
Hams	lbs.	700,369	$ 10,555
Pork	bbls.	28,173	563,470
Beef	bbls.	34,966	454,558
Cheese	lbs.	1,148,380	114,838
			Carried forward $ 1,143,421
			Brought forward $1,143,421
Sheep		8,445	21,113
Hogs		2,324	13,944
Poultry		1,184	3,552
Indian corn	bushels	1,086,762	815,072
Wheat	do.	82,065	103,581
Rye	do.	67,605	54,084
Barley	do.	3,047	3,047
Oats	do.	23,284	11,642
Beans	do.	21,162	37,034
Peas	do.	41,400	72,600
Potatoes	do.	76,506	38,253
Apples	barrels	8,253	24,759
Flour	do.	750,660	6,500,000
Meal, rye	do.	48,388	241,940
Indian	do.	135,271	608,720
Buckwheat	do.	203	812
Ship stuff	cwt.	828	4,968
Biscuit	bbls.	54,603	273,015
Do.	kegs	44,184	33,138
Rice	tierces	76,523	<u>2,142,644</u>
Total of eatable articles			<u>$ 12,147,339</u>

CHAPTER XIII

Calumnious claimour against the manufacturers on the ground of extortion. Destitute of the shadow of foundation. Take the beam out of thine own eye. Rise of merino wool 400 per cent. Great rise of the price of merchandize after the declaration of war.

The most plausible argument used to defeat the applications of the manufacturers for relief, and to consign those that have hitherto escaped ruin, to the fate that has befallen so many of their brethren, is the "*extortion*" they are said to have practised during the late war, which, if they have an opportunity, they will, it is asserted, repeat. The justice of this accusation is as firmly believed by a large portion of the people of the United States, as if it were supported by "*proofs from holy writ.*" Great zeal and address have been employed by persons whose interests are subserved by exciting hostility against the manufacturers, to disseminate this prejudice. Unfortunately their efforts have been crowned with success. The accusation, it is true, has been refuted times without number; but, regardless of the refutation, it is still advanced with as much confidence as if disproof had never been attempted, and, indeed, as if it were impossible.

This reproachful charge has been recently advanced by a respectable body of planters, whose opportunities and situation in life should have shielded them from falling into such an error. The general meeting of delegates of the United Agricultural Societies of Virginia, in a memorial adopted on the 10th of January, deprecate the idea of being placed

"At the mercy of an association, who, competition being removed, will no longer consider the intrinsic value of an article, or what price would afford a fair profit to the manufacturer, but *how much the necessities of the consumer would enable them to extort. Of this spirit we had a sufficient specimen during the late war with Great Britain.*"

This very gentlemanly, decorous, and veracious accusation is the act of:

Thomas Cocke,	W. J. Cocke,	Roger A. Jones,
Edmund Ruffin,	Nicholas Fanleon,	Theophilus Field,
John Edmonds,	Charles H. Graves,	John Jones, and Esqrs.,
George Blow,	Richard Cocke,	Henry Jones.
W. P. Ruffin,	John Pegram,	

When these gentlemen were thus denouncing "the extortion practised in consequence of the necessities of the consumer," it is wonderful they did not pause a little, and reflect on the price of fifteen dollars per cwt. which they received in 1818 for their tobacco, in consequence of *the necessities* of the shippers, whereby so large a portion of those shippers were ruined, and so many illustrious families reduced from a state of affluence to penury and dependence! They might also turn their attention to the extravagant price of two and three dollars per bushel for wheat, and eleven, twelve, thirteen, and fourteen dollars per barrel for flour. These reminiscences would have been rather malapropos, and deranged some of the flowery paragraphs of their memorial. Our own offences are easily forgotten. "They are marked in sand"—while those of our neighbours are "engraven on marble."

As the prejudice on this subject has produced the most deleterious consequences, not merely on the happiness and prosperity of the manufacturers generally, but on the power and resources of the nation, I hope for a candid hearing, while I investigate it, and undertake to prove—

1.   That the charge is not only not true, but the reverse of truth; that the rise of price was perfectly justifiable; and that the shadow of extortion did not attach to the procedure.
2.   That the charge of extortion would apply with infinitely greater force and propriety to the farmers, planters, and merchants, who in this case are the accusers, than it does to the manufacturers.

The accusation has been more frequently predicated on the rise of the price of broad cloths, than of any other article. As in this case it comes before us in a tangible form, and subject to the talisman of figures, I shall therefore confine myself to this prominent and conspicuous case; observing, *en passant*, that the facts and reasoning apply equally to other branches. They all stand on nearly the same ground. In every case, in which a rise of price took place, it arose from a cause similar to that which operated on broad cloth. Therefore if the charge be disproved in this instance, it falls to the ground on the whole; just as when, during the late war, several vessels were captured in circumstances exactly similar, the trial of one decided the fate of the rest.

The facts of the case are, superfine broad cloth was sold previous to the war at from eight to nine dollars per yard—during the war it rose to twelve, thirteen, and fourteen.

On this "*extortion*" the changes have been rung from New Hampshire to Georgia—from the Atlantic to the Mississippi. It is considered as a set off against, and justification of, the widespread scene of desolation, the sacrifice of capital to the amount of millions, the ruin of hundreds of capitalists, and the extreme distress of thousands whose sole dependence is on the labour of their hands—on which congress have for years looked with unfeeling indifference, without taking a single effectual step to relieve the sufferers, or to remove their sufferings.

The value of every manufactured article depends on the price of the raw material—the cost of workmanship—and the profit of the capitalist by whom it is produced.

That a rise in the price of either or both of the two first will justify a rise in the price of the article, is too manifest to require proof.

Now, to the senseless and calumnious outcry against "*extortion*," on this subject, it would be sufficient to state the simple fact, that the raw material experienced a most extraordinary rise, as will appear from the following statement of the prices at different periods—

Prices of Merino wool.

1812.	May 1.	per lb.	75 cents.
	July 20.		75 to 100
	Oct. 1.		75 to 150
1814.	May 1.		300 to 400
	Aug. 29.		300 to 400
	Nov. 14.		300 to 400*

This alone would settle the question beyond the power of appeal.

Let it be observed, that it requires two pounds of wool to make a yard of superfine cloth. Therefore the difference in the price of the raw material accounts for and fully justifies the rise in the price of the cloth. Two pounds in May, 1812, cost one dollar and fifty cents; in May, 1814, they averaged seven dollars. It follows, that the per centage of profit was not so great on the cloth at fourteen dollars as at eight.

I do not know the expense of workmanship; but shall suppose it five dollars per yard—Any other sum would answer equally well.

1812. May 1.		1814. May 1.	
2 lbs. wool	1 50	2 lbs. wool	$ 7
Workmanship	5 00	Workmanship	5
	6 50		12
Profit	1 50	Profit	2
Price of cloth	$ 8 00	Price of cloth	$ 14
Profit about 20 per cent.		Profit 16 2/3 per cent.	

---

*   Grotjan's Price Current.

Wages, too, rose considerably in consequence of the increased demand for workmen; for however extraordinary it may seem to Colonel Pegram and his friends, it is nevertheless true, that a workman thinks he has as clear a right to raise his wages in case of an increased demand, as a planter has to raise the price of his tobacco or cotton in similar circumstances.

There is, moreover, another item of considerable importance to be taken into view.

Owing to the utter impolicy of our government, and the want of adequate protection to the woollen manufacture, the business had not been carried to any extent previous to the war. The establishments were at that time to be erected, at an enormous expense, and under considerable disadvantages. This warranted an extra price, in the shape of interest.

I now proceed to prove, that had the woollen and other manufacturers raised the prices of their fabrics, without any rise in the raw materials, or wages, or without any extraordinary expense of buildings, neither the farmer nor the merchant could justly censure them, without at the same time pronouncing their own condemnation.

So far as respects the farmer, I might rest the question on the case stated, of the Merino wool. The rise on this article, from seventy-five cents to three and four dollars, in two years, was among the most extravagant advances ever known in the annals of trade. And if the charge of "*extortion*" would ever fairly lie against a rise in price, it would in this case indubitably. Never was the admonition—

"*First cast the beam out of thine own eye—and then thou shalt see clearly to cast out the mote out of thy brother's eye*,"[49]

more appropriate. Had the Pharisee in the gospel, reproached the publican with pride, he would not have been more culpable than the farmer, who raised his wool four hundred per cent. and reproaches the manufacturer with "*extortion*" for raising the cloth, made of that wool, fifty per cent. Indeed in all the exuberant stock of human folly, there cannot be found any thing more extraordinary or extravagant.

But the defence does not rest on this ground alone. It is corroborated by almost every article of agricultural produce, which has always risen in consequence of an increased demand. To remove all doubt, if doubt could have existed, I state from the Philadelphia price current the various prices of four articles at different periods, with the very extraordinary advances on them.

Flour.	1809.	Jan.	16.	per bbl.	$ 5 50
		March	6.		7 50
	1810.	May	1		8 00
		Aug.	1		11 00

Tar.	1813.	Jan.	9.		2 10
		May	8.		4 00
Pitch.	1813.	Jan.	9.		2 50
		May	8.		4 50
		Oct.	9.		5 00
Hams.	1813.	Jan.	9.	per lb.	9½
		May	8.		11
		Oct.	9.		14½

So much for the farmers. Let us now examine how far they are kept in countenance by the proceedings of the merchants.

War was declared on the 18th of June, 1812. An immediate rise of price took place in every article in the market which was either scarce or likely to become so. Some were at once raised fifty, sixty, and seventy per cent.

	1812.	June 9.	1812.	July 13.
Imperial tea	per lb.	$1 30		$1 87 ½
Hyson		96		1 35
Coffee		15 ½		20
White Havanna sugar,	per cwt.	14 75		18 50
Brown do. do.		12 75		16 00

All these advances took place in less than five weeks.

	1812.	June 9.	1812. Aug. 10.
Russia hemp	per ton	$ 242 50	$ 300 00
Havanna molasses		56	72 ½
Souchong tea		50	75

*   *   *   *   *

This was all regarded as perfectly fair, honest and honourable. There was not the shadow of "*extortion*" supposed to be in it. The merchant, who raised his souchong tea fifty per cent., was so deeply engaged in clearing the manufacturer's eye of the "*mote*," that he quite forgot to "*take the beam out of his own*."

Can the citizen, who buys flour at six dollars, and sells it occasionally in the West Indies for twenty, twenty-five, or thirty dollars, without a deep blush reproach the manufacturer with "*extortion*" for raising broad cloth, from eight to fourteen dollars, when the raw material rose so extravagantly? or even had the price of the latter remained stationary?

Rise of price, in consequence of scarcity or increased demand, is, or is not, "*extortion.*" This is a dilemma, on the horns of which the farmers, planters and merchants are caught. If it be "*extortion,*" they have been and are "*extortioners*" in the fullest sense of the word; as they always have and always do raise the price of their produce or merchandize, in consequence of scarcity or increased demand. Indeed, if this be extortion, all mankind are extortioners—lawyers, doctors, apothecaries, house owners, ship owners, money lenders, planters, and farmers, without distinction; for they all raise their prices in consequence of an increased demand. But if this be not extortion, as it certainly is not, then every man, woman, or child in the nation, from the highest, proudest, haughtiest, and wealthiest, down to the lowest scullion, who has advanced the charge of "*extortion*" against the manufacturers, has broken the eighth commandment of the decalogue, and "*borne false witness against his neighbour.*"

I trust, therefore, that there is no man of liberality in the country, who considers the subject with due attention, but will allow that the incessant clamour against the manufacturers for extortion, is illiberal and disgraceful to the age—utterly destitute of foundation—in direct hostility with that brotherly regard which fellow citizens owe each other, and which is the surest foundation of harmony and happiness in a community; and that it produces a system of conduct inconsistent with the soundest principles of political economy— as well as destructive to the permanent wealth, power, and resources of the nation.

CHAPTER XIV

The agricultural the predominant interest in the United States. Great advantages to agriculture from the vicinity of manufacturing establishments. Case of Aberdeen. Of Harmony. Of Providence. Fall of lands the result of the decay of manufactures.

As the agriculturists are now, and are likely to be for a century at least, the predominating interest in this country, and have a decided influence in its legislation, it is of immense importance that they should form correct views on the system best calculated to promote the general welfare. And it is much to be regretted that the endeavours to persuade them, that there is an hostility between their interests and those of their manufacturing fellow citizens, have been but too successful. Never was there a prejudice much more unfounded, or more pernicious to their prosperity and to that of the nation at large.

It is proved, (page 123) that the annual consumption of the city of Philadelphia in food and drink, amounts to about $ 11,000,000, all paid to the farmers, which is more than one-fifth part of all the domestic exports of the United States for the last year; within ten per cent., of the whole of the articles of food exported within that year; and almost thirty per cent. of the average domestic exports of the nation for the last thirty years.

To the farmer and planter the home market is incomparably more advantageous than the foreign. Woeful experience proves that the latter is subject to ruinous fluctuations. Whereas the former is permanent and steady, little liable to vicissitude. It furnishes demand for the farmer's vegetables, his poultry, his fruit, his fuel, and various other articles, which are too perishable, or too bulky in proportion to their value, for exportation. The income from all these forms an important item in the prosperity of the farmer. This is true, even in small countries, as England, Ireland, and Scotland, of which every part is contiguous to, or not far distant from the advantages of navigation. But it has ten-fold weight in a country like the United States, of which a large and important portion is from three to fifteen hundred miles distant from the emporium to which its productions must be transported before they are put on shipboard to be forwarded to a market. The difference, to these portions of this country, between a foreign and domestic market, is probably equal to fifty per cent. of the whole profits of farming.

As theories, however plausible, are liable to great errors, unless supported by the bulwark of facts, I presume that it cannot be unacceptable to the reader, to have these important views supported by facts of undeniable authenticity. I therefore submit for consideration the case of the neighbourhood of Aberdeen, in Scotland, and that of the settlement of Harmony, in the state of Pennsylvania.

"Have we not opportunities of observing every day, that *in the neighbourhood of a ready market, no inducements are necessary to excite the common farmer to become industrious, and carry on improvements of every sort with success?* A particular case occurs to me just now, that is so directly in point, that I cannot resist the temptation of producing it, *as an example of the rapid progress with which improvements in agriculture are made when circumstances are favourable.*

"The town of ABERDEEN HAS MADE GREAT ADVANCES IN TRADE AND MANUFACTURES WITHIN THESE THIRTY OR FORTY YEARS PAST. The number of inhabitants has increased greatly within that period. *Money has become more plenty there than formerly.* Their manner of living is now more elegant and expensive; articles of luxury have increased. In consequence of good roads having become more common, horses and wheel-carriages have also become extremely numerous. On all which accounts, *the demand for fresh vegetables has greatly increased* in that place within the period above-mentioned."

"But on account of the particular situation of that town, it was a matter of some difficulty to augment the produce of the fields in that neighbourhood, and supply the daily increasing demand for these. *This city is placed in the midst of a country that is naturally the most sterile that can possibly be imagined.* For, unless it be a few hundred acres of ground that lie between the mouths of the rivers Dee and Don, close by the town, *there was not an inch of ground for many miles around it that could supply the inhabitants with any of the necessaries of life.* On the east is the German Ocean. On the south the Grampian Mountains come close to the river, terminating in a head-land on the south side of the harbour, called the *Girdle Ness*: and on the west and north, it is environed for many miles with an extended waste, the most dismal that can be conceived, in which nothing can be discovered but large masses of stone heaped upon one another, interspersed here and there with a few bushes of starved heath, or disjoined by uncomfortable bogs and spouting marshes, the most unpromising to the views of the farmer that can possibly be imagined.

"But what is it that human industry cannot perform! what undertaking is too bold for man to attempt *when he has the prospect of being repaid for his labour!* Even these dismal wastes, it was imagined, might be converted into corn-fields. The ground was trenched; the stones were blasted by gunpowder, and removed at an immense expense; manures were purchased: and *thousands of acres of this sort of ground are now waving with the most luxuriant harvests, and yield a rent from five to eight pounds sterling per acre.*

"In any other part of the world that I have seen, it would be reckoned impossible to convert such soils to any valuable use; and the most daring improver that I have met with any where else, would shrink back from attempting to cultivate a field which an Aberdeensman would consider as a trifling labour. Long habit has familiarised them to such arduous undertakings—undertakings which could not be attempted any where else; as, unless in such a particular situation as I have described, the improver could never be repaid. For in what other part of Europe could a man lay out one hundred pounds sterling, or upwards, on an acre of ground, before it could be put under crop, with any prospect of being repaid? yet this is no uncommon thing in that neighbourhood.

"Nor is this all: For to such a height is the spirit for improvement risen in that part of the world, that they are not only eager to cultivate those barren fields, but even purchase these dreary wastes at a vast expense, for that purpose. *The last spot of ground of this sort that was to be disposed of in that neighbourhood, was feued off by the town of Aberdeen in the year 1773, for ever, at an annual quit-rent, or, as we call it,* feu-duty, *of thirty-three or thirty-four shillings sterling per acre, although it was not then, and never could have been worth six pence per acre, if left in its native state*—nor could be converted into corn-ground but at an expense nearly equal to that above-mentioned.

"Could I produce a more satisfactory proof, that A GOOD MARKET WILL ALWAYS PRODUCE A SPIRITED AGRICULTURE?"*

To this Scotch case, which is nearly as strong and conclusive as the mind can conceive, I shall add a more recent American one, which has a peculiar interest.

The settlement at Harmony, in the state of Pennsylvania, was begun in the fall of 1804, and is probably the only settlement ever made in America, in which from the outset agriculture and manufactures proceeded hand-in-hand together. The progress to wealth and prosperity, therefore, has been far beyond any previous example in this country.

*   *   *   *   *

The original stock, in 1804, was 20,000 dollars, which was expended in the purchase of land, and in supporting themselves till they commenced their operations. And, in 1811, their property amounted to the wonderful sum of 220,000 dollars.

---

*   Anderson on the means of exciting a spirit of National industry, p. 63.

900 acres of land	$ 90,000
Stock of provisions	25,000
Mills, machinery, and public buildings	21,000
Dwelling houses	18,000
Horses, cattle, hogs, and poultry	10,000
1000 sheep, one-third of them merinoes, of which one ram cost 1000 dollars	6,000
Stock of goods, spirits, manufactures, leather, implements of husbandry, &c. &c	50,000
	$220,000*

To this delightful picture of the blessed effects of a judicious distribution of industry, the statesman ought to direct his eyes steadily. It holds out a most instructive lesson on the true policy to promote human happiness, and to advance the wealth, power, and resources of nations. The history of the world may be examined in vain for any instance of such rapid strides made by any body of men, wholly unaided by bounties, premiums, loans or immunities from government. The Harmonists were true practical political economists. They did not, like so large a portion of the rest of the people of the United States, lavish their wealth on the manufactures of a distant hemisphere, nor buy abroad cheap those articles which they could procure at home. In the sound and strong language of Mr. Jefferson, they "placed the manufacturer beside the agriculturist;"[50] and they have reaped the copious harvest which such a policy cannot fail to secure. One such practical example outweighs volumes of the visionary theories of those closet politicians, who are the dupes of their heated imaginations.

Mr. Gallatin's[51] report on manufactures, dated April, 17,1810, contains an important statement of the situation of a manufactory in Providence, Rhode Island, which sheds great light on this subject, and which is entitled to the most serious attention.

In this manufactory there were employed, males	24
Females	29
And besides the above, there were employed for the establishment, in neighbouring families, males	50
Females	75
	178

Thus, out of one hundred and seventy-eight persons, there were one hundred and four females. The report is so far deficient, that it does not detail the

---

*   Melisch's Travels, 80.

respective ages of the work people; but judging from the state of other manufactories, we may assume that at least half of the whole number were children.

If this be admitted, it will follow, that there were men   37
Women   52
Male and female children   89
                                                               178

To the farmer this statement presents itself in a peculiarly striking point of light. Of the whole number of persons to whom this manufactory afforded employment, more than two-thirds belonged to the circumjacent farm-houses, who were thus enabled to gather up fragments of time, which would otherwise have been inevitably lost. It is not improbable that the profits of their labour were nearly equal to the profits of the farming.

I might cite the cases of Brandywine, Wilmington, Pittsburg, Providence, Lancaster, and a hundred other places in the United States, where the establishment of manufactories, by affording an extensive and advantageous market to the farmer, doubled and trebled the price of the lands in their neighbourhood—and increased in an equal degree the comforts and prosperity of the farmers. And on the contrary, numberless instances are to be met with, in which the recent decline of manufactures has reduced the lands to one-third, or one-fourth, of the previous price. The average reduction of the price of land in the neighbourhood of Pittsburg is one-half of what it was bought and sold for in 1813, 14, and 15.

The farmers of the United States have been induced to oppose protection to their manufacturing fellow citizens, lest they should be obliged to purchase domestic, at a higher rate than imported manufactures. This erroneous policy has carried its own punishment with it. The reduction in the price of the farmer's produce, which can be obviously traced to the prostration of the manufactories, has in many cases been quadruple the saving in the price of the articles he purchased. I take as examples, raw wool and woollen cloth, and suppose that the farmer could buy foreign cloth for six dollars, and would have to pay, in consequence of protecting duties, nine for American—a difference that never existed in regular trade. The prices of goods purchased at auction, cannot with propriety be taken into account. They baffle all calculation.

Merino wool now sells for fifty cents per pound: of course it would require twelve pounds to pay for a yard of British cloth. But had the woollen manufacture been duly protected, wool would be at least one dollar. Thus nine pounds of wool would pay for a yard of domestic cloth, at the presumed advance of price.

Let it be added, moreover, that the farmer would probably sheer twice or three times the quantity of wool, were the price one dollar, that he does at present: for had the woollen manufacture been protected, the merino sheep, in which such immense sums were invested, would have been preserved, instead of so large a portion of them being consigned to the slaughter-house.

*   *   *   *   *

CHAPTER XV

The extent and value of the commerce of the United States have long been prolific themes for orators in congress, and writers of newspapers— and it appears generally assumed to be only second to our agriculture, and far beyond manufactures in importance. It has had incomparably more attention bestowed on it by our government, than either agriculture or manufactures. A candid investigation of those sounding pretensions, whereby they may have the seal of certainty imprinted on them, if they be correct; or, if otherwise, may be reduced to their proper standard, cannot fail to be interesting.

That commerce, properly conducted, on fair and reciprocal terms, is highly beneficial, has never been doubted by any sound mind. It tends to civilize, and increase the comforts of, the great family of mankind.

But that it may be, and is occasionally, very injurious, is equally clear. When one nation receives only luxuries from another, and pays for them in necessaries of life, or specie, or in raw materials which would find employment for its own people, it is eminently pernicious.

To make the matter more clear, I will suppose that England were to furnish France with her raw wool, lead, tin, iron, flax and hemp, and to receive in return Merino shawls, silks, satins, pearl necklaces, diamond watches, &c. the most devoted advocate for commerce would allow this species of it to be extremely pernicious.

Again. If England furnished wool, flax, hemp, and iron, and received in return even necessary articles, such as broadcloths, linen, duck, hardware, &c. it would be highly disadvantageous; as she would give the produce of the labour of five, ten, or twenty persons for that of one.

But such a commerce would be transcendently pernicious, if England had a large portion of her population wholly unemployed, and capable of manufacturing those articles for her own consumption.

If this reasoning be correct, as applicable to Great Britain, it is difficult to prove why the system should not be equally pernicious to the United States. It is as absurd, as impolitic, and as cruel to our citizens, who are suffering for want of employment, and who could manufacture cotton goods for us, to export such quantities of raw cotton, and receive cambrics and muslins in return, as it would be for England to export her wool, and import her woollen manufactures.

———————

"*Strike, but hear*," said a general, about to offer some unpalatable opinions to a friend. As the views I am going to take of the subject of commerce, however true, are likely to be as unpalatable to the merchants as the opinions of the general to his friend, I say to them "strike, but hear."

I shall attempt to prove—

1. That a large proportion of the productive manufacturing industry of this country has been sacrificed to our commerce.
2. That the commerce of the United States has been carried on, upon very unequal terms—and that it has produced most injurious results upon the national prosperity.
3. That its extent and advantages have been overrated. And
4. That the numerous bankruptcies among our merchants have chiefly arisen from the want of protection to manufactures.

These views are so repugnant to the feelings and prejudices of a numerous class of citizens, that I can scarcely hope for a fair discussion. More than half my readers will at once pronounce me deranged—and be disposed to throw the book into the fire. Again, therefore, I say, "strike, but hear."

———————

I. Sacrifice of productive industry.

To prove the sacrifice of productive industry, I refer the reader to the tariffs of 1789,* 1791, 1792, and 1804, where he will find that the duties on seven-eighths of the manufactured goods imported into this country

———————

*   See page 55.

were originally at five—then seven and a half—then ten—then twelve and a half—and at length fifteen per cent., the advance not the result of the applications of the manufacturers for protection, but to meet the increasing demands of the treasury. Hence, with every possible advantage of water power, raw materials, machinery, talents, enterprize, industry, and capital, until the declaration of war, three-fourths of the clothing of the inhabitants of all our towns and cities were of foreign fabrics—and the wealth of the nation was lavished to support foreign workmen, and foreign governments, while we had hundreds, nay thousands of citizens capable of supplying them, who were driven in many cases to servile and far less profitable labour.

The experience of our late war, and the immense spring it gave to the industry and manufactures of the country, prove that one-half the protection afforded to the merchants in the China trade would have enabled our citizens to have established the cotton and woollen branches on a liberal scale, and saved many millions of dollars to the country annually. This was unhappily sacrificed by the system of low duties, which was advocated by the merchants and adopted by congress to promote the interests of commerce. The influence of the former has been successfully exerted at all times, to prevent prohibitions and prohibitory duties.

The unsoundness of the policy this country has pursued, by which it has been virtually placed in the situation of a colony to Great Britain and the other manufacturing nations of Europe, appears palpable from the following considerations:

So far as respects the cotton and woollen branches, on a large scale, we were almost as completely excluded from them by the impolicy of our tariff until 1812, as if a law had been passed to render their establishment penal. This declaration may surprize—but is nevertheless susceptible of proof. The two strong facts already stated—that with all our advantages for the manufacture of cotton, we consumed only 30,000 pounds in the year 1800, although we exported about 30,000,000—and that in 1812, we were so dependent on Europe for woollens, that we had not a supply of blankets for our army, nor were our manufactories at that time in a situation to make provision for the emergency, place the matter beyond doubt. He that will not be convinced by these facts, of the ruinous policy we pursued—and the wanton waste of our resources, would not be convinced, though one were to rise from the dead.

The tariff of 1789, which established the five per cent. duty, might as well have had the following preface, as the one which was prefixed to it:

"Whereas, although this country has become independent of Europe in its government, and by its arms—it is expedient that it should still continue in the colonial state, so far as respects its supplies of all the essential articles for comfort and convenience:

Therefore be it enacted, &c. that the duties to be levied on the importation of manufactures of cotton, wool, linen, pottery, lead, iron, steel, brass, and wood, be no more than five per cent. ad valorem."

However ludicrous this may appear, it only gives body and substance to the virtual effects of the tariff.

II.

In order to prove my second position, I subjoin a view of our exports and imports, and a statement of the various species of the former for fifteen years.

Our exports have consisted chiefly of four different species of articles—

1. Necessaries of life.
2. Raw materials, which we ourselves could have manufactured, and which constituted one-fourth part of our exports.
3. Naval stores, of indispensable necessity for the nations which purchased them.
4. The luxury of tobacco, which is about one-eighth part of the whole amount.

Our imports consist principally of—

1. Tea, coffee, wines, spices, cocoa, chocolate, almonds, raisins, &c. which we do not raise, and which of course do not affect our national industry.
2. Spirits, sugar, cotton, indigo, hemp, malt, lead, &c. which interfere with the best interests of our farmers and planters.
3. Manufactures of cotton, wool, leather, iron, &c. &c. which interfere with the interests of our manufacturers, and of which we could, by proper protection, supply ourselves with the greater part.
4. Luxuries, which tend to introduce extravagance, and deprave our morals.

*   *   *   *   *

A cursory glance at our exports, will satisfy the reader, that few nations have carried on commerce to more disadvantage, than we have done a large portion of ours. We have exchanged the most valuable productions of nature in the rudest state, with the least possible degree of labour—and received in return every species of merchandize in its most finished form—of which labour constituted two-thirds, three-fourths, and four-fifths of the value. This more particularly applies to cotton, which we have shipped at an average of about twenty-five cents per pound, except Sea Island, and received back at an advance about five-fold—thus enabling foreign nations to pay for the whole crop with one-fifth part of it—and wantonly throwing away the remaining four-fifths. And a large portion of the manufacture being performed by machinery, we have given the labour of twenty or thirty persons for one. Never was there a system more admirably calculated to stunt the growth of a nation; to destroy the effect of the advantages bestowed on it by nature; and to render its inhabitants hewers of wood and drawers of water to other nations.

One view of this subject is so appalling, that it will make the heart ache of every man who has any regard for the real interests of this country, or a wish to advance its wealth, power, and resources.

The increase by manufacture of the value of the raw material of cotton, was in 1811, according to Colquhoun, about five-fold. Let us see the operation of this portion of our commerce tested by that scale.

We exported, it appears, in fifteen years, cotton to the amount of	$ 154,179,117
This, according to Colquhoun, produced	$ 770,895,585
Leaving to foreign nations the enormous profit of	$ 616,716,468
Or an annual average of	$ 41,114,431

Two-thirds of which we might by a sound policy have retained among ourselves.

There can be no doubt that Great Britain defrayed the whole expense of the war against us by the profits she derived from this single article, in a few preceding years.

Thus our short-sighted policy tends to aggrandize, at our own expense, foreign nations with which we have had, and may have, most perilous collisions.

It now remains to give a general but concise view of the injurious effects produced by our commerce. I shall confine myself to facts of such universal notoriety as to preclude controversy.

Commerce has—

1. Carried away our raw materials, and deluged us with manufactures, whereby millions of capital invested in manufacturing establishments have been lost—hundreds of the proprietors ruined—and thousands of workmen reduced to idleness, and exposed to the lures of dissipation and crime.
2. Subjected us to an expense for foreign intercourse and for the Barbary powers[32] to the amount of nearly 12,000,000 of dollars in twenty years.*

---

* Seybert, 712, 713.

3. Bankrupted an immoderate proportion of those who pursued it.
4. Caused a war, by which there is entailed on us a heavy debt of nearly 80,000,000 of dollars, and an annual interest of above 4,700,000 dollars.
5. Rendered a navy necessary, which creates an expense of above 3,500,000 dollars for the present year.
6. Given a prodigious spring to luxury and extravagance, by the superfluous articles it has introduced among us.
7. Drained away the circulating medium of the country, whereby every kind of business is paralized, and the nation impoverished.
8. Rendered us dependent on foreign nations for many of the comforts, and even some of the necessaries of life.

That these consequences have resulted from our commerce, I trust will be admitted. They are considerable drawbacks on its advantages, which ought to be immensely great to countervail them.

It behoves us then to examine the extent and value of this commerce, so highly prized and so dearly bought.

––––––––––

III.
I now proceed to my third point, to prove that the extent and advantages of our commerce have been greatly overrated.

To simplify as much as possible a complicated subject, I shall consider the commerce of the United States under five several heads.

1. The exportation of our superfluous productions.
2. The importation of necessary supplies.
3. The carrying trade.
4. The coasting trade.
5. The shipping.

The first is beyond comparison the most important. In it the whole nation is deeply interested. Much of its prosperity depends on procuring suitable markets for its surplus productions. This affords a strong stimulus to industry, which would otherwise pine and languish.

To enable the reader to judge correctly on this subject, I annex a table of our exports from the organization of the government. For the first six years there was no distinction between foreign and domestic. I have assumed that there were two-fifths of the former, and three-fifths of the latter, which is about the average proportion of the whole of the subsequent period.

Exports from the United States from 1790 to 1819, inclusive.[*]

Year.	Domestic.	Foreign.	Total.
1790	[†]12,123,094	[‡]8,082,062	20,205,156
1791	[†]11,407,225	[‡]7,604,816	19,012,041
1792	[†]12,451,860	[‡]8,301,238	20,753,098
1793	[†]15,665,744	[‡]10,443,828	26,109,572
1794	[†]19,815,741	[‡]13,210,492	33,026,233
1795	[†]28,793,684	[‡]19,195,788	47,989,472
1796	40,764,097	26,300,000	67,064,097
1797	29,850,206	27,000,000	56,850,206
1798	28,527,097	33,000,000	61,527,097
1799	33,142,522	45,523,000	78,665,522
1800	31,840,903	39,130,877	70,971,780
1801	47,473,204	46,642,721	94,115,925
1802	36,708,189	35,774,971	72,483,160
1803	42,205,961	13,594,072	55,800,033
1804	41,467,477	36,231,597	77,699,074
1805	42,387,002	53,179,019	95,566,021
1806	41,253,727	60,283,236	101,536,963
1807	48,699,592	59,643,558	108,343,150
1808	9,433,546	12,997,414	22,430,960
1809	31,405,702	20,797,531	52,203,233
1810	42,366,675	24,391,295	66,757,970
1811	45,294,043	16,022,790	61,316,833
1812	30,032,109	8,495,127	38,527,236
1813	25,008,152	2,847,845	27,855,997
1814	6,782,272	145,169	6,927,441
1815	45,974 403	6,583,350	52,557,753
1816	64,781,896	17,138,556	81,920,452
1817	68,313,500	19,358,069	87,671,569
1818	73,854,437	19,426,696	93,281,133
1819	50,976,838	19,165,683	70,142,521
	$1,058,800,898	$ 710,510,800	$1,769,311,698
Average	$ 35,293,363	$ 23,503,600	$ 58,977,056

The surplus productions of the United States, the great and legitimate basis of our foreign trade, are, as appears from this table, far below what might

---

[*]   Seybert, 93.

[†]   Estimated at three-fifths of the whole.

[‡]   Estimated at two-fifths.

have been expected from the population, and the resources of the country. They average, as we see, only about 35,000,000 of dollars, or about 8,500,000 pounds sterling per annum, from the organization of the government to the close of the last year. The average population of that period has been about 6,500,000 souls. It therefore appears that we have exported only about five dollars and a half per head of our whole population. This nearly corresponds with our recent experience.

During the last five years we exported of domestic productions about 305,000,000 dollars—or 61,000,000 per annum. Our population during that period has probably averaged about 9,500,000 souls; which gives an export of only six dollars and a half per head.

It is thus indubitable that this department of our commerce, obviously the most important, has been vastly overrated, and sinks into insignificance, on a comparison with our domestic trade, which, as may be seen (page 123) is nearly fifteen hundred per cent. beyond it. The food and drink of Philadelphia, New York, Boston and Baltimore, supposing them to contain only 370,000 souls, at a quarter of a dollar per head daily, amount to nearly as much as the average of the whole of our domestic exports!

370,000 persons at a quarter of a dollar per day,
    consume per annum $ 33,300,000

Yet there are hundreds and thousands of citizens of the United States that are unalterably convinced that the United States owe all their prosperity, all their improvements, all their wealth, to commerce!!

I have in vain sought for a general statement of our imports. It is not to be found either in Seybert or Pitkin.[53] The former, however, gives one for seven years, from 1795 to 1801, viz.

1795	$ 69,756,258
1796	81,436,164
1797	75,379,406
1798	68,551,700
1799	79,069,148
1800	91,252,768
1801	111,363,511
	$ 576,808,935
Average	$ 82,401,276

It is not easy to calculate the amount of foreign goods consumed in this country. The foreign exports for the preceding seven years were 236,792,386 dollars. Deducted from the above sum of 576,808,935 dollars, there is a balance for home consumption for that period, of 340,016,549 dollars, being an average of above 48,000,000 dollars. But during this time our commerce was far more flourishing than in other years. I shall, therefore, assume an average consumption of foreign merchandize to the amount of 40,000,000 per annum, which will not be regarded as far from the fact.

Dr. Seybert has hazarded a calculation, that the profits of navigation, are at the rate of fifty dollars per ton—and he therefore sets down an average annual profit of 34,459,350 dollars! which would amount to 1,033,780,500 dollars in thirty years!

It is easy to perceive how extravagantly erroneous this calculation must necessarily be. A vessel of three hundred tons would make, by freight alone, a profit to her owner annually of 15,000 dollars. Yet many of our merchants have had two, three, four, five, and six vessels of this size constantly employed for years—have not lived extravagantly—and yet have finally become bankrupts.

Were the doctor's statement correct, the great body of ship-owners would have become as wealthy as Cosmo de Medici.

Ten per cent. is regarded as a fair average of the profits of commerce. For freight I shall assume an equal sum.

Hence is deduced the following result—

Average annual domestic exports	$ 35,293,363
Foreign goods consumed here, estimated at	40,000,000
	$ 75,293,363
Ten per cent. profit	7,529,336
Add an equal sum for profit on freight	7,529,336
Total	$ 15,058,672

The carrying trade is far less important. Without much participation in it, the nation might have enjoyed, and may still enjoy, a most enviable state of prosperity. And it will probably appear, in summing up its advantages and disadvantages, during the whole of our career, that the latter greatly outweigh the former.

To form a decision on this point, it is necessary to ascertain its extent.

It consists of two distinct branches. In the first, the foreign merchandize *in transitu* touches at our ports. In the second, the voyages are made from one foreign port to another.

Of the first branch we have an accurate account. The treasury returns distinguish between the exports of foreign and domestic articles. But of the second we can only form an estimate.

The foreign exports from the United States, as appears by the preceding table, have averaged 23,683,000 dollars per annum for thirty years.

It is probable that the other branch of the carrying trade is about one-half this amount. Some intelligent merchants whom I have consulted, estimate it at from 10 to 15,000,000 dollars annually. But to afford the utmost latitude to the contrary side of the question, I shall suppose it equal to the other branch.

Thus then stands the account of the carrying trade—

Foreign exports	$ 23,680,000
Voyages from one foreign port to another, estimated at	23,680,000
	$ 47,360,000
Profit, ten per cent.	$ 4,736,000
Add an equal profit for freight	4,736,000
Total profit of carrying trade	$ 9,472,000

Summary.

Profits of trade in exports, and in imports for home consumption	$ 15,058,672
Of carrying trade	9,472,000
Coasting trade, supposed	3,500,000
	$ 28,040,672[51]

These profits are the utmost that can be claimed on the most liberal calculation. But I must observe that it is difficult to conceive that half of them could have ever accrued; as so large a portion of the merchants who are supposed to have acquired them, have been reduced to bankruptcy. This strong fact is utterly incompatible with the idea of such profits, and I am persuaded would warrant a reduction of fifty or sixty per cent. of the amount.

The offsets have been immense. Shipwrecks—falling markets—and depredations to the amount of probably one hundred millions by the belligerants[sic], under orders in council, decrees, &c The aggregate of all these would probably amount to thirty per cent. on the assumed profits.

But even admitting that the whole sum of twenty-eight millions has been gained annually by commerce, it is worth while to consider whether it has not been like the Indian's gun.[55]

It has cost us from 1796 to 1815—

For foreign intercourse	$ 9,615,140
Naval department	52,065,691
Barbary powers	2,349,568
War debt	78,579,022
	$ 142,609,421*
Average per annum	$ 7,130,471

---

*   Seybert, 713.

The expenses chargeable to this account at present, and likely to continue, are—

Interest on war debt of $78,579,022	$4,714,741
Secretary's estimate for the navy, 1820	3,527,600
	$ 8,242,381

This is above twenty-five per cent. in perpetuity on those profits of commerce, which are *supposed* to have accrued during the whole of the period in which it had every possible advantage that its warmest advocates could desire. It is moreover, nearly twenty per cent. of the whole average amount of the exports of the country embracing the period in which our staples commanded exorbitant prices, which we are never likely to receive again.

I therefore confidently rely, that those who have condescended to "*hear*," though they may have "*struck*," will, however reluctantly, acknowledge that at the touch of the talisman of truth, the boasted advantages of commerce have greatly diminished in amount—and that it has indubitably cost the country more than it was worth.

In taking an account of the numerous offsets—the collisions with the belligerents—the chief part of the expense of the navy—our war—the war debt—and its interest, it would be unfair not to draw a line of distinction between the different branches of commerce. That important one which consists in the exportation of our surplus productions and procuring necessary supplies in return, ought probably to be exonerated from any portion of these heavy items. It might be carried on for a century, without producing any of those consequences. They have sprung almost altogether from the extraneous trade in the colonial productions of the belligerents, which arose from the general state of warfare of Europe, and from the cupidity with which it was pursued by our merchants. If this point of view be correct, then the account is reduced within a narrow compass.

It may be useful to hazard a calculation on the present and probable future profits of commerce, in order more fully to prove my position, that it has cost too dear.

The domestic exports of 1819, were	$ 50,976,838
Foreign exports	19,165,683
Foreign goods consumed here, suppose	60,000,000
	$ 130,142,521
As our markets have stood lately, a profit of	
five per cent. is a large allowance	6,507,126
Present profits on freights	1,000,000
Coasting trade	1,500,000
	$ 9,007,126

Thus it appears, that for every dollar of the present gain of the merchants by commerce, the nation at large pays nearly a dollar of tax entailed on it by that commerce!

I now invite the attention of the reader to my last position, which is—

IV. That the numerous bankruptcies among our merchants have chiefly arisen from the want of protection to manufactures.

That an immoderate number of our merchants have been reduced to bankruptcy, is universally admitted. The exact proportion cannot be ascertained. It has been carried as high as nine-tenths. This I believe extravagant. I assume two-thirds, which is supposed to be a low calculation. It remains to enquire how this calamitous result has taken place, under what is so generally styled a flourishing state of our commerce.

Various causes have conspired to produce this effect.

Commerce in this country has partaken of the nature of a lottery. The prizes were often immense, but rare—the blanks numerous. It has been attended occasionally with immoderate profits, which have been succeeded by great losses. The profits fostered a spirit of extravagance and luxury, which wasted all the previous temporary advantages, and rendered the merchants unable to contend with the storms of adversity.

But the chief source of the misfortunes of our merchants has been the extravagant number of them—which has proceeded from the ruinous policy of our tariff, as I hope to make appear.

Had the great, leading manufactures of cotton, wool, and iron, with some others, which were arrested by foreign importation, been duly protected, as a sound policy dictated, during the thirty years of the existence of our government, thousands of young men in every part of the United States, who have been brought up to the mercantile profession, and increased its numbers immoderately, would have been devoted to those branches.

Many parents have destined their children to the pursuit of commerce, merely for want of other suitable employment, and without either the talents, the credit, or the friends requisite. Hence most of our merchants have generally had two or three, and some as many as four apprentices, who, when free, have become supercargoes, or commenced a profession for which they were wholly incompetent, and thus added to the long list of bankrupts.

The effect of this state of things is, that there are probably more shipping and importing merchants in the United States than in the British dominions in Europe. Almost every little port from Passamaquoddy to St. Mary's, has its body of merchants, and importers, more or less numerous, who are constantly supplanting each other in the home and foreign markets, to their mutual ruin. The West Indies have thus proved the grave of the fortunes and happiness of half the merchants that have carried on trade with them. The trade to that quarter affords neither certainty nor security; as the prices are constantly fluctuating. The markets are either overstocked, or visited by a dearth. When the latter takes place, prices rise extravagantly. Intelligence arrives in this country. Our markets are crowded with shippers, who outbid each other, and raise the prices. Vessels are dispatched from all our ports, with full cargoes. The first, perhaps the second or third, is sold at a great profit. The glut sinks the price, and all the remainder sell at and often far below cost. The business is almost wholly a lottery, or species of gambling. Regular commerce disclaims it altogether.

The price of flour in the West Indies frequently rises, and as frequently falls to the amount of three, four, five and six dollars per barrel, in the course of two, three, or four weeks. Hence the merchant whose vessel sails at the rate of nine knots an hour, often makes a fortune—while his less fortunate neighbour, whose rate of sailing is only eight knots, is ruined.

Thus the inordinate competition at home and abroad, has produced the effect of obliging the merchants to buy our staples dear and sell them cheap. The competition likewise operates ruinously in the purchase of return cargoes, the prices being thereby greatly enhanced. These are among the most striking causes of the ruin of so large a portion of the mercantile class, and have obviously resulted chiefly, if not altogether, from the depression of manufactures.

I offer a calculation on the subject, which, even if somewhat erroneous, may prove useful.

Suppose the whole number of merchants in the United States, since the year 1789, to have averaged constantly 18,000—and that two-thirds of them have failed. Had manufacturing establishments been properly patronized, there probably would not have been more than 12,000; to the mass of whom the profession would have afforded a decent subsistence. In this case, it is probable that the bankruptcies would not have exceeded 2,000. Of course, 10,000 would have prospered out of 12,000; whereas, only 6,000 have succeeded out of 18,000. Whatever deduction from, or addition to, this calculation, may be made, the inference cannot fail to be highly favourable to the general scope of my argument, and to pronounce a strong sentence of condemnation on the ruinous policy this nation has pursued.

Another view may be taken of the subject.

It appears that a large portion of our commerce consists in the transportation of the merchandize and manufactures of other nations from the places of production to this country, and hence to those of consumption respectively. But might not our merchants employ themselves as well in lending facilities to the industry of their fellow citizens, as to that of foreign nations? Would not broadcloths from Young's, or Dupont's, or Sheppard's manufactories—or shirtings and sheetings from Schenck's or from Waltham, load a vessel as well, and pay as good a freight, as from Leeds or Manchester?[56] Would it not be at least as profitable to themselves, and as useful to their fellow citizens and to their country, to export cargoes of home-made goods to South America, and import specie, as to deluge their native country with foreign goods, drain it of its specie, and destroy its productive industry?

As I believe that the want of correct views on this point has been among the primary causes of the present distresses of the country, I hope to be pardoned for once more presenting it to the reader. The idea that the want of protection to manufactures has proved highly pernicious to the merchants, by an undue increase of their numbers, will appear plain to those who reflect, that, when by the restrictive system, and the war, there was a market open for, and protection afforded to, domestic manufactures, great numbers of respectable merchants, in all our cities, devoted their time, their talents, and their capital to the cotton and woollen branches, very advantageously for themselves and for the country, while this protection continued—but ultimately to the ruin of many of them. It is obvious that the inducements to commence a career in manufacturing are greater than to quit another business, and enter on this at an advanced period of life. And therefore I think it irresistibly follows, that the successful opposition to the establishment of manufactures has been the great cause of the superabundance of merchants, and that from this superabundance has flowed the bankruptcy of so large a proportion of them.

It is frequently asserted, that though so many of the merchants have been reduced to bankruptcy, the country has gained even by their ruin. This doctrine, which I have tried to develope [*sic*], I do not understand. Let us investigate it.

Suppose a farmer to sell 5000 bushels of wheat at two dollars per bushel. The miller grinds it—pays the farmer, and sells the flour to the merchant, who sells to the shipper. The latter becomes bankrupt, and pays three, five, or ten shillings in the pound, as the case may be. Of course the flour merchant suffers a heavy loss. I cannot see how, from a transaction of this kind, which is an epitome of a large proportion of our mercantile business for years past, the country can be said to have gained. Money, it is true, is put into the pocket of one man, but it is withdrawn from the pocket of another. There is no increase of the national wealth.

Having in this chapter taken ground wholly new, with no former lights to illuminate my path, I may have occasionally wandered into error. But I trust the wandering, whatever it may have been, has not led me far astray—and that the positions I have assumed, and the inferences I have deduced, if not wholly right, are not materially wrong.

CHAPTER XVI

Fostering care of commerce by congress. Monopoly of the coasting and China trade secured to our merchants from the year 1789. Revolting partiality. Wonderful increase of tonnage. Act on the subject of plaster of Paris. Law levelled against the British navigation act. Rapidity of legislation.

The records of American legislation bear the most satisfactory testimony of the transcendent influence of the mercantile interest, and of the unceasing exertions made to fence it round with every species of protection the government could bestow. No fond mother ever indulged a beloved child more than congress has indulged commerce—attended to all its complaints—and redressed all its wrongs.

My limits forbid a detail of the great variety of acts passed for the exclusive benefit of commerce, with which the statute book abounds. I shall confine myself to a few of the most prominent and important.

I.   The second act passed by the first congress contained clauses which secured to the tonnage of our merchants, a monopoly of the whole of the China trade—and gave them paramount advantages in all the other foreign trade. The duties on teas were as follow:

	In American vessels.	In foreign vessels.
Bohea teas per lb.	*Cts.* 9	*Cts.* 15
Souchong and other black teas	10	22
Hyson teas	20	45
All other green teas	12	27

The annals of legislation furnish no instance of grosser or more revolting partiality than is displayed in this act, which established the first tariff. A pound of hyson tea, which cost fifty-six cents, imported in a foreign, paid *twenty five cents more duty than in an American vessel.* Whereas a yard of broad cloth, or two yards of silk, cambric, or muslin, value five dollars, *paid but twenty-five cents*, all together, or five per cent. Thus the foreign ship-owner was at once shut out of our ports, beyond the power of competition, for the benefit of the American merchant; whereas the foreign manufacturer was invited in by a low duty: and the possibility of competition on the part of the American manufacturer wholly precluded! Let me not be misunderstood, as if I regarded as incorrect the decided preference given to the American merchant. By no means. My object is to point out the immense inequality of the treatment of the two bodies of men, which, to the great discredit of our legislation, and the incalculable injury of our country, as I hope I have proved in the preceding chapter, runs through our statute book. This is a digression, which the occasion called for. I return.

II. The same act gave our merchants an additional decisive advantage, by allowing a discount of ten per cent. on the duties upon goods imported in American vessels.

III. Such was the fostering care bestowed on the mercantile interest, that the third act was directed wholly for their security. By this act the tonnage duty on vessels belonging to American citizens was fixed at six cents per ton; on American built vessels, owned wholly or in part by foreigners, thirty cents; and on all other foreign vessels, fifty cents.

IV. In order to exclude foreign vessels from the coasting trade, they were subjected to a tonnage duty of fifty cents per ton for every voyage; whereas, our vessels paid but six cents, and only once a year.

These four features of decisive protection, were enacted in a single session, the first under the new government. They placed the mercantile interest on high ground, and gave it overwhelming advantages over foreign competitors. In fact, they almost altogether destroyed competition. I shall state their effects at the close of this chapter.

It is not difficult to account for this parental care. The mercantile interest was ably represented in the first congress. It carried the elections pretty generally in the seaport towns, and had made a judicious selection of candidates. Philadelphia was represented in the senate by Robert Morris, and in the house of representatives by Thomas Fitzsimons and George Clymer,[37] three gentlemen of considerable talents, and great influence. The representation in congress was divided almost wholly between farmers, planters, and merchants. The manufacturing interest was, I believe, unrepresented; or if it had a few representatives, they were not distinguished men, and had little or no influence.

The tariff bears the most unequivocal marks of this state of things. Agriculture and commerce engrossed nearly the whole attention of congress. Their interests were well guarded. Manufactures, as may be seen, (page 201) were abandoned to an unequal conflict with foreign rivalship, which consigned a large portion of them to ruin.

V. 1817. An act imposing two dollars per ton on all foreign vessels arriving from ports to which American vessels are not allowed to trade.

I have shewn the revolting neglect with which the applications of the manufacturers were treated, so highly discreditable to congress. It now remains to contrast this procedure with the kind attention and fostering care bestowed on the merchants, and the rapidity of motion in their concerns.

On the 29th of July, 1816, the governor of Nova Scotia, by proclamation, announced the royal assent to an act of the legislature of that province, whereby the trade in Plaster of Paris was intended to be secured to British or colonial vessels.

To counteract this insidious measure, Mr. Rufus King,[58] on the 17th February, 1817, moved in the house of representatives of the United States, "that the committee on foreign relations be instructed to report such measures as they may judge necessary to regulate the importation of Plaster of Paris, and to countervail the regulations of any other nation, injurious to our own, relating to that trade."

In four days afterwards, viz. on the 21st, Mr. Forsyth,[59] chairman of that committee, reported a bill to regulate the trade in Plaster of Paris, which was read the first and second time on that day, and the third on the 3d of March. The yeas and nays were called, and it was passed by a majority of eighty to thirty-nine. *It was then sent to the senate;* there read three times on the same day, and passed with some amendments—then returned to the house of representatives, who concurred in the amendments, and finally passed the bill. Thus it was *actually read four times, amended, and passed in one day*—a case probably without example. It was only fourteen days from its inception to its approbation by the president.

Let it be observed further, that the hostile measure which called forth this spirited act, was only about seven months and a half in existence, when it was thus decisively counter-acted. What a contrast between this celerity of operation and the lame policy observed towards manufactures!

The all-important act prohibiting the entry into our ports of British vessels arriving from places from which American vessels are excluded, was reported and twice read in senate on the 1st of April, 1818. On the 4th it was read the third time, and passed. On the same day it was read twice in the house of representatives. On the 11th it was read a third time, and passed. On the 16th it was presented to the president—and approved by him on the 18th.

Let any man, however hostile to manufactures or manufacturers, compare the progress of these two bills, involving such important principles, particularly the latter, with the snail's pace of any bill for the relief of manufacturers, and he will be obliged to confess that congress is actuated by a very different spirit towards the two different descriptions of citizens. Both acts are manly and dignified, and worthy of the legislature of a great nation, determined to assert a reciprocity of advantage in its intercourse with foreign nations. The latter is an attempt to uproot the British navigation act, in one of its most important features, to which that nation is most devotedly attached. Considering its magnitude and importance, it may be justly doubted whether it was not too precipitately passed. It was only four days on its passage in the senate—and eight in the house of representatives. Be this, however, as it may, my present object is only once more to place in contrast the paternal care of commerce and the frigid and withering indifference, not to say hostility, towards manufactures, displayed in that body, which ought to "look with equal eye" upon, and to dispense equal justice to, all classes of citizens.

And to close the catalogue, a bill for the protection of commerce is now before congress, and not likely to meet with much opposition, which cannot fail to affect the agricultural interest severely, by very materially abridging the markets for their productions. It is calculated to effect the object of the last mentioned act, which has failed to answer the purpose intended.

More detail is unnecessary. The position is fully established, that commerce has steadily enjoyed all the protection the government could afford. Every hostile movement on the part of foreign nations, to the injury of our merchants, has been decidedly met and counteracted.

The consequence of this system has been to insure our merchants—

I.   The whole of the coasting trade, amounting to 400,000 tons per annum.
II. Eighty-six per cent. of the tonnage engaged in the foreign trade, viz.

Total tonnage in the foreign trade for twenty-two years,
      from 1796 to 1817,   tons 18,201,541
Of which there was American   15,741,632
Foreign   2,458,909
                                       18,201,541

And III. An increase of tonnage unexampled in the history of navigation:—

Tonnage of the United States.

	Tons.		Tons.
In 1789	201,562	In 1804	1,042,402
1790	478,377	1805	1,140,366
1792	564,437	1806	1,207,733
1794	628,816	1807	1,268,545
1796	841,700	1808	1,242,443
1798	898,428	1809	1,350,178
1801	1,033,218	1810	1,442,781
1802	892,102	1811	1,232,502
1803	949,171	1812	1,269,997

CHAPTER XVII

Erroneous views of the tariff. Protection of Agriculture in 1789. Prostrate state of the staples of South Carolina and Georgia. Ninety per cent. on snuff, and one hundred on tobacco. Striking contrast. Abandonment of manufactures.

The farmers and planters of the United States are under a strong impression—

I. That the tariff affords a decided protection to the manufacturers.
II. That it operates as a "heavy tax on the many for the benefit of the few."
And III. That there is no reciprocity in the case—as agriculture is not protected.

That the first position is radically erroneous, is self-evident from the lamentable situation of so large a proportion of the manufactures and manufacturers of the United States, on which I have already sufficiently descanted.

The second is disproved in the eleventh chapter.

To the discussion of the third, I devote the present one.

There are not many of the productions of agriculture which require protection, as there are few of them that are imported. Their bulk, in general, and the consequent expense of freight, afford them tolerable security. But such as are imported, or likely to be, have been subject to high duties from the commencement of the government to the present time.

The products of the earth imported into the United States do not much extend beyond hemp, cotton, malt, tobacco, cheese, indigo, coals and potatoes, which, by the tariff of 1789, were subject to the following duties.

		Cents.			*Cents.*
Hemp	per cwt.	60	Snuff	per lb.	10
Malt	per bushel	10	Indigo	do.	16
Coals	do.	2	Cotton	do.	3
Cheese	per lb.	4	Potatoes	per cent.	5
Manufactured tobacco	do.	6			

The duty on cheese was equal to *fifty-seven per cent.*; on
Indigo about *sixteen*; on
Snuff, *ninety*; on
Tobacco, *one hundred*; on
Coals about *fifteen per cent.*

The duty on the raw materials, hemp and cotton, demand particular attention. They were about twelve per cent.—imposed, in compliance with the suggestions of Mr. Burke, to aid the agriculturists of South Carolina and Georgia, *because they hoped to be able to raise those articles.*

South Carolina and Georgia at that period were at a very low ebb. Their great staples, rice and indigo, had greatly sunk in price—and they had not as yet entered on the culture of cotton.

Ædanus Burke,[60] in a debate on the tariff, on the 16th April, 1789, to induce the house to lay a considerable duty on hemp and cotton, gave a melancholy picture of the situation of those states—

"The staple products of South Carolina and Georgia," he observed, "were hardly worth cultivation, on account of their fall in price. The lands were certainly well adapted to the growth of *hemp*: and he[61] had no doubt but its culture would be practised with attention. *Cotton was likewise in contemplation among them: and if good seed could be procured,* HE HOPED MIGHT SUCCEED!! But the low strong rice lands would produce hemp in abundance, many thousand tons even this year, if it was not so late in the season."*

In a debate on the same subject, Mr. Tucker,[62] another of the representatives from that state, reechoed the plaintive strains of his colleague:—

"The situation of South Carolina was melancholy. While the inhabitants were deeply in debt, *the produce of the state was daily falling in price.* Rice and indigo were become so low, as to be considered by many not objects worthy of cultivation. Gentlemen" he added, "will consider that it is not an easy thing for a planter to change his whole system of husbandry in a moment. But accumulated burdens will drive to this, and increase their embarrassments."†

The duty on manufactured tobacco was intended to operate as an absolute prohibition—and was liberally proposed with this view by Mr. Sherman, a representative from Connecticut.

"Mr. Sherman moved six cents per pound on manufactured tobacco; as he thought *the duty ought to amount to a prohibition.*"‡

---

*   Debates of Congress, vol. I. p. 79.
†   Idem, 70.
‡   Idem, 93.

While these high duties were imposed upon such of the productions of the farmer and planter, as were likely to be imported, all the great leading articles of manufactures, as may be seen, (page 202) were subject to only *five per cent.!!!*

A striking contrast in the tariff for 1789.

	Per cent.		Per cent.
Snuff	90	Woollens	5
Tobacco	100	Cottons	5
Indigo	16	Pottery	5
Coals	15	Linen	5
Cotton	12	Manufactures of iron	5
Hemp	12	lead	5
		copper	5

In the last chapter, I gave a sketch of the fostering care of commerce: Here we see in the very outset of the government the same care extended to agriculture, and an equal degree of neglect of manufactures—the germ of that cruel and withering system, which has, I repeat, placed this country nearly in the state of a colony to the manufacturing nations of Europe—which, without expending a single cent for our protection, have enjoyed more benefits from our commerce than ever were enjoyed by the mother country, during the colonial state of this continent—and more benefits than any nation ever enjoyed from colonies, except Spain. Perhaps even this exception is superfluous.

In 1790, the tariff was altered, when indigo was raised to twenty-five cents per pound, and coals to three cents per bushel.

In 1792, it was again altered, and hemp raised to twenty dollars per ton, and coals to four and a half cents per bushel.

This was about *twenty per cent.* on hemp, and *twenty-five* on coals—whereas the leading manufactures of cotton, wool, leather, steel, brass, iron, and copper, were only raised to *seven and a half per cent.*

Passing over the intermediate alterations of the tariff, which all bear the same stamp, I shall notice the protection afforded at present to those agricultural articles usually imported.

	Price.*	Rate of duty.	Duty. Per cent.
Hemp, per ton	$ 114.00	$ 30.00	26
Cotton, per lb.	.10	.3	30
Cheese in Holland	.10	.9	90
Coals, per bushel	.13	.5	38 ½

---

*   At the places of exportation respectively.

Snuff, average per lb.	.16	.12	75
Manufactured tobacco	.10	.10	100
Segars per M	5.00	2.50	50
Geneva, per gallon	.42	.42	100
Jamaica rum do.	.70	.48	68
Brown sugar, per lb.	.8	.3	37 ½

All the other productions of agriculture are subject to fifteen per cent. duty; which, be it observed, is the same as on more than half the manufactures imported into this country.

We find the staple article of South Carolina and Georgia, of which the freight is about thirty per cent. secured by thirty per cent. duty—the staple of Virginia by seventy-five, and one hundred—and the peach brandy and whiskey, of the farmers generally, by sixty-eight and one hundred, while the cotton and woollen branches are exposed to destruction, and have been in a great measure destroyed, for want of a duty of forty-five or fifty per cent.!!!

To display the monstrous partiality of this procedure—I shall contrast the duty and freight of a few articles of both descriptions—

	Duty.	*Freight.*	*Total*		*Duty.*	*Freight.*	*Total*
	Per ct.	Per ct.			Per ct.	Per ct.	
Hemp	26	24	50	Cotton stockings	25	2	28
Cotton	30	30	60	Cambrics	25	2	27
Cheese	90	15	105	Superfine cloth	25	2	27
Geneva	100	10	110	Silks	15	1	16
Rum	68	10	78	Woollen stockings	20	2	22
Snuff	75	5	80	Thread stockings	15	2	17
Tobacco	100	5	105	Gold leaf	15	1	16
Coals	38 ½	12	50 ½	Linens	15	2	17
Sugar	37 ½	6	43 ½				

It is hardly possible to conceive of a more revolting arrangement—or one that more completely violates the holy, the golden rule—

"All things whatsoever ye would that men should do to you, do you even so to them."

Now, in the face of this nation, I venture to ask, is there a respectable man in society, who considers the above items, and will not allow that the protection of agriculture is incomparably more complete, than of manufactures?

And yet, wonderful to tell, the extravagant protection bestowed on the manufacturers, and the want of protection to agriculturists—the insatiable appetite of the former, and the liberality and disinterestedness of the latter, are preached in long-winded speeches in, and memorials to, congress, and as long-winded newspaper essays, and are received as sacred and undeniable.

*   *   *   *   *

Objections have been made to the classification of manufactured tobacco and snuff among the articles dutied for the benefit of agriculture; as they fall under the denomination of manufactures. They are, it is true, manufactures. But that they are so extravagantly taxed, is not from any partiality towards the manufacturers of them—but to protect the planters. It requires no moderate share of modesty to assert, and of credulity to believe, that regard for the manufacturers leads to lay a duty of one hundred per cent. on manufactured tobacco, when for five years the manufacturers of woollens and cottons have in vain implored to have the duty on superfine cloth, muslins, and cambrics, raised beyond twenty-five per cent. Even the Jew Apella,[63] capacious as was his gullet, would not be able to swallow this fiction.

I wish it distinctly understood, that as the prices of hemp, Geneva, rum, coals, &c. are subject to frequent fluctuations in foreign markets, I do not pretend to vouch for the critical exactness at the present time, of the preceding quotations. I have collected my information from merchants of character, on whom reliance may be placed, and have every reason to believe that it is substantially correct.

CHAPTER XVIII

An awful contrast. Distress in Great Britain, because she cannot engross the supply of the world. Distress in the United States, because the home market is inundated with rival manufactures.

This shall be a short chapter. But I hope it will make a deep and lasting impression. The subject is of vital importance.

I have drawn several contrasts between our policy, and that of foreign nations, to evince the unsoundness and pernicious consequences of the former. To one more I request attention.

Great distress pervades the manufacturing districts of Great Britain, in which commerce largely partakes. And whence does it arise? Because her merchants and manufacturers cannot engross the supply of the world; for their capacity of producing every article made by machinery is commensurate with the wants of the whole human race; and, could they find a passage to the moon, and open a market there, they would be able to inundate it with their fabrics.

Their government, with a fostering and paternal care, which by the contrast reflects discredit on ours, secures them the *unlimited range of the domestic market*; and loses no opportunity, by bounties, drawbacks, and every other means which can be devised, to aid them in their efforts to engross our and all other markets. But the wisdom of the other nations of Europe, guarding the industry of their subjects, excludes them from various markets which they were wont to supply—and baffles their skill and sagacity. The great mass of their surplus productions is, therefore, disgorged on us, to the destruction of our manufacturers and the impoverishment of the nation.

What a lamentable contrast we exhibit! Our manufacturers suffer equally. Their capital is mouldering away—their establishments falling to ruins— themselves threatened with bankruptcy, and their wives and children with dependence—their workmen dispersed and driven to servile labour and mendicity—and why? Not because they are excluded from foreign markets. They aspire to none. Their distress arises from being debarred of their home market, to which our mistaken policy invites all the manufacturers of the earth!

Thus, while the British government uses all its energies to enable the manufacturers of that nation to monopolize the markets of the United States, our government looks on with perfect indifference, while the ill-fated, depressed, and vilified American, defeated in the unequal struggle with powerful rivals and an energetic government, is bankrupted or beggared—or in danger of bankruptcy or beggary—and in vain invokes its protection! In a word, the representatives of the freest people on the globe, have less regard for, and pay less attention to the happiness of, their fellow citizens, than the monarchs of the old world to their subjects!

Our citizens merely seek a portion of that protection which the most despotic monarchs in Europe afford their subjects. But they seek in vain. Pharaoh did not turn a more deaf ear to the applications of the Israelites, than congress have, for five years, to those of their fellow citizens who have contributed to elevate them to the honourable stations they occupy—and who pay their proportion for services from the benefit of which they are in a great measure precluded.

What a hideous, what a deplorable contrast! What a libel on republican government! What a triumph for the friends of monarchy—for those who hold the appalling heresy, to which our career affords some countenance, that man was not made for self-government.

This is so shocking a state of things, that with all the evidence of the facts before my eyes, I can scarcely allow myself to credit it! Would to God, it were not true—but alas! it is a most afflicting reality.

CHAPTER XIX

Encouragement and patronage of immigrants by England and France. Advantages of the United States. Great numbers of immigrants. Their sufferings. Return of many of them. Interesting table.

Some political economists have asserted that the strength of a nation consists in the number of its inhabitants. This, without qualification, is manifestly erroneous. A numerous population, in a state of wretchedness, is rather a symptom of debility than of strength. Such a population is ripe for treason and spoil. But a dense population, usefully and profitably employed, and in a state of comfort and prosperity, constitutes the pride and glory of a statesman, and is the basis of the power and security of nations. Hence there is scarcely any object which the most profound statesmen and monarchs of Europe, have for ages more uniformly pursued than the encouragement of immigrants possessed of useful talents.

Under all the governments of Europe, therefore, even the most despotic, inducements have been frequently held out to invite a tide of population of this description. And the wealth, power, and prosperity of some of the first rate nations, date their commencement from migrations thus promoted and encouraged. The decay and decrepitude of the nations from which the immigrants have removed, have been coeval and proceeded pari passu with the prosperity of those to which they have migrated.

The woollen manufacture, the great source of the wealth and prosperity of England, owes its introduction there to the wise policy of Edward III.[sic] who invited over Flemish workmen, and accorded them most important privileges.

The horrible persecutions of D'Alva in the Netherlands, and the repeal of the edict of Nantz,[64] in France, at a more recent period drove thousands of artists of every kind, possessed of great wealth, and inestimable talents, to England, whence she derived incalculable advantages.

Spain, whose policy we despise, repeatedly encouraged settlements of immigrants to establish useful manufactures, which had a temporary success. But the radical unsoundness of her system, and her spirit of persecution, blasted all these promising attempts.

France, under Louis XIV.[sic] pursued this system to a greater extent than any other nation. That king gave titles of nobility—pensions and immunities, to various artists and manufacturers, who introduced new branches of industry into his dominions: and a great portion of the wealth which he squandered in the splendor of his court, and the ambitious projects of his reign, arose from his protection of those immigrants, and the manufactures they introduced.

If this policy was wise, and had the sanction of the statesmen of nations of which the population was comparatively dense, how much more forcibly does it apply to countries like the United States and Russia, of which the population bears so small a proportion to the territory!

No country affords more room for immigrants—none would derive more benefit from them—none could hold out so many solid and substantial inducements—and there is none to which the eyes and longings of that active and energetic class of men who are disposed to seek foreign climes for the purpose of improving their condition, are more steadily directed. We have the most valuable staples—the greatest variety of soil, climate, and productions—an almost unlimited extent of territory—and the most slender population in proportion to that territory, of any nation in the world, except the Indians, and perhaps the wandering Tartars. And had manufactures, particularly the cotton, woollen and iron, instead of the paltry duty of five per cent. been early and decisively taken under the protection of the government, at its first organization, after the example of other nations, there is no doubt but we should have had a tide of immigration beyond any that the world has ever witnessed.

From the oppression and misery that prevail in various parts of Europe—from the high idea entertained of the advantages of our form of government—and from a variety of other circumstances, it is fair to presume, that had immigrants been able at once to find employment at the occupations to which they were brought up, we might have had an annual accession of 30 or 40,000 beyond the numbers that have settled among us. But I shall only suppose 20,000.

To evince what might have been, from what has taken place, I annex the only two tables of immigration I have been able to find. And let it be observed that the first is necessarily very imperfect; as there was no governmental regulation to enforce the collection of accurate statements.

In 1817, 22,240 immigrants arrived in ten ports:—

			18,114
In Boston	2,200	In Baltimore	1,817
New York	7,634	Norfolk	520
Perth Amboy	637	Charleston	747
Philadelphia	7,085	Savannah	163
Wilmington, D.	558	New Orleans	879
	18,114		22,240[*]

---

[*]   Seybert, 29.

In New York, from March 2, 1818, to Dec. 11, 1819, the numbers reported at the mayor's office, were 18,929.[*]

			18,532
English	7,539	Portuguese	54
Irish	6,062	Africans	5
French	922	Prussians	48
Welsh	590	Sardinians	3
Scotch	1,942	Danes	97
Germans	499	Russians	13
Spaniards	217	Austrians	8
Hollanders	255	Turk	1
Swiss	372	Polander	1
Italians	103	Sandwich Islanders	2
Norwegians	3	Europeans not described	52
Swedes	28	Passengers do. do.	113
	18,532		18,929

The mayor of New York[†] has given a calculation, that these were but two-thirds of the whole number that arrived. Admitting this estimate, the whole number in twenty-one months was about 28,000, or 16,000 per annum.

Twenty-thousand, which I have assumed, as what might have been annually added to our population by a sound policy on the subject of manufactures,will be regarded as probable on a consideration of the preceding tables— particularly that of the enormous arrivals in New York, notwithstanding a variety of discouraging circumstances, of which the tendency was to repress or even to destroy the spirit of immigration.

Among these, the principal one has been the calamities and wretchedness endured by most of those immigrants, whose fond hopes and expectations were wholly blasted on their arrival here. Thousands and tens of thousands of artists, mechanics, and manufacturers, with talents beyond price, and many of them with handsome capitals, escaped from misery and oppression in Europe, and fled to our shores as a land of promise, where they expected to find room for the exercise of their industry and talents. But the fond delusion was soon dispelled. As soon as they arrived, they sought employment at their usual occupations. None was to be found. Those whose whole fortune was their industry, wandered through our streets, in search even of menial employments, to support a wretched existence. And numerous instances have

---

[*] Report of the society for the prevention of pauperism, p. 67.
[†] "The chief magistrate of this city has calculated that this number does not include more than two-thirds of the real number." Idem, p. 20.

occured, of cotton weavers and clothiers, as well as persons of other useful branches, who have sawed and piled wood in our cities—and some of whom have broken stones on our turnpikes for little more than a bare subsistence. Many hundreds have returned home, heart-broken, and lamenting their folly, after having exhausted all their funds in the double voyage and their inevitable expenses. Their misfortunes operate as a beacon to their countrymen, to shun the rocks on which they have been shipwrecked.

It is easy to estimate the effects that must have been produced by the dismal tales in the letters written by those who remained, and the verbal accounts of those who returned. It is not extravagant to suppose that every returned immigrant prevented the immigration of twenty persons, disposed to seek an asylum here. And the melancholy letters, transmitted by those who had no means of returning, must have had nearly equal influence.

Many of those who were unable to return, rendered desperate by distress and misery, have proved injurious to the country, to which they might have produced the most eminent advantages.

I hazard an estimate of the gain that might have been made by a sound policy, which would have encouraged manufacturing industry, and promoted immigration, to the extent I have assumed, viz. 20,000 additional per annum, since the commencement of our present form of government.

I will suppose the value of the productive labour of each individual to be only a quarter of a dollar per day beyond his subsistence, which for 20,000 would have amounted to $1,500,000 per annum. The whole number that would have arrived in the thirty years, would have been 600,000. The annexed table exhibits a result, which petrifies with astonishment, and sheds a new and strong stream of light on the impolicy of our system.

	No. of immigrants.	*Value of labour.*		*No. of immigrants.*	*Value of labour.*
					180,000,000
1st year	20,000	$ 1,500,000	16th do.	320,000	24,000,000
2d do.	40,000	3,000,000	17th do.	340,000	25,500,000
3d do.	60,000	4,500,000	18th do.	360,000	27,000,000
4th do.	80,000	6,000,000	19th do.	380,000	28,500,000
5th do.	100,000	7,500,000	20th do.	400,000	30,000,000
6th do.	120,000	9,000,000	21st do.	420,000	31,500,000
7th do.	140,000	10,500,000	22d do.	440,000	33,000,000
8th do.	160,000	12,000,000	23d do.	460,000	34,500,000
9th do.	180,000	13,500,000	24th do.	480,000	36,000,000
10th do.	200,000	15,000,000	25th do.	500,000	37,500,000
11th do.	220,000	16,500,000	26th do.	520,000	39,000,000

12th do.	240,000	18,000,000	27th do.	540,000	40,500,000
13th do.	260,000	19,500,000	28th do.	560,000	42,000,000
14th do.	280,000	21,000,000	29th do.	580,000	43,500,000
15th do.	300,000	22,500,000	30th do.	600,000	45,000,000
		$ 180,000,000			$ 697,500,000

The natural increase of the immigrants by generation, at five per cent. per annum, would make the number amount to 1,288,000. Of the addition I take no account. I barely mention, that an immigration of 10,000 annually, would, according to this increase, have produced the same result as the assumed number 20,000.

Let us then state the results of different numbers:—

The labour of 10,000, with the natural increase of five per cent. per annum, at a quarter of a dollar per day, would produce in 30 years	$ 697,500,000
That of 5,000 with the same increase	$ 348,750,000
It is fair to suppose that the articles produced by them would be worth double the labour, or, in the first case,	$ 1,395,000,000
In the second	$ 697,500,000

These immense advantages we blindly threw away, while we were scuffling through the world at every point of the compass, and "in every bay, cove, creek, and inlet," to which we had access, for a precarious commerce, which ruined the great mass of the merchants who pursued it—exposed our hardy seamen to stripes and bondage—involved us in unnecessary collisions with the belligerant powers—and finally in war—and entailed on us a host of foreign ministers—a wasting navy that will cost above 3,500,000 dollars this year—and a debt of nearly 80,000,000 of dollars!

Other views of the subject present themselves.

Although a large proportion of the immigrants who arrive in this and other countries, are dependent on their labour for support, yet many capitalists immigrate; and there would be double the number, could they employ their capitals advantageously. I will assume an average of one hundred and fifty dollars for each immigrant, in money and property. This would amount in the whole to 3,000,000 dollars per annum, or in the whole thirty years, to 90,000,000 of dollars.

The consumption of the productions of agriculture by those immigrants, according to the calculation in page 119, at the rate of a quarter of a dollar per day, would be at present per annum 54,000,000 of dollars, and their clothing at 40 dollars per annum, 24,000,000.

Calculations have been made of the value to a state of an active, efficient individual. In England it was formerly, I believe, supposed to be about 100*l.* sterling. I will suppose each immigrant to be worth three hundred dollars— this would make the amount of the 600,000 immigrants assumed above, $ 180,000,000.

These calculations are all necessarily crude—and admit of considerable drawbacks. But whatever may be the drawbacks, sufficient will remain to prove to the world, that there probably never was a nation which had so many advantages within its grasp—and never a nation that so wantonly threw its advantages away.

Summary.

Suppose 10,000 immigrants annually, with the
    natural increase of five per cent.

Amount of labour in thirty years	$ 697,500,000
Value of their productions	$ 1,395,000,000
Amount of property imported	$ 90,000,000
Present annual consumption	$ 78,000,000

As this chapter drew to a close, I met with a report made to the house of representatives of the United States, on the subject of immigrants, which deserves some notice.

An application was made to congress by a body of Swiss, for a quantity of land, on more advantageous terms than those on which they are sold by law. The committee, after stating the necessity of lessening the existing indulgences in the sale of the public lands, add—

"If the public interests should ever justify a relaxation from them, it would be in favour of American citizens:"

And recommend to the house the following resolution—

"*Resolved,* that the prayer of the petitioners ought not to be granted."

So far there is reason and propriety in the report. The terms on which lands are sold by the United States are sufficiently favourable for foreigners as well as natives. But when the committee notice the depressed situation of American manufactures, and assign it as a reason against encouraging the immigration of such a useful body of men, possessed of invaluable talents, it is a full proof that they did not study the subject profoundly.

"In answer to that part of the petition which declares that one of the principal objects is 'the domestic manufacture of cotton, wool, flax, and silk;' the committee will only say, that it may be well considered, *how far it would comport with sound policy to give a premium for the introduction of manufacturers, at the moment when, by the almost unanimous declaration of our manufacturers, it is said they cannot live without further protection.*"

A more obvious idea would have been to have suggested such encouragement of manufactures, as would have relieved our citizens actually engaged in those branches, and held out due inducements for accessions to our population of the sterling character of the applicants in question.

THE END.

ADDRESSES

OF

THE PHILADELPHIA SOCIETY

FOR

THE PROMOTION

OF

NATIONAL INDUSTRY.

———◆———

"A trade is disadvantageous to a nation which *brings in things of mere luxury or pleasure,* which are entirely or for the most part consumed among us.

"Much worse is that trade which brings in a commodity that is not only consumed among us, but *hinders the consumption of the like quantity of ours.*

"That trade is eminently bad, which *supplies the same articles as we manufacture ourselves, especially if we can make enough for our consumption.*"—British Merchant, vol. i. p. 4.

"Foreign luxuries, and needless manufactures, imported and used in a nation, *increase the people of the nation that furnishes them, and diminish the people of the nation that uses them.*

"Laws, therefore, that prevent such importations, and, on the contrary, promote the exportation of manufactures, to be consumed in foreign countries, may be called, (with respect to the people that make them,) *generative laws; as, by increasing subsistence, they encourage marriage.*

"Such laws, likewise, *strengthen a nation doubly,* by increasing its own people, and diminishing its neighbours."—*Franklin's Works,* vol. iv. pp. 188, 189.

———◆———

SIXTH EDITION.

———◆———

PHILADELPHIA.

....

1822.

Addresses of the Philadelphia Society for the Promotion of National Industry

Mathew Carey

PREFACE TO THE *ADDRESSES*

In presenting our fellow citizens with these addresses, collected together, we cannot refrain from expressing our high sense of the very favourable reception they have experienced. The various defects of style and arrangement which pervade them, have been overlooked, in consideration of the magnitude of the subject they embrace.

We feel persuaded that the cause we advocate yields to none in importance. It is a great error to suppose, as unhappily is too frequently done, that it is the cause of the manufacturers alone. Nothing can be more foreign from the real fact. It is the cause of the nation. It is the mighty question, whether we shall be really or nominally independent—whether we shall persevere in a policy, which, in four or five years, has done more to prostrate our strength and resources, than a fierce war of equal duration could have done—a policy similar to that which has sunk and degraded Spain for centuries, notwithstanding her immense internal and colonial resources—a policy which has never failed, and never can fail, to debilitate and impoverish every country where it has prevailed or may prevail—a policy discarded by every wise nation in Europe—a policy in direct hostility with that of England, Russia, Austria, France, and Denmark—a policy, in a word, that fosters and promotes the wealth, power, resources, industry, and manufactures of foreign nations, and represses and paralizes those of our own country.

If there be any one truth in political economy more sacred and irrefragable than another, it is, that the prosperity of nations bears an exact proportion to the encouragement of their domestic industry—and that their decay and decrepitude commence and proceed *pari passu* with their neglect of it. The wonderful resources of England, so far beyond her intrinsic advantages, and the prostrate state of Spain and Portugal, notwithstanding the numberless blessings bestowed on them by nature, place these great truths on the most impregnable ground.

The United States pursue a wayward and short-sighted policy, of which the world affords few examples, and which evinces how little we have profited by the experience of other nations— and how much we neglect the maxims of the wise statesmen of Europe, as well as of our own country.

With a capacity to raise cotton to supply the whole world, our treasures are lavished in Hindostan to purchase cotton of inferior quality, which is now manufactured in the United States,* to the injury of our cotton planters. And with skill, talents, water-power, capital, and machinery to supply our utmost demand for cambrics and muslins, millions of money are in a similar manner lavished in Hindostan and England, to procure those articles; while tens of thousands of our own citizens, capable of furnishing them, are pining in indigence; their employers ruined; and machinery, which cost millions of dollars, rusting and rotting; and while hundreds of manufacturers, invited to our shores by the excellence of our form of government, are unable to earn a subsistence at their usual trades, and are forced to go to Canada or Nova Scotia, or to return to Europe.† About fifty sailed from hence in one vessel, a few days since.

Under the influence of such a mistaken system, is it wonderful, that distress and embarrassment pervade the nation—that the enlivening sound of the spindle, the loom, and the hammer, has in many places almost ceased to be heard—that our merchants and traders are daily swept away by bankruptcy, one after another—that our banks are drained of their specie—that our cities exhibit an unvarying scene of gloom and despair—that confidence between man and man is almost extinct—that debts cannot in general be collected— that property cannot be sold but at enormous sacrifices—that capitalists have thus an opportunity of aggrandizing themselves at the expense of the middle class of society, to an incalculable extent—that money cannot be borrowed, but at an extravagant interest—in a word, that with advantages equal to any that Heaven has ever bestowed on any nation, we exhibit a state of things at which our enemies must rejoice—and our friends put on sackcloth and ashes?‡

We trust the day is not far distant, when we shall cast a retrospective eye on this lamentable folly, with as much astonishment, as we now do at the folly and wickedness of our ancestors in hanging and burning witches. The folly in both cases is about equal. Theirs, however, was limited to a narrow sphere, out of which it was perfectly innocuous. But ours extends its baneful influence to the remotest extremities of the nation.

---

*   At the time this was written, there were large quantities of East India cotton used by the manufacturers of the U. S.

†   It is probable, that above one thousand emigrants returned from the U. S. to their native countries in 1819.

‡   For a statement of the distress of this period, see the New Olive Branch, Chapter VII.

We are gravely told, by writers on whom, unfortunately, great reliance is placed, that our circumstances as a nation being materially different from those of other nations, we require a totally different policy—and that, however proper or necessary it may be for England or France, to encourage manufactures, sound policy dictates a different course for the United States.

These maxims are the reverse of truth; and having had great influence on the operations of our government, have proved highly pernicious. We are, on the contrary, more imperiously called on to encourage manufactures than most other nations, unless we be disposed wantonly to sacrifice the interests of a most important and numerous portion of our population, those farmers and planters who are remote from the seaboard. We request a patient hearing while we offer our reasons.

In a compact country, like England, where inland navigation is carried to such a wonderful extent, there are few parts of the kingdom that are not within one or two days' carriage of the seaboard—and consequently their productions can be transported to foreign markets at a moderate expense. Whereas a large portion of our agricultural citizens are from three hundred to a thousand miles distant from any seaport, and therefore almost wholly debarred from all foreign markets, especially at the present and all probable future prices.

Flour has been forwarded to the Philadelphia market from Pittsburg, at a freight of four dollars per barrel. Some of it was probably brought to Pittsburg, from fifty to a hundred and fifty miles, at considerable expense. Deduct the expenses and profits of the Pittsburg merchants, from six or seven dollars, and in what a lamentable situation it places the farmer—how miserable a remuneration he has for his labour—and how "*dear he pays for the whistle*," in buying his goods cheap in Hindostan, and depending on European markets for the sale of his productions!

The consequences of this system are so pernicious, that it requires a little further notice. A farmer in the neighbourhood of Pittsburg, sends his produce to that city, whence it is conveyed to Philadelphia, three hundred miles by land—or to New Orleans, two thousand by water. It is thence conveyed four thousand to Liverpool, from whence he receives his china, his delftware, and his pottery. From the amount of his flour as sold in England, all the expenses of transportation are to be deducted—and to the price of his china and other articles, the expenses of the return voyage are to be added. What a frightful view of the situation of a large portion of the people of the western country does this sketch exhibit? Is it difficult to account for the prostrate state of affairs in that part of the union, and under a government, which, emanating more completely from the mass of the people than any other that ever existed, might have been expected to have extended a more paternal care over its citizens than the world ever witnessed!

It is therefore indubitable, that to the reasons for encouraging manufactures, existing in England and France, all of which apply here, is to be added a powerful one peculiar to the United States, arising from the distance between so large a portion of our territory and any seaport towns, as well as the immense distance from those towns to the countries from whence we draw our supplies.

Let us suppose for a moment, that the western farmer, instead of purchasing his pottery and delftware in England, had, in his own neighbourhood, manufactories of those articles, whence he could procure them free of the enormous expenses of sea and land carriages, amounting in many instances to treble the first cost—and that in return, he supplied the manufacturer, of whom he purchased them, with his wheat and corn and other articles! —What a different face that country would wear!—What rapid strides it would then make in the career of prosperity!— What additional allurements it would hold out to immigrants!

We offer for reflection, fellow-citizens, an important fact, that sheds the strongest light on this theory. The settlement of Harmony in the western country, was conducted on this plan.[1] This little commonwealth depended wholly on itself for supplies. It had, to use the cogent language of Mr. Jefferson, *"placed the manufacturer beside the agriculturist."*[2] What was the consequence? The settlement made more rapid advances in wealth and prosperity, than any equal body of men in the world at any period of time—more, in one year, than other parts of the United States, which depend on foreign markets for the sale of their produce and the supply of their wants, have done in ten.

It is frequently stated, that as some of the cotton manufacturers in the eastern states have prospered, the protection to the manufacture is abundantly adequate. If this argument warranted the inference drawn from it, it would prove that the policy of Spain is sound, and fraught with wisdom; for notwithstanding the decay of that nation, there are in it many prosperous manufactures, which, from particular circumstances, are, like some of those in the eastern states, enabled to struggle against foreign competition.—But the decay of so large a portion of the manufacturing establishments in the middle and eastern states, notwithstanding the enterprise, large capital, and industry of the proprietors, is a full proof that there is not sufficient protection to this important branch.

Public attention has unfortunately been diverted from the real sources of our prostrate state, by certain trite common places, re-echoed throughout the union,—that it is a time of general suffering—that distress and embarrassment pervade the whole civilized world—that we are no worse than other nations— and that we cannot hope for an exemption from the common lot of mankind.

This appears plausible—but will not stand the test of examination. It is not wonderful, that the nations of Europe, exhausted by a twenty years' war—pillaged and plundered by hostile armies—with expensive governments and immense armies to support in time of peace—and groaning under the weight of enormous debts, and grinding tithes and taxes, should be in a state of suffering. But there is no parallel between their situation and ours. Our short war,[3] far from exhausting our resources, developed them. We retired from it, prosperous and glorious. Our fields are as fertile—our citizens as industrious and ingenious—our capacity for manufacturing as great as ever—and our taxes are comparatively insignificant. Our distresses cannot therefore be traced to the same source as theirs. They flow wholly from our own mistaken policy, which leads us to purchase abroad what we could produce at home—and, like thoughtless prodigals and spendthrifts, to incur debts beyond our utmost means of payment.

The restoration of peace, however, as might have been naturally expected, greatly affected our commerce, particularly the carrying trade, of which the war had given us an inordinate share. An immense capital, invested in commerce, was thus rendered wholly unproductive; and, had manufactures been encouraged, as sound policy dictated, hundreds of our merchants, whose property has since wasted away, and who have been swallowed up in the vortex of bankruptcy, would, as was the case during the war, have transferred their talents, their industry, and their capital to that department, to the advancement of their own interest and the general welfare; instead of a vain struggle in a branch which was so overstocked, that it could not afford support to more than half the persons engaged in it.—Those that remained in the mercantile profession, after such a transfer of a portion of its members to profitable employment of another description, might and probably would have prospered. And thus it is as clear as the noon-day sun, that an efficient protection of manufactures would have been highly advantageous to the merchants; although many of them, from taking a superficial view of the subject, have been under an opposite impression, and have, unfortunately, been hostile to such protection.

The advocates of the system of Adam Smith ought to be satisfied with the fatal experiment we have made of it. It is true, the demands of the treasury have not allowed us to proceed its full length, and to discard import duties altogether. But as our manufactures are paralized, so large a portion of our manufacturers ruined, and our country almost wholly drained of its metallic medium, to pay for foreign merchandize, notwithstanding the duties imposed *for the purpose of revenue*,[1] it is perfectly reasonable to conclude, that the destruction would have been more rapid and complete, had those duties not existed. This, we hope will be regarded as decisive; for, if our woolen manufacture, for instance, protected, as it is termed, by a duty of 27 1–2 per cent., has been more than one half destroyed, so that it was no longer an object to preserve the invaluable breed of Merino sheep,[5] in which millions of dollars were invested, and of which the greater part have been consigned to the shambles, to the great and manifest injury of the proprietors, it cannot be doubted, that, without such duty, it would have been at once wholly annihilated, as our citizens would, in that event, have been utterly unable to maintain a struggle against foreign rivals. If argument were of avail against the dazzling authority of great names, and against ingrained, inveterate prejudice, this case would settle this question forever. Where are now, we ask, the *"collateral branches"* to which the thousands of our artists, mechanics, and manufacturers, *"thrown out of their ordinary employment, and common method of subsistence"* can *"easily transfer their industry,"** as Dr. Smith asserts?[26]

Another part of Dr. Smith's theory, is, that when a particular branch of industry is destroyed by *"the home market being suddenly laid open to the competition of foreigners,"* *"the stock will still remain in the country, to employ an equal number of people in some other way."* And, therefore, *"the capital of the country remaining the same, the demand for labour will still be the same, though it may be exerted in different places, and for different occupations."*† These maxims are now fairly tested in the United States, as they have been for centuries in Spain. The cotton, woollen, pottery, glass, and various other manufactures, have been in a great measure suspended in the middle states, by *"the home market being suddenly laid open to the competition of foreigners"* at the close of the war. Is there a man who will venture to assert, that *"the demand for labour is the same?"* that *"the stock remains the same?"* or that it *"employs an equal number of people in some other way?"* We flatter ourselves that the most decided advocate of the doctor's system will admit, on calm reflection, that these maxims are utterly destitute of even the shadow of foundation.

We urge this point on the most sober and serious reflection of our fellow citizens. It is a vital one, on which the destinies of this nation depend. The freedom of commerce, wholly unrestrained by protecting duties and prohibitions, is the keystone of the so-much-extolled system of the doctor, which, though discarded, as we have stated, in almost every country in Europe, has, among our most enlightened citizens, numbers of ardent, zealous, and enthusiastic admirers. We have made an experiment of it as far as our debt and the support of our government would permit. We have discarded prohibitions; and, on the most important manufactured articles, wholly prohibited in some countries, and burdened with heavy prohibitory duties in others, our duties are comparatively low, so as to afford no effectual protection to the domestic manufacturer. *The fatal result is before the world*—and, in almost every part of the union, is strikingly perceptible. In addition to the example of Spain and Portugal, it holds out an awful beacon against the adoption of theories, which, however splendid and captivating on paper, are fraught with ruin when carried into practice.

There is one point of view, in which, if this subject be considered, the egregious errors of our system will be manifest beyond contradiction. The

---

*   Wealth of Nations, Hartford Edition, I. 329–30.

†   Ibid.

policy we have pursued renders us dependent for our prosperity on the miseries and misfortunes of our fellow-creatures! Wars and famines in Europe are the keystone on which we erect the edifice of our good fortune! The greater the extent of war, and the more dreadful the famine in that quarter, the more prosperous we become! Peace and abundant crops there undermine our welfare! The misery of Europe ensures our prosperity! its happiness promotes our decay and prostration!! What an appalling idea! Who can reflect without regret on a system built upon such a wretched foundation!

What a contrast between this system and that developed with such ability by Alexander Hamilton, which we advocate! Light and darkness are not more opposite to each other. His admirable system would render our prosperity and happiness dependent wholly on ourselves. We should have no cause to wish for the misery of our fellow men, in order to save us from the distress and embarrassment which at present pervade the nation. Our wants from Europe would, by the adoption of it, be circumscribed within narrower limits, and our surplus raw materials be amply adequate to procure the necessary supplies.

Submitting these important subjects to an enlightened community, and hoping they will experience a calm and unbiased consideration, we ardently pray for such a result as may tend to promote and perpetuate the honour, the happiness, and the real independence of our common country.

To the legislature of the United States, on whose decision depends the perpetuation of existing distress, or the restoration of the country, to that high grade of prosperity from which a false policy has precipitated her, we present the following luminous maxims; viz.

"*The uniform appearance of an abundance of specie, as the concomitant of a flourishing state of manufactures, and of the reverse where they do not prevail, afford a strong presumption of their favourable operation on the wealth of a country.*"[*]

"*Considering a monopoly of the domestic market to its own manufactures, as the reigning policy of manufacturing nations, a similar policy, on the part of the United States, in every proper instance, is dictated, it might almost be said, by the principles of distributive justice; certainly, by the duty of endeavouring to secure their own citizens a reciprocity of advantages.*"[†]

"*The United States cannot exchange with Europe on equal terms.*"[‡]

"*That trade is eminently bad which supplies the same goods as we manufacture ourselves; especially, if we can make enough for our own consumption.*"[§]

---

[*] Hamilton's Works, vol I. p. 217.
[†] Idem, p. 225.
[‡] Idem, 186.
[§] British Merchant, vol. I. p. 4.

NO. I

Philadelphia, March 27, 1819.
Definition of political economy. Its importance. Influence of great names. Leading feature of
Adam Smith's theory. Pernicious consequences of its adoption.

FRIENDS AND FELLOW CITIZENS,

The Philadelphia Society for the Promotion of National Industry, respectfully
solicit your attention to a few brief essays on topics of vital importance to your
country, yourselves, and your posterity. They shall be addressed to your reason
and understanding, without any attempt to bias your feelings by declamation.

Political economy shall be the subject of these essays. In its broad and
liberal sense, it may be correctly styled the 'science of promoting human
happiness;' than which a more noble subject cannot occupy the attention of
men endowed with enlarged minds, or inspired by public spirit.

It is to be regretted that this sublime science has not had adequate attention
bestowed on it in this country. And unfortunately, so many contradictory
systems are in existence, that statesmen and legislators, disposed to discharge
their duty conscientiously, and for that purpose to study the subject, are liable
to be confused and distracted by the unceasing discordance in the views of
the writers.

It is happily true, nevertheless, that its leading principles, calculated to
conduct nations safely to the important and beneficent results, which are its
ultimate object, are plain and clear; and, to be distinctly comprehended, and
faithfully carried into effect, require no higher endowments than good sound
sense and rectitude of intentions.

It is a melancholy feature in human affairs, that imprudence and error often
produce as copious a harvest of wretchedness as absolute wickedness. Hence
arises the imperious necessity, in a country where so many of our citizens may
aspire to the character of legislators and statesmen, of a more general study of
this science, a thorough knowledge of which is so essential a requisite, among
the qualifications for those important stations.

To remove all doubt on this point, numberless instances are to be found
in history, in which single errors of negotiators and legislators have entailed

full as much, and in many cases more misery on nations, than the wild and destructive ambition of conquerors. Unless in some extraordinary instances, a sound policy, on the restoration of peace, heals the wounds inflicted by war, and restores a nation to its pristine state of ease and comfort. But it has frequently occurred, that an article of a treaty, of ten or a dozen lines, or an impolitic or unjust law, has produced the most ruinous consequences for a century.

It is our intention,

1. To review the policy of those nations which have enjoyed a high degree of prosperity, with or without any extraordinary advantages from nature; and likewise of those whose prosperity has been blasted by fatuitous counsels, notwithstanding great natural blessings.
2. To examine the actual situation of our country, in order to ascertain whether we enjoy the manifold blessings to which our happy form of government and numerous local advantages entitle us; and, if we do not, to investigate the causes to which the failure is owing.
3. To develop the true principles of political economy, suited to our situation and circumstances, and calculated to produce the greatest sum of happiness throughout the wide expanse of our territory.

In this arduous undertaking, we request a patient and candid hearing from our fellow-citizens. We fondly hope for success; but, if disappointed, we shall have the consolation of having endeavoured to discharge a duty every good citizen owes to the country which protects him; the duty of contributing his efforts to advance its interest and happiness.

As a preliminary step, we propose to establish the utter fallacy of some maxims, supported by the authority of the name of Adam Smith, author of The Wealth of Nations, but pregnant with certain ruin to any nation by which they may be carried into operation. This course is prescribed to us by the circumstance, that the influence of these maxims has been most sensibly and perniciously felt in our councils; has deeply affected our prosperity; and been the main source whence the prevailing distress of the nation has flowed.

This writer stands so pre-eminent in the estimation of a large portion of Christendom, as the Delphic Oracle of political economy, and there is such a magic in his name, that it requires great hardihood to encounter him, and a high degree of good fortune to obtain a fair and patient hearing for the discussion.

But at this enlightened period, we trust our citizens will scorn to surrender their reason into the guidance of any authority whatever. When a position is presented to the mind, the question ought to be, not who delivered it, but what is its nature? and, how is it supported by reason and common sense, and especially by fact? A theory, how plausible soever, and however propped up by a bead-roll of great names, ought to be regarded with suspicion, if unsupported by fact—and, *a fortiori*, if contrary to established fact, ought to be unhesitatingly rejected. This course of procedure is strongly recommended by the decisive circumstance, that, in the long catalogue of wild, ridiculous, and absurd theories on morals, religion, politics, or science, which have domineered over mankind, there is hardly one that has not reckoned among its partisans, men of the highest celebrity.* And in the present instance, the most cogent and conclusive facts bear testimony against the political economist, how great soever his reputation.

We hope, therefore, that our readers will bring to this discussion, minds wholly liberated from the fascination of the name of the writer whose opinions we undertake to combat, and a determination to weigh the evidence in the scales of reason, not those of prejudice.

In order to render Dr. Smith full justice, and to remove all ground for cavil, we state his propositions at length, and in his own language:

1. "To give the monopoly of the home market to the produce of domestic industry, in any particular art or manufacture, is in some measure to direct private people in what manner they ought to employ their capitals; and must, in almost all cases, be either a useless or a hurtful regulation. If the domestic produce can be brought there as cheap as that of foreign industry, the regulation is evidently useless. If it cannot, it must generally be hurtful.

2. "It is the maxim of every prudent master of a family, never to attempt to make at home what it will cost him more to make than to buy. The tailor does not attempt to make his own shoes, but buys them of the shoemaker. The shoemaker does not attempt to make his own clothes, but employs a tailor. The farmer neither attempts to make one nor the other, but employs those different artificers. All of them find it for their interest to employ their whole industry in a way in which they have some advantage

---

* Montesquieu, whose reputation was as great as that of Dr. Smith, and whose Spirit of Laws has had as extensive a currency as the Wealth of Nations held the absurd idea, which remained uncontroverted for half a century, that the habits, manners and customs, and even the virtues and vices of nations, were in a great measure governed by climate; whence it would result that a tolerable idea might be formed of those important features of national character, by consulting maps, and ascertaining latitudes and longitudes! Bacon studied judicial astrology! All the great men of his day believed in magic and witchcraft! Johnson had full faith in the story of the Cocklane-Ghost! So much for great names.

over their neighbours; and to purchase with a part of its produce, or, what is the same thing, with the price of a part of it, whatever else they have occasion for.

3.   "That which is prudence in the conduct of every private family, can scarcely be folly in that of a great kingdom. If a foreign country can supply us with a commodity cheaper than we ourselves can make it, better buy it from them, with some part of the produce of our country, employed in a way in which we have some advantage.

4.   "The general industry of the country being in proportion to the capital which employs it, will not thereby be diminished, any more than that of the above-mentioned artificers; but only left to find out the way in which it can be employed with the greatest advantage. It is not so employed, when directed to an object which it can buy cheaper than it can make. The value of its annual produce is certainly more or less diminished, when it is thus turned away from producing commodities evidently of more value than the commodity which it is directed to produce. According to the supposition, that commodity could be purchased from foreign countries cheaper than it can be made at home. It could, therefore, have been purchased with part only of the commodities, or, what is the same thing, with a part only of the price of the commodities, which the industry employed by an equal capital would have produced at home, had it been left to pursue its natural course."[*]

There is in the subordinate parts of this passage much sophistry and unsound reasoning, which we may examine on a future occasion; and there is likewise, as in all the rest of the doctor's work, a large proportion of verbiage, which is admirably calculated to embarrass and confound common understandings, and prevent their forming a correct decision. But, stripped of this verbiage, and brought naked and unsophisticated to the eye of reason, the main proposition which we at present combat, and to which we here confine ourselves, is, that:

"If a foreign country can supply us with a commodity cheaper than we ourselves can make it, better buy of them, with some part of the produce of our own industry, employed in a way in which we have some advantage."

The most rational mode of testing the correctness of any maxim or principle is, to examine what have been its effects where it has been carried into operation, and what they would be in any given case where it might be applied. This is the plan we shall pursue in this investigation.

Great Britain affords a felicitous instance for our purpose. Let us examine what effect the adoption of this maxim would produce on her happiness and prosperity.

---

[*]   *Wealth of Nations*, Hartford, 1818, vol. I, p. 319.

There are above a million of people, of both sexes and of all ages, employed in that country, in the woollen and cotton manufactures.[*] By their industry in these branches, they make for themselves and families a comfortable subsistence. They afford a large and steady market for the productions of the earth, giving support to, probably, at least two millions of persons engaged in agriculture, who furnish the one set of manufacturers with the raw materials, and both with food. They moreover, enrich the nation by bringing into it wealth from nearly all parts of the earth. The immense sums of money they thus introduce into their native country afford means of employment, and ensure happiness to other millions of subjects—and thus, like the circles made on the surface of the stream by the central pebble thrown in, the range of happiness is extended so wide as to embrace the whole community.

From this cheering prospect, let us turn the startled eye to the masses of misery, which Dr. Smith's system would produce; and we shall then behold a hideous contrast, which, we trust, escaped the doctor's attention; for the acknowledged goodness and benevolence of his character, will not allow us to believe that he would have been the apostle of such a pernicious doctrine, had he attended to its results. We fondly hope, that, like many other visionary men, he was so deeply engaged in the fabrication of a refined theory, that he did not arrest his progress to weigh its awful consequences.

The East Indies could at all times, until the recent improvements in machinery, have furnished cotton goods at a lower rate than they could be manufactured in England, which had no other means of protecting its domestic industry, but by a prohibition of the rival fabrics. Let us suppose that France, where provisions and labour are much lower than in England, has possessed herself of machinery, and is thus enabled to sell woollen goods at half, or three-fourths, or seven-eighths of the price of the English rival commodities. Suppose, further, that articles manufactured of leather are procurable in Germany, and iron wares in Sweden, below the rates in England. Then, if the statesmen of the last nation were disciples of Adam Smith, as "foreign countries could supply them with those commodities cheaper than they themselves can make them," they must, according to the doctor, "buy from them with some part of the produce of their own country," and accordingly open their ports freely to those various articles, from these four particular nations. Who can contemplate the result without horror? What a wide spread scene of ruin and desolation would take place? The wealth of the country would be swept away, to enrich foreign, and probably hostile

---

[*]   Dr. Seybert states, that in 1809, there were 800,000 persons in Great Britain engaged in the cotton manufacture alone. It has since increased considerably. It is, therefore, probable that the two branches employ at least 1,300,000 persons—*Statistics*, p. 92.

nations, which might, at no distant period, make use of the riches and strength thus fatuitously placed in their hands, to enslave the people who had destroyed themselves by following such baneful counsels. The labouring and industrious classes would be at once bereft of employment; reduced to a degrading state of dependence and mendicity; and, through the force of misery and distress, driven to prey upon each other, and upon the rest of the community. The middle classes of society would partake of the distress of the lower, and the sources of the revenues of the higher orders be dried up.* And all this terrific scene of woe, and wretchedness, and depravity, is to be produced for the grand purpose of procuring broadcloth, and muslins, and shoes, and iron ware, in distant parts of the earth, a few shillings per yard, or piece, or pound, cheaper than at home! The manufacturers of Bombay, and Calcutta, and Paris, and Lyons, and Frankfort, and Stockholm, are to be fed, and clothed, and fostered by English wealth, while those of England, whom it ought to nourish and protect, are expelled from their workshops, and driven to seek support from the overseers of the poor. We trust this will not be thought a fancy sketch! Such a view of it would be an extravagant error. It is sober, serious reality; and puts down forever this plausible, but ruinous theory. Ponder well on it, fellow citizens.

Let us suppose another strong case. The cotton produced in this country, amounts, probably, to thirty millions of dollars annually at present prices—but to forty at least, at the prices of 1815 and 1816. We will suppose the minimum of the price, at which it can be sold, to pay for the labour and interest on the capital employed in its culture, to be twelve cents per pound. We will further suppose, that the southern provinces of Spanish America have established their independence, and are able to supply us with this valuable raw material at the rate of ten cents. Ought we, for the sake of saving a few cents per pound, to destroy the prospects, and ruin the estates of nearly 800,000 inhabitants of the southern states—to paralize a culture so immensely advantageous, and producing so large a fund of wealth, and strength and happiness? Should we, for such a paltry consideration, run the risk of consequences which cannot he regarded without awe, and which could not fail eventually to involve in ruin, even those who might appear in the first instance to profit by the adoption of the system?

It may be well worth while to proceed a step further, and take the case of a nation able to supply us fully and completely with wheat and other grain at a lower rate than our farmers can furnish them. Thus then we should find ourselves pursuing Adam Smith's sublime system; buying cheap bargains of wheat or flour from one nation; cotton from another; hardware from a third;

---

* No small portion of this picture is (1819) rapidly realizing in this country.

and, to pursue the system throughout, woollen, and cotton, and linen goods from others; while our country was rapidly impoverishing of its wealth, its industry paralized, the labouring part of our citizens reduced to beggary, and the farmers, planters, and manufacturers, involved in one common mass of ruin. The picture demands the most sober, serious attention of the farmers and planters of the United States.

It may be asserted, that the supposition of our country being fully supplied with cotton and grain, by foreign nations, is so improbable, as not to be admissible even by way of argument. This is a most egregious error; our supposition, so far as it respects cotton, is in "the full tide of successful experiment." That article, we repeat, to a great amount, is even at present[*] imported from Bengal, and sold at a price so far below our own, (difference of quality considered) that our manufacturers find the purchase eligible. Let it be considered, that in 1789, doubts were entertained whether cotton could be cultivated in the United States;[†] that in the year 1794, there were exported from this country, of foreign and domestic cotton, only seven thousand bags;[‡] and yet, that in 1818, the amount exported was above ninety-two millions of pounds. No man can be so far misled as to suppose that Heaven has given us any exclusive monopoly of the soil and climate calculated for such extraordinary and almost incredible advances. The rapid strides we have made, may be also made by other nations. Cotton is said to be shipped at Bombay for three pence sterling per lb.; and therefore, setting South America wholly out of the question, it can hardly be doubted, from the spirit with which the culture of that plant is prosecuted in the East Indies, and the certainty that the seeds of our best species have been carried there, that in a few years that country will be able, provided Adam Smith's theory continues to be acted upon here, to expel our planters from their own markets, after having driven them from those of Europe.

It is not, therefore, hazarding much to assert, that the time cannot be very remote, when southern cotton industry will be compelled to supplicate congress for that legislative protection, for which the manufacturing industry of the rest of the union has so earnestly implored that body in vain; and which, had it been adequately afforded, would have saved from ruin numerous manufacturing establishments, and invaluable machinery, which cost millions of dollars—now a dead and irreparable loss to the enterprising proprietors. Had these establishments been preserved, and duly protected, they would have greatly lessened our ruinously unfavourable balance of trade, and of

---

[*] 1819.
[†] Seybert's Statistics, page 84.
[‡] Idem, p. 94.

course prevented that pernicious drain of specie, which has overspread the face of our country with distress, and clouded (we trust only temporarily) as fair prospects as ever dawned on any nation.*

We have given a slight sketch of the effects the adoption of this system would produce in England and the United States, if carried into complete operation; and also glanced at the consequences its partial operation has already produced here. We now proceed to cast a very cursory glance (reserving details for a future occasion) at its lamentable results in Spain and Portugal, where the statesmen are disciples of Adam Smith, and where the theory, which now goes under the sanction of his name, has been in operation for centuries. As "foreign countries can supply them with commodities cheaper than they themselves can make them," they therefore consider it "better to buy from them, with some part of the produce of their own country."

These countries are in a forlorn and desperate state, notwithstanding the choicest blessings of nature have been bestowed on them with lavish hand; industry is paralized, and the enormous floods of wealth, drawn from their colonies, answer no other purpose but to foster and encourage the industry, and promote the happiness of rival nations; and all obviously and undeniably the result of the system of "*buying goods where they are to be had cheapest,*" to the neglect and destruction of their domestic industry. With such awful beacons before your eyes, can you contemplate the desolating effects of the system in

---

* This view may appear too gloomy. Would to heaven it were! A cursory glance at some of the great interests of the United States, will settle the question. Cotton, the chief staple of the country, is falling, and not likely to rise:† as the immense quantities from the East Indies have glutted the English market, which regulates the price in ours. Affairs in the western country, on which so many of our importers depend, are to the last degree unpromising.—The importers, of course, have the most dreary and sickening prospects before them. They are deeply in debt, their resources almost altogether suspended, and a large proportion ultimately precarious. Our commerce and navigation languish every where, except to the East Indies, the most ruinous branch we carry on. Further, notwithstanding nearly eight millions of specie were imported by the Bank of the U. States at a heavy expense, in about one year; so great has been the drain, that the banks are generally so slenderly provided, as to excite serious uneasiness. We are heavily indebted to England, after having remitted immense quantities of government and bank stock, whereby we shall be laid under a heavy and perpetual annual tax for interest. Our manufactures are in general drooping, and some of them are one-half or two-thirds suspended. Our cities present the distressing view of immense numbers of useful artizans, mechanics, and manufacturers, willing to work, but unable to procure employment. We might proceed with the picture to a great extent; but presume enough has been stated to satisfy the most incredulous, that the positions in the text are by no means exaggerated.

† At the time this was written, the price in Liverpool was for Uplands, about 16d sterling—for Sea Islands, 34d. It is now for the former, 10d.—for the latter, 18d.

those two countries, without deep regret, that so many of our citizens, and some of them in high and elevated stations, advocate its universal adoption here, and are so far enamoured of Dr. Smith's theory, that they regard as a species of heresy the idea of appealing to any other authority, on the all-important and vital point of the political economy of nations!

To avoid prolixity, we are obliged to postpone the consideration of other positions of Dr. Smith on this subject; and shall conclude with a statement of those maxims of political economy which we shall endeavour to inculcate, the soundness of which is established by the experience of the wisest as well as of the most fatuitous nations of the earth.

1. Industry is the only sure foundation of national virtue, happiness, and greatness; and, in all its useful shapes and forms, has an imperious claim on governmental protection.
2. No nation ever prospered to the extent of which it was capable, without due protection of domestic industry.
3. Throughout the world, in all ages, wherever industry has been duly encouraged, mankind have been uniformly industrious.
4. Nations, like individuals, are in a career of ruin when their expenditures exceed their income.
5. Whenever nations are in this situation, it is the imperious duty of their rulers to apply such remedies, to correct the evil, as the nature of the case may require.
6. There are few, if any, political evils, to which a wise legislature, untrammelled in its deliberations and decisions, cannot apply an adequate remedy.
7. The decay and distress, for a long series of years, of Spain, Portugal, and Italy, prove, beyond controversy, that no natural advantages, how great or abundant soever, will counteract the baleful effects of unsound systems of policy; and the cotemporaneous prosperity enjoyed by Switzerland, Holland, and Scotland, equally prove, that no natural disadvantages are insuperable by sound policy.
8. Free government is not prosperity. It is only the means, but, wisely employed, is the certain means of insuring prosperity.
9. The interests of agriculture, manufactures, and commerce, are so inseparably connected, that any serious injury suffered by one of them must materially affect the others.
10. The home market for the productions of the earth and manufactures, is of more importance than all the foreign ones, even in countries which carry on an immense foreign commerce.
11. It is impossible for a nation, possessed of immense natural advantages, in endless diversity of soil and climate—in productions of inestimable

value—in the energy and enterprize of its inhabitants—and unshackled by an oppressive debt—to suffer any great or general distress, in its agriculture, commerce, or manufactures, (war, famines, pestilence and calamities of seasons excepted) unless there be vital and radical errors in its system of political economy.

NO. II

Philadelphia, April 7, 1819.
Further review of Adam Smith's maxims. Their pernicious consequences admitted by himself. Proposed remedy in collateral manufactures and country labour. Futility of the proposition. Ignorance of the nobility, country gentlemen and merchants, asserted by Dr. Smith. Position utterly unfounded.

Dr. Smith's maxim, discussed in our first number, inevitably involves in its consequences, as we have proved, the destruction of those manufacturing establishments, which produce articles that can be purchased "cheaper abroad than they can be made at home;" and its necessary result is, to deprive those engaged in them of employment. The doctor, after having inflicted a deadly wound by this maxim, undertakes to provide a sovereign and infallible remedy for the evil, which, to do him and his system justice, we shall exhibit in his own words:—It remains to examine how far the prescription applies a remedy to the evil.

I. "Though a number of people should, *by restoring the freedom of trade, be thrown all at once out of their ordinary employment, and common method of subsistence*, it would by no means follow, that they would thereby be deprived either of employment or subsistence."*

II. "To the *greater part* of manufactures, there are other *collateral manufactures* of so familiar a nature, that a workman can easily *transfer his industry* from one to the other.

III. "The greater part of such workmen, too, are occasionally employed in *country labour*.

IV. "The stock, which employed them in a particular manufacture before, will still remain in the country, to employ an equal number of people in some other way.

---

* Wealth of Nations, I. 329.

V.   *"The capital of the country remaining the same, the demand for labour will still be the same,* though it may be exerted "in different places, and for different occupations."*

Here are five distinct prepositions, more clear and plain than Dr. Smith's usually are; but, as we hope to make appear, all highly erroneous, calculated to lead those statesmen astray, who square their systems by them, and pregnant with ruin to those nations which may be impolitic enough to carry them into operation.

The main point is the facility of *"transferring industry"* from one branch to a *"collateral manufacture."* All the rest are but subsidiary to, or explanatory of this fallacious assumption.

Two questions arise here, both important, and both demanding affirmative answers, in order to support the doctor's hypothesis.

I. Are there such *"collateral manufactures,"* as he assumes, in which men, bereft of employment in those departments of manufacture, which are to be destroyed by the doctor's grand and captivating idea of *"restoring the freedom of commerce,"* may *"transfer their industry?"*

It may be conceded, that there is a species of affinity between the weaving of cotton and woollen, and a few other manufactures. But this cannot by any means answer the doctor's purpose. Where will he, or any of his disciples, find *"collateral manufactures,"* to employ printers, coach-makers, watch-makers, shoemakers, hatters, paper-makers, book-binders, engravers, letter-founders, chandlers, saddlers, silver-platers, jewellers, smiths, cabinet-makers, stone-cutters, glass-makers, brewers, tobacconists, potters, wire-drawers, tanners, curriers, dyers, rope-makers, brick-makers, plumbers, chair-makers, glovers, umbrella-makers, embroiderers, calico-printers, paper-stainers, engine-makers, turners, wheelwrights, and the great variety of other artists and manufacturers? There are no such collateral manufactures as he has presumed. And it may be asserted, without scruple, that if, by what the doctor speciously styles *"restoring the freedom of trade,"* five hundred, or a thousand, or ten thousand hatters, shoemakers, printers, or chandlers, are "thrown out of their ordinary employment," there is no *"collateral manufacture of so familiar a nature,"* that they *"can easily transfer their industry from one to another."* For the truth of this assertion we freely appeal to the common sense of an enlightened public.

We state a case, plain and clear. We will suppose five hundred workmen, and a capital of five hundred thousand dollars, employed in the manufacture of watches, coaches, and silver-plate; and that Switzerland, or Paris, or London, fills our markets at such rates as to overwhelm at once all competition, and

---

*   Wealth of Nations, I. 330.

suppress the home manufactories, as has often been the case in various branches, in this and other countries. Where are the "*collateral manufactures*," to receive and employ those oppressed and forlorn workmen, whose prospects, and those of their families are thus blasted? Are they to become hatters, or shoemakers, or tailors, or saddlers, or weavers, or smiths, or carpenters? Is there a man who can persuade himself into the belief of such an order of things? Is there a man fatuitous enough to suppose, that "*the general industry of the country will not thereby be diminished?*" No: and it is a matter of inexpressible astonishment, that such an idea could have ever been hazarded, in a sober and serious book, which has been so long regarded as a guide to statesmen and legislators, and as the infallible oracle of political economy. It will not stand the test of a moment's investigation. As well might we suppose, that, on shutting up the courts of justice, and expelling the whole corps of lawyers, they might at once commence the medical or clerical profession, without any previous study, as that hatters, or tailors, or shoemakers, or weavers, or watch-makers, or printers, whom the grand system of "*purchasing commodities cheap*," and the equally grand system of "*restoring the freedom of commerce*," might bereave of employment, should find those "*collateral manufactures*," which Dr. Smith has so kindly provided for them.

We explicitly declare, that we are far from charging the doctor with an intention to mislead or deceive. We believe him, like many other theorists, to have been deluded by his own system. But be this as it may, we trust it will appear that a more deceptious ground never was assumed. We use strong and unequivocal language; as the political heresy we combat is of the most pernicious tendency; is supported by the most imposing and formidable name in the whole range of political science; and, as has been observed, embraces among its disciples a large portion of those of our citizens whose situations as legislators of the Union and of the several states, render their errors on this vital point pregnant with the most destructive and ruinous consequences.

II. Suppose every branch of manufactures, without exception, to have some "*collateral manufacture*," can those who are devested of employment by what is speciously and captivatingly styled "*restoring the freedom of trade*," "*transfer their industry*" so "*easily*" as Dr. Smith assumes?

We answer distinctly, No: or, at all events, on so very small and insignificant a scale, as to be unworthy of notice, in discussions involving the best interests and the happiness of nations. To test the correctness of this opinion, let it be observed, that, in manufacturing countries, all the departments are generally full, and not only full, but there are almost always supernumeraries in abundance: and therefore, even did these "*collateral manufactures*" really exist, to the full extent the doctor's theory would require, and not been "fancy sketches," derived from his fertile imagination, there would be no vacancy, to which the objects of the doctor's care could "*transfer their industry*."

Although this appears so plain and palpable, as not to admit contradiction or dispute, yet, on a point of such magnitude, it cannot be time ill-spent, to illustrate it by example.

There are scarcely any branches between which there is so much affinity as the cotton and woollen. And if the doctor's theory would ever stand the ordeal of examination, it would be in the case of these two "*collateral manufactures.*" Suppose, then, that, by the introduction of East India muslins, four or five hundred thousand persons, (about one-half of the whole number engaged in the cotton manufacture) in England, are at once thrown out of employment:— can any man be led to believe, that they could find a vacuum in the "*collateral*" woollen "*manufacture*" to which "*they could easily transfer their industry?*" Fatuity alone could harbour the supposition. They would find all the situations in that branch full and overflowing.

But the strongest argument against the doctor's "*collateral manufactures*" and "*transfers of industry,*" remains. He obviously did not calculate the results of his own system, nor take into consideration, that, to give it free operation, its pernicious effect would not be confined to one or two branches of industry. It would extend to the whole mass. The flood of importation on the "*restoration*" of the Doctor's "*freedom of trade,*" would bear down in one common ruin, all those manufactures, of which the articles fell within his description being "purchased cheaper elsewhere." What then becomes of his "*collateral manufactures?*" and "*transfer of industry,*" and "*employment of capital,*" and all those elegant, sounding phrases, with which he rounds off his paragraphs? Are they not swept away, "like the baseless fabric of a vision," not leaving "a trace behind?"[7]

The doctor with great gravity informs us, that "*the greater part of such workmen are occasionally employed in country labour.*" This is most extravagantly erroneous; for of all the manufacturers of England or any other country, there is not probably one in five, who has ever been in his life twelve months at "*country labour.*" Their habits and manners wholly incapacitate them for that kind of employment. A jeweller, a watchmaker, a hatter, a shoemaker, or a weaver, would be almost as unfit for "*country labour,*" as a ploughman, or a gardener, or a shepherd, to make hats or coats.

But suppose, for a moment, through courtesy, that we admit with Dr. Smith, that all these different manufacturers are so much accustomed to "*country labour,*" as to be adepts at it, what inference is to be drawn from the admission? Did the doctor believe, did he intend the world to believe, or does there live a man who can believe, that when, by the grand project of "*restoring the freedom of trade,*" and "*buying commodities from foreign countries,*" which can supply us with them "*cheaper than we ourselves can make them,*" thousands and tens of thousands of people are "*all at once thrown out of their ordinary employment,*" *and common means of subsistence*," they can find employment at "*country labour?*" However extravagant and childish the idea is, the doctor must have meant this, or the words were introduced without any meaning whatever.

But it is well known, that except in harvest time, there is in the country no want of auxiliaries. The persons attached to farms are generally, at all other seasons, amply adequate to execute all the necessary "*country labour*" without "transferring" to that department the industry of those "manufacturers" who are "*all at once thrown out of their ordinary employment, and common means of subsistence.*"

Dr. Smith, in order to prove the impropriety of those laws, whereby rival manufactures are wholly excluded, observes,

"*If the domestic produce can be brought there as cheap, the regulation is evidently useless. If it cannot, it is evidently "hurtful."*"*

This passage is written in a style very different from that usual with Dr. Smith, who is as lavish of words as any writer in the English language, and equally lavish of explanations and amplifications. But here he falls into the contrary extreme, and his brevity renders his positions ambiguous; as he does not condescend to give us the reason for those assertions. He leaves the reader to divine why "*the regulation is useless?*" why "*hurtful?*" We must, therefore, endeavour to explore the meaning. It appears to be, if we understand the first sentence, that "all restrictions or regulations," in favour of domestic industry, to the exclusion of rival manufactures, are "*useless,*" if "*the articles can be made at home as cheap,*" as the imported ones; because, in that case, the domestic manufacturer is secure from injury by the competition.

This is extravagantly erroneous. Suppose our woollen manufacturers sell their best broadcloth at eight dollars per yard, and that foreign broadcloth to an immense amount, is imported "*as cheap.*" Is it not obvious, that the glut in the market, and the ardent competition between the two parties, would produce the effect which such a state of things has never failed to produce, that is, a reduction of the price below the minimum at which the manufacturer could support himself by his labours, and that he would therefore be ruined?

We now proceed to consider the last proposition:—

"*The capital of the country remaining the same, the demand for labour will still be the same, though it be exerted in different places and in different occupations.*"†

To prove the extreme fallacy of this position, we will take the case of any particular branch, in which there are one hundred master manufacturers, each worth ten thousand dollars, forming together, "*a capital,*" of one million, whose business is destroyed by the "*restoration of the freedom of commerce,*" and "*the purchase of articles from abroad cheaper than we ourselves can make them.*"

---

*   Wealth of Nations, I. 319.
†   Wealth of Nations, I. 330.

It is well known that the property of manufacturers generally consists in buildings for their works, machinery, raw materials, manufactured goods, and outstanding debts. The result of *"the restoration of the freedom of commerce"* on Dr. Smith's plan, would be to reduce the value of the four first items, from twenty to fifty per cent., and to bankrupt a large proportion of the proprietors.

As this is a point of considerable importance, we shall take a single instance, which is always more easily comprehended than a number, and yet affords as clear an illustration.

We will suppose the case of a tanner, worth thirty thousand dollars, of which his various vats, buildings, and tools amount to ten thousand; his hides and leather, ten thousand; and his outstanding debts, an equal sum. By the inundation of foreign leather, sold, we will suppose, far below the price which affords him a reasonable profit, or even a reimbursement of his expenses, he is unable to carry on his business, which sinks the value of his vats and buildings three fourths, and of his stock one-half. At once, his fortune is reduced above twelve thousand dollars: and thus, with a diminished capital and broken heart, perhaps in his old age, he has to go in quest of, but will not find, a *"collateral manufacture,"* to employ that diminished capital.—Analogous cases without number would occur, by the doctor's system of *"restoring the freedom of trade:"* and let us add, as we can with perfect truth, and we hope it will sink deep into the minds of the citizens of the United States, that throughout this country there are numberless cases equally strong, which no man of sound mind and heart can regard without the deepest sympathy for the ill-fated sufferers, and regret at the mistaken policy which produced such a state of things.

It therefore irresistibly follows, that Dr. Smith's idea, that *"the capital of the country will be the same,"* after the destruction of any branch of manufacture, is to the last degree unsound: and, of course, that the superstructure built on it partakes of its fallacy.

The doctor gravely informs us, *"The tailor does not make his own shoes, but buys them of the shoemaker. The shoemaker does not attempt to make his own clothes, but employs a tailor."*[*] And he adds farther:

"By means of glasses, hot-beds, and hot-walls, very good grapes can be raised in Scotland, and very good wine too can be made of them, at about thirty times the expense for which at least equally good can be brought from foreign countries. Would it be a reasonable law to prohibit the importation of all foreign wines, merely to encourage the making of Claret and Burgundy in Scotland?"[†]

---

[*]   Wealth of Nations, I. 320.

[†]   Idem, 320.

From these positions, to which no man can refuse assent, he deduces the specious, but delusory maxim of *"restoring the freedom of trade,"* which, in fact and in truth, is nothing more or less than opening the door to the admission of foreign goods to an unbounded extent, to the ruin of the citizens or subjects engaged in the manufacture of articles of a similar description—and thereby impoverishing the nation and sacrificing its domestic industry at the shrine of avarice, in order to purchase goods *"cheaper than they can be made at home."*

But by what process of sound reasoning does it follow, because the shoemaker will not become a tailor, or the tailor a shoemaker; or because it would be extravagant folly to exclude foreign wines, in order to introduce the culture of the vine into Scotland, a country wholly unfit for that object; that therefore thousands of men employed in useful branches of business, diffusing happiness among tens of thousands of workmen and their numerous families, and enriching their country, are to have their usefulness destroyed, their prospects blasted, their workmen with their families reduced to distress, and the country exposed to a ruinous drain of specie?

These maxims are the basis on which a large portion, indeed the most important part of Dr. Smith's work, depends. If the basis be solid and impregnable, the fabric will stand firm: but if the foundation be sandy, the superstructure will crumble into ruins. We trust we have fully proved that the foundation is sandy; and that the necessary and inevitable consequence follows, that the theory itself is wholly untenable and pernicious.

With one more extract, we shall conclude this review:

"That foreign trade enriched the country, experience demonstrated to the nobles and country gentlemen, as well as to the merchants; but, *how, or in what manner, none of them knew!* The merchants knew perfectly in what manner it enriched themselves. It was their business to know it. But *to know in what manner it enriched the country, was no part of their business!* The subject never came into their consideration, but when they had occasion to apply to their country for some change in the laws respecting foreign trade."[*]

It is hardly possible to conceive a passage more absurd or erroneous than this. That *"the nobles, and country gentlemen, and merchants,"* were ignorant *"how foreign trade enriched their country,"* is almost too ludicrous to be assailed by argument, and is a strong instance of the delirium, in which enthusiastic theorists are liable to be involved, by the ignis fatuus of their visionary views. Can there be found a man, in the wide extent of the United States, to believe that Sir Joshua Gee, Josiah Child, Theodore Janssen, Charles King, Thomas Willing, Robert Morris, George Clymer, Thomas Fitzsimons, Governeur and Kemble,[8] and the thousands of other merchants, of equal mind, who have

---

[*]   Wealth of Nations, I. 303.

flourished in Great Britain and this country, could be ignorant "*in what manner foreign commerce enriched a country*," without the aid of the Wealth of Nations? It is impossible. Take any man of sound mind, who has followed the plough, or driven the shuttle, or made shoes all his life, and clearly state the operations of trade to him, and he will rationally account for the "*manner in which foreign trade enriches a country*." Indeed a merchant's apprentice of six months standing, could not mistake "*the manner*." Any one of them would at once pronounce, that foreign trade enriches a country, exactly as farmers, planters, or manufacturers are enriched; that is, by the very simple process of *selling more than they buy*. No nation ever was, none will ever be enriched in any other way. And it is unaccountable that Dr. Smith should have supposed that it was reserved for him to make the grand discovery. The principle was well understood by the merchants of Tyre 3000 years before Adam Smith was born. And if Spain be one of the most forlorn and wretched countries in Europe, it has not arisen from ignorance of the true principles of political economy, but from neglecting them, as well as the counsels of her wisest statesmen. Ustariz,[9] who flourished about a hundred years ago, in that ill-fated and impoverished country, has ably developed the grand principles of that noble science, in a system as far superior to Dr. Smith's as the constitution of the United States is superior to the form of government of Spain.

APPENDIX TO *THE NEW OLIVE BRANCH*

Chapter II

[And as distress and embarrassment equally pervaded those states where there were none, it is absurd to ascribe the evil to those institutions where they existed.]

In North Carolina there were two emissions of paper money, with a legal tender, from 1783 to 1787. They depreciated fifty per cent. in a short time.

The following extracts will convey a tolerably adequate idea of the state of affairs during the period embraced in this chapter, and exonerate me from the charge of exaggeration. They cannot fail to be worthy the attention of such of our statesmen as are disposed to trace national calamities to their proper causes, in order to guard against their return at a future period.

"In every part of these states, the scarcity of money has become a common subject of complaint. This does not seem to be an imaginary grievance, like that of hard times, of which men have complained in all ages of the world. The misfortune is general, and in many cases it is severely felt. The scarcity of money is so great, or the difficulty of paying debts has been so common, that *riots and combinations have been formed in many places, and the operations of civil government have been suspended.*"*

"*Goods were imported to a much greater amount than could be consumed or paid for.*"†

"Thus was the usual means of remittance by articles the growth of the country, almost annihilated, and little else than specie remained, to answer the demands incurred by importations. *The money, of course, was drawn off; and this being inadequate to the purpose of discharging the whole amount of foreign contracts, the residue was chiefly sunk by the bankruptcies of the importers.* The scarcity of specie, arising principally from this cause, was attended with evident consequences; it checked commercial intercourse throughout the community, and furnished reluctant debtors with an apology for withholding their dues both from individuals and the public."‡

---

*   Dr. Hugh Williamson.
†   Minot's history of the Insurrection in Massachusetts, p. 2.
‡   Idem, p. 13.

"On opening their ports, an immense quantity of foreign merchandize was introduced into the country, and they were tempted by the sudden cheapness of imported goods, and by their own wants, to purchase beyond their capacities for payment. Into this indiscretion they were in some measure beguiled by their own sanguine calculations on the value which a free trade would bestow on the produce of their soil, and by a reliance on those evidences of the public debt which were in the hands of most of them. So extravagantly too did many estimate the temptation which equal liberty and vacant lands would hold out to emigrants from the old world, as to entertain the opinion that Europe was about to empty itself into America, and that the United States would derive from that source such an increase of population, as would enhance their lands to a price heretofore not even conjectured."[*]

"The bonds of men, whose competency to pay their debts was unquestionable, could not be negociated but at a discount of *thirty, forty, and fifty per centum: real property was scarcely vendible;* and sales of any articles for ready money could be made only at a ruinous loss. The prospect of extricating the country from those embarrassments was by no means flattering. Whilst every thing else fluctuated, some of the causes which produced this calamitous state of things were permanent. The hope and fear still remained, that the debtor party would obtain the victory at the elections; and instead of making the painful effort to obtain relief by industry and economy, many rested all their hopes on legislative interference. *The mass of national labour and national wealth was consequently diminished."*[†]

"But the public treasury did not afford the means of keeping this force (under Lincoln) in the field a single week: and the legislature not being in session, the constituted authorities were incapable of putting the troops in motion. This difficulty was removed by individual patriotism!"[‡]

"Property, when brought to sale under execution, sold at so low a price as frequently ruined the debtor without paying the creditor. A disposition to resist the laws became common: assemblies were called oftener and earlier than the constitution or laws required.'[§]

"Laws were passed by *which property of every kind was made a legal tender in the payment of debts,* though payable according to contract in gold or silver. Other laws installed the debt, so that of sums already due, only a third, and afterwards only a fifth, was annually recoverable in the courts of law."[¶]

"Silver and gold, which had circulated largely in the latter years of the war, were returning by the usual course of trade, to those countries, whence large quantities of necessary and unnecessary commodities had been imported. Had any general system of impost been

---

[*]   Marshal's Life of Washington, I. p. 75.
[†]   Idem, p. 88.
[‡]   Idem, p. 121.
[§]   Ramsay's S. Carolina, II. p. 428.
[¶]   Belknap's History of New Hampshire, II. p. 352.

adopted, some part of this money might have been retained, and some part of the public debt discharged; but the power of Congress did not extend to this object; and the states were not united in the expediency of delegating new and sufficient powers to that body. The partial imposts, laid by some of the states, were ineffectual, as long as others found their interest in omitting them."*

"The people of New Hampshire petitioned; and to gratify them the legislature enacted, that *when any debtor shall tender to his creditor, in satisfaction of an execution for debt, either real or personal estate sufficient,* the body of the debtor shall be exempt from imprisonment, and the debt shall carry an interest of six per cent.; the creditor being at liberty either to receive the estate, so tendered, at a value estimated by three appraisers, or to keep alive the demand by taking out an alias, within one year after the return of any former execution, and levying it on any estate of the debtor which he can find."†

Chapter III

1. 1789 Federal Tariff Schedule *[Its protection of agriculture is reserved as the subject of another chapter.]*

At 7 1/2 per cent.

Blank books,	Tin and pewter ware,
Paper,	Canes,
Paper hangings,	Whips,
Cabinet wares,	Ready made clothing,
Buttons,	Brushes,
Saddles,	Gold, silver, and plated ware,
Tanned leather,	Jewelry,
Anchors,	Paste work,
Wrought iron,	Manufactures of leather,
Gloves,	Hats.
Millenery,	

At 10 per cent.

Looking glasses,	Buckles,
Window and other glass,	Gold and silver lace,
Gunpowder,	Gold and silver leaf,
China, stone and earthen ware,	Paints.

At 15 per cent.

Coaches, chariots, chaises, solos, &c.

---

*   Idem, p. 356.

†   Idem, p. 429.

Subject to specific duties.

	Cents.		Cents.
Boots, per pair	50	Untarred cordage and yarn, per cwt.	90
Leather shoes	7	Twine or pack thread, per cwt.	200
Silk shoes or slippers	10	Wool and cotton cards, per dozen	50
Cables, per cwt.	75		
Tarred cordage, do.	75		
Unwrought steel, per lb.	56		

Non-enumerated articles, subject to 5 *per cent.*

Bricks,	Cannon,
Brass in sheets,	Cutlery,
Brazing copper,	*Cotton goods of all kinds,*
Combs,	Fire arms,
Clocks,	Gilt wares,
Copper bottoms,	Hempen cloth,
Hair powder,	*Iron manufactures,*
Inkpowder,	Japanned wares,
Linens and other manufactures of flax,	*Lead manufactures*
	Muskets,
Maps and Charts,	Printing types,
Paints,	*Pottery,*
Printed books,	Pins,
Paintings,	Steel manufactures,
Silks,	Stone ware,
Slates,	Side arms,
Starch,	Sail cloth,
Sealing wax,	Tin wares,
Worsted shoes,	Wood manufactures,
Brass manufactures,	*Woollen goods of every kind!!*
China ware,	&c. &c.

2. *Samuel Smith statement* *[but they experienced the same degree of slight as they have done in 1816–17]*

On the eleventh of April, 1789, Samuel Smith, Esq. of Maryland, presented to congress a memorial from the manufacturers of Baltimore, stating—

"That since the close of the late war, and the completion of the revolution, they have observed with serious regret the manufacturing and the trading interest of the country rapidly declining, and the attempts of the state legislatures to remedy the evil, failing of their object; that in the present melancholy state of our country, the number of poor increasing for want of employment, foreign debts accumulating, houses and lands depreciating in value, and trade and manufactures languishing and expiring; they look up to the supreme legislature of the United States, as the guardians of the whole empire, and from their united wisdom and patriotism, and ardent love of their country, expect to derive that aid and assistance, which alone can dissipate their just apprehensions, and animate them with hopes of success in future; by imposing *on all foreign articles, which can be made in America, such duties as will give a just and decided preference to their labours;* discountenancing that trade which tends so materially to injure them and impoverish their country; measures which in their consequences may contribute to the discharge of the national debt, and the due support of government; that they have annexed a list of such articles as are, or can be manufactured amongst them, and humbly trust in the wisdom of the legislature to grant them, in common with other mechanics and manufacturers of the United States, that relief that may appear proper."*

3. Pennsylvania Tariff Preamble [*The sound policy, the fostering care of its citizens, and of the resources of the state displayed in the latter, form a strong and decisive contrast with the utter impolicy of the tariff.*]

SECT. I. "Whereas divers useful and beneficial arts and manufactures have been gradually introduced into Pennsylvania, and the same have at length risen to a very considerable extent and perfection, insomuch that *during the late war between the United States of America and Great Britain, when the importation of European goods was much interrupted, and often very difficult and uncertain, the artisans and mechanics of this state, were able to supply in the hours of need, not only large quantities of weapons and other implements, but also ammunition and clothing, without which the war could not have been carried on, whereby their oppressed country was greatly assisted and relieved.*"

SECT. II. "And whereas, although *the fabrics and manufactures of Europe and other foreign parts, imported into this country in times of peace, may be afforded at cheaper rates than they can be mdde*[sic] *here, yet good policy and a regard to the well being of divers useful and industrious citizens, who are employed in the making of like goods in this state, demand of us that moderate duties be laid on certain fabrics and manufactures imported, which do most interfere with, and which (if no relief be given) will undermine and destroy the useful manufactures of the like kind in this country: For this purpose,"* &c. &c.

Chapter IV

Importation of clothing [*fans, fringes, glue, tassels and trimmings, limes and lemons, mittens, gloves, powders, pastes, washes, tinctures, plums, prunes, toys, wafers, &c. &c.*]

---

* Debates of Congress, I. 29.

As few persons are aware of the extravagant extent of the importations of clothing, I annex the amount for five years, of articles subject to 15 per cent. duty, of which about nine-tenths were cotton and woollen goods.

1804	$ 30,285,267
1805	37,137,598
1806	43,115,367
1807	46,031,742
1808	23,780,758
	$ 180,350,732[*]

The re-exportation of articles of
the same description for these years, was—

1804	$ 000,000	
1805	1,587,801	
1806	2,075,601	
1807	2,197,383	
1808	755,085	
		6,615,870[†]
Balance		173,737,862
Deduct for sundries, say ten per cent.		17,373,786
Cotton and woollen goods consumed in five years		$156,364,076

Had the duty been twenty-five per cent., and the imports 100,000,000, the revenue would have gained, and there would have been an immense saving to the nation of above 50,000,000 of dollars in four years! When will statesmen learn the grand secret of "*transforming taxes into useful regulations?*"

During these five years, we exported of raw cotton—

1804	lbs. 36,034,175
1805	38,390,087
1806	38,657,465
1807	63,944,559
1808	10,630,445
	lbs. 183,656,713

---

[*]   Seybert, 164.

[†]   ed. Note: Carey inserted the footnote marker but no footnote here. Presumably the source was also Seybert.

Chapter V

*1. **Elbridge Gerry speech** [felt deep distress at the bitter draught of the dregs of the chalice of humiliation swallowed at this crisis by the government of the United States, and brought the affair before the legislature of that state.]*

"It being officially announced, that the Indians complain they cannot receive the usual supplies of goods, by reason of the non-importation act, and that they were not to be purchased within the United States."

"I submit to your consideration, whether it is not incumbent on this state, to use the means in its power for *enabling the national government to rise superior to such a humiliating circumstance!* In the year 1775, when our war with Great Britain commenced, and when, immediately preceding it, a non-importation act had been strictly carried into effect, the state of Massachusetts apportioned on their towns, respectively, to be manufactured by them, articles of clothing wanted for their proportion of the army, which besieged Boston; fixed the prices and qualities of those articles, and they were duly supplied within a short period."

"Thus, before we had arrived at the threshold of independence, and when we were in an exhausted state, by the antecedent, voluntary and patriotic sacrifice of our commerce, *between thirteen and fourteen thousand cloth coats were manufactured, made and delivered into our magazine, within a few months from the date of the resolve which first communicated the requisition.*"

"Thirty six years have since elapsed, during twenty-nine of which we have enjoyed peace and prosperity, and have increased in numbers, manufactures, wealth and resources, beyond the most sanguine expectations."

"All branches of this government have declared their opinion, and I conceive on the most solid principle, that as a nation *we are independent* of any other, for the necessaries, conveniences, and for many of the luxuries of life."

"Let us not, then, at this critical period, admit any obstruction, which we have power to remove, to discourage or retard the national exertions for asserting and maintaining our rights; and above all, let us convince Great Britain that we can and will be independent of her for every article of commerce whilst she continues to be the ostensible friend, but the implacable foe of our prosperity, government, union, and independence."

*2. **Cotton manufacturing** [How much more instructive than Condorcet, Smith, Say, Ricardo, and the whole school of economists of this class!]*

I am aware that from local circumstances, cotton and some other articles were at reduced prices at the places of production during the war, from the difficulty and expense of transportation. The fall of cotton was a natural consequence of the impolicy of the planters in not having previously secured themselves a domestic market.

The following tables exhibit a statement of the great advancement made; and prove that our citizens only require half the patronage of government, which is afforded by England, France, Austria, and Russia, to enable them to enter into competition with the whole world.

State of the *cotton manufacture within thirty miles of Providence, R. I. in 1815, extracted from a memorial to congress.*

Cotton manufactories	140
Containing in actual operation	spindles 130,000
Using annually	bales of cotton 29,000
Producing yards of the kinds of cotton goods usually made	27,840,000
The weaving of which at eight cents per yard amounts to	$ 2,227,200
Total value of the cloth	$ 6,000,000
Persons steadily employed	26,000

State of the cotton manufacture throughout the United States in 1815, from a report of the Committee of Commerce and Manufactures.

Capital	$ 40,000,000
Males employed, from the age of seventeen and upwards	10,000
Women and female children	66,000
Boys, under seventeen years of age	24,000
Wages of one hundred thousand persons, averaging $150 each	$15,000,000
Cotton wool manufactured, nine thousand bales, amounting to lbs.	27,000,000
Number of yards of cotton, of various kinds,	81,000,000
Cost, per yard, averaging 30 cents	$ 24,300,000

State of the woollen manufacture throughout the United States in 1815, from the same.

Amount of capital supposed to be invested in buildings, machinery, &c.		$12,000,000
Value of raw material consumed annually	7,000,000	
Increase of value by manufacturing	12,000,000	
Value of woollen goods manufactured annually		$ 19,000,000
Number of persons employed		
constantly		50,000
occasionally		50,000
		100,000

In the city and neighbourhood of Philadelphia, there were employed—

In the cotton branch	2325 persons.
In the woolen	1226 do.
In iron castings	1152 do.
In paper making	950 do.
In smithery	750 do.

The value of the manufactures of the city of Pittsburg, which in 1815 employed 1960 persons, was 2,617,833 dollars. And every part of the country displayed a similar state of prosperity. How deplorable a contrast our present state exhibits!

Chapter VI

Tariff of 1816 *[I annex a statement of various articles, with the duties as reported by Mr. Dallas, and as finally adopted.]*

ARTICLES.	Mr. Dallas's Tariff. Per cent.	Tariff adopted. Per cent.
Blank books	35	30
Bridles	35	30
Brass ware	22	20
Brushes	35	30
Cotton manufactures of all sorts	33 1-3	25
(Those below 25 cts. per square yard, to be dutied as at 25 cents.)		
Cotton stockings	33 1-3	20
China ware	30	20
Cabinet ware	35	30
Carriages of all descriptions	35	30
Canes	35	30
Clothing, ready made	35	30
Cutlery	22	20
Cannon	22	20
Earthen ware	30	20
Glass ware	30	20
Harness	35	30
Iron ware	22	20
Leather and all manufactures of leather	35	30
Linens	20	15

Manufactures of wood	35	30
Needles	22	20
Porcelain	30	20
Parchment	35	30
Printed books	35	15
Paper hangings	35	30
Paper of every description	35	30
Printing types	35	20
Pins	22	20
Silks	20	15
Silk stockings	20	15
Sattins	20	15
Stone ware	30	20
Saddles	35	30
Thread stockings	20	15
Vellum	35	30
Walking sticks	35	30
Whips	35	30
Woollen stockings	28	20
Woollen Manufactures generally	28	25
Boots, per pair	200 cts.	150 cts.
Iron in bars and bolts, per cwt.	75	45
Shoes and slippers of silk, per pair	40	30
—— of leather	30	25
—— for children	20	15

Chapter VII

1. Memorials Presented to Congress 1816–1817 *[The Pittsburg memorial was, it is true, printed for the use of the members.]*

The following is a list of the applications—

No.	1816.	*Memorials.*	*Subjects.*
1	Dec. 16.	From New York	Iron manufactures.
2	16.	New Jersey	do.
3	20.	New York	Umbrellas.
4	27.	Massachusetts	do.
5	30.	New Jersey	Iron manufactures.
6	1817, Jan. 6.	New Jersey	do.
7	8.	New York	do.
8	9.	Philadelphia	do.

9	10.	Connecticut	Iron manufactures.
10	10.	New Jersey	do.
11	13.	Pennsylvania	do.
12	13.	New Jersey	do.
13	14.	Boston	do.
14	16.	Kentucky	Bar iron.
15	20.	Pennsylvania	Bar iron.
16	22.	Pennsylvania	Iron manufactures.
17	27.	New Jersey	Bar iron.
18	28.	Pennsylvania	Iron manufactures.
19	29.	Berkshire, Manufactures generally.	
20	29.	New York	do.
21	30.	New Jersey	Iron manufactures.
22	30.	N. York, Manufactures generally.	
23	30.	Oneida County	do.
24	31.	New York	do.
25	Feb. 1.	Pennsylvania	Iron manufactures.
26	3.	New York	do.
27	4.	Pennsylvania	do.
28	4.	N. York, Manufactures generally.	
29	4.	New York	do.
30	6.	Connecticut Iron manufactures.	
31	6.	New York and Vermont do.	
32	8.	Pennsylvania	do.
33	11.	N. Jersey, Manufactures generally.	
34	11.	New York	Iron manufactures
35	Feb. 13.	From Rhode Island.	Cotton and woollen.
36	13.	Connecticut	do.
37	17.	Pittsburg, Manufactures generally.	
38	20.	Illinois Lead.	
39	24.	Baltimore, Manufactures generally.	
40	26.	Philadelphia	do.
41	28.	Oneida	do
42	28.	Berkshire	do.

2. Pittsburgh Memorial *[and rendered tributary to foreign powers, whose interests are in direct hostility with ours."]*

From the Pittsburg Memorial.

"The committee have found that *the manufacture of cottons, woollens, flint glass, and the finer articles of iron, has lately suffered the most alarming depression.* Some branches which had been several years in operation, have been destroyed or partially suspended; and others, of a more recent growth, annihilated before they were completely in operation.

"The tide of importation has inundated our country with foreign goods. Some of the most valuable and enterprizing citizens have been subjected to enormous losses, and others overwhelmed with bankruptcy and ruin. The pressure of war was less fatal to the hopes of enterprize and industry, than a general peace with the calamities arising from the present state of our foreign trade."

"*It was confidently believed, that the destinies of the United States would no longer depend on the jealousy and caprice of foreign governments, and that our national freedom and welfare were fixed on the solid basis of our intrinsic means and energies. But these were 'airy dreams.' A peace was concluded with England, and in a few months we were prostrate at her feet. The manufacturers appealed to the general government for the adoption of measures that might enable them to resist the torrent that was sweeping away the fruits of their capital and industry. Their complaints were heard with a concern which seemed a pledge for the return of better days. The tariff of duties, established at the last session of congress, and the history of the present year, will demonstrate the falsity of their expectations.*"

"England never suffered a foreign government, or a combination of foreign capitalists, by glutting her own market, to crush in the cradle, any branch of her domestic industry. She never regarded, with a cold indifference, the ruin of thousands of her industrious people, by the competition of foreigners. The bare avowal of such an attempt would have incurred the indignant resistance of the whole body of the nation, and met the frowns, if not the instant vengeance of the government. The consequences of this policy in England are well known; her manufactures have become a source of wealth incalculable; the treasures of Spanish America are poured into her lap; her commerce is spread over every ocean, and, with a population comparatively small, she is the terror and the spoiler of Europe. Take from England her manufactures, and the fountains of her wealth would be broken up; her pre-eminence among nations would be lost for ever."

"For a speedy redress of such pressing evils, we look to the government of the union. *Will they uphold the sinking manufactures of the country, or will they not?* are their late assurances of aid and protection forgotten with the crisis that gave them birth? Let them realize the hopes of the country, and act with decision before it be too late."

"In the United States we have the knowledge of the labour-saving machinery, the raw material, and provisions cheaper than in Britain; but the overgrown capital of the British manufacturer, and the dexterity acquired by long experience, make a considerable time, and heavy duties necessary for our protection.—We have beaten England out of our market in hats, shoes, boots, and all manufactures of leather: we are very much her superior in ship building; these are all the works of the hands, where labour-saving machinery gives no aid; so that *her superiority over us in manufactures, consists more in the excellence and nicety of the labour-saving machinery, than in the wages of labour.* With all their jealousy, and restrictions upon the emigrations of workmen, the distresses and misfortunes of England will, by due encouragement, send much of her skill and knowledge to our shores; let us be ready to take full benefit of such events, as England herself did when despotic laws in Germany, and other parts of Europe, drove their manufacturers into Britain, which laid the foundation of her present eminence."

"That the cotton trade and manufacture is a concern of vast importance, and even of leading interest to the country, is a truth, your memorialists conceive, too palpable, to be denied or doubted. Were not our own constant observation and daily experience sufficient to establish it, the prodigious exertions of our ever-vigilant and indefatigable rival, directed against this particular interest, would place the matter beyond a question. For where a judicious and enterprizing opponent (as England undoubtedly is in this respect) directs her strongest engines of hostility, we have reason to conclude there lies our vital and most important concerns. This consideration is coming home to us with more and more force; and *the cotton planter, as well as the manufacturer, must have before this time discovered the alarming fact, that our great rival has become possessed of both our plants and seeds of cotton, which she is employing all her vast means to propagate in the East Indies and other British possessions, with an energy and success which threaten the most alarming consequences.* When your memorialists consider that the article thus jeopardized is the great staple of the country, they cannot but hope the people and their representatives will be generally convinced, that it is not the interest of individuals alone that is at stake, but that of the whole community."

"An appeal is made to the equity, to the patriotism of the southern statesman: his aid and co-operation is invoked for the relief of the suffering manufacturers of the northern and middle states."

"In the interior of the United States, few articles can be raised which will bear a distant transportation; products much more valuable when the grower and consumer are near each other, are therefore excluded from cultivation. A dependence on foreign markets in the most prosperous times necessarily restricts the labours of agriculture to a very few objects; a careless, decrepit, and unprofitable cultivation is the known result."

"The propriety of these observations may, in some degree, be illustrated by the difference in value between the land in the vicinity of a large town, and at a greater distance from it. The labour which produces the greatest quantity of subsistence is bestowed in the culture of articles too cumbrous for transportation; and in general a farm which will subsist fifty persons in its vicinity, would not subsist the fifth of that number three hundred miles off.

If the value of land be so much enhanced by the proximity of a market, and so rapidly diminished by the distance of transportation, the introduction of manufactories, and the creation of an interior market, ought to be regarded as peculiarly auspicious to the interest of agriculturists."

"Confining our views to the western country, we might emphatically ask, with what exportable commodities shall we restore the balance of trade, now fast accumulating against us? How arrest the incessant drain of our capital? *Our manufactures are perishing around us, and already millions have escaped, never to return."*

It will remain an eternal blot on the escutcheon of the fourteenth congress, that this pathetic address received no more attention than if it had been from a party of field negroes to a marble-hearted overseer.

From the Oneida Memorial.

"That the above county contains a greater number of manufacturing establishments, of cotton and woollen, than any county in the state, there being invested in said establishments at least 600,000 dollars."

"That although the utmost efforts have been made by the proprietors to sustain those establishments, their efforts have proved fruitless, and more than three-fourths of the factories remain necessarily closed, some of the proprietors being wholly ruined, and others struggling under the greatest embarrassment.

"In this alarming situation, we beg leave to make a last appeal to the congress of the United States. While we make this appeal, our present and extensive embarrassments in most of the great departments of industry, as well as the peculiar difficulty in affording immediate relief to manufacturers, are fully seen and appreciated. Yet your petitioners cannot believe that *the legislature of the union will remain an indifferent spectator of the wide-spread ruin of their fellow citizens, and look on, and see a great branch of industry, of the utmost importance in every community, prostrated under circumstances fatal to all future attempts at revival, without a further effort for relief.* We would not magnify the subject, which we now present to congress, beyond its just merits, when we state it to be one of the utmost importance to the future interests and welfare of the United States."

"It is objected that the entire industry of the country may be most profitably exerted in clearing and cultivating our extended vacant lands. But *what does it avail the farmer, when neither in the nation from which he purchases his goods, or elsewhere, can he find a market for his abundant crops?* Besides, the diversion of labour from agriculture to manufactures, is scarcely perceptible. Five or six adults, with the aid of children, will manage a cotton manufactory of two thousand spindles."

Chapter VIII

Passage of Acts of Congress *[But be that allowance what it may, it cannot remove the accusation of a most ruinous waste of time, and a most culpable and shameful procrastination of public business in congress.]*

In the first session of the twelfth congress, which commenced on the 4th of November, 1811, and terminated on the 6th of July, 1812, there were one hundred and thirty-eight acts passed, which were signed by the president in the following chronological order—

In November	2
December	8
January	9
February	14
March	14
April	26
May	21
June	17
July 1st	8
July 6th	<u>29</u>
	<u>138</u>

Twelfth congress.—Second session. From November 2, 1812, to March 3, 1813. —Sixty-two acts.

November	1
December	4
January	11
February	23
March 3d	<u>23</u>
	<u>62</u>

Thirteenth congress.—First session. From May 24, to Aug 2, 1813.—Fiftynine acts.

May	00
June	3
July	32
August 2d	<u>24</u>
	<u>59</u>

The twenty-four acts signed on the 2d of August, contain *forty-six pages of close print.* The act imposing the direct tax, is in the number, and contains *twenty-two pages.*

Thirteenth congress.—Second session. From December 6, 1813, to April 18, 1814.—Ninety-five acts.

December	2
January	7
February	7
March	27
April 1st to 16th	18
April 18th	34
	95

Thirteenth congress.—Third session. From September 19, 1814, to March 3, 1815.—One hundred acts.

September	00
October	1
November	6
December	11
January	9
February	38
March 1st	4
March 3d	31
	100

The thirty-one acts signed on the **3d** of March, contain thirty-five pages.

This was the ever memorable session of congress, in which the imbecility of the majority and the factious violence of the minority, brought the nation to the jaws of destruction, previous to the close of the war.

Fourteenth congress—First session. From December 4, 1815, to April 30, 1816.—One hundred and seventy-three acts.

December	2
January	4
February	15
March	14
April 2d to the 24th	39
26th and 27th	59
29th	31
30th	8
	173

Fourteenth congress.—Second session. From December 2, 1816, to March 3, 1817.—One hundred and fourteen acts.

In December	00
In January	8
In February	10
On Saturday, March 1st	14
March 3d	<u>82</u>
	<u>114</u>

The acts of this session are comprised in one hundred pages. Those signed in January occupy three pages and a half—those in February four—those on the first of March nine—and those on the **3d** seventy-three!

Fifteenth congress.—First session. From November 16, 1817, to April 20, 1818.— One hundred and thirty acts.

November	00
December	1
January	7
February	6
March	10
April 3d to 18th	54
April 20th	<u>52</u>
	<u>130</u>

The fifty-two acts signed on the **20th** of April, contain of J. E. Hall's edition, no less than eighty-seven pages. In this session there were, it appears, one hundred and six acts passed in seventeen days—and only twenty-four in the preceding four months and a half!

The annals of legislation may be challenged for any parallel case.

Fifteenth congress.—Second session. From November 16,1818, to March 3, 1819.— One hundred and seven acts.

November	00
December	7
January	4
February	33
March 2d	8
March 3d	<u>55</u>
	<u>107</u>

Chapter IX

Branches with no return in Philadelphia *[No returns were procured from twenty-six branches.]*

Bookbinders	***Manufacturers of gun-powder***
Brewers	Painters and glaziers
Brickmakers	Plumbers
Carpenters	Shoemakers
Coopers	Shotmakers
Chocolate makers	Sugar bakers
Calico printers	Snuff and tobacco manufacturers
Curriers	Stonecutters
Chair makers	Turners
Dyers	Tanners
Engravers	Umbrella makers
Embroiderers	Wheelwrights, &c. &c.
Glovers	Glass manufacturers

Chapter XIII

Additional price increases *[Souchong tea 50 75]*

Salt,	per bushel	1812.	May 1.	55
			Aug. 1.	85
		1813.	Oct. 1.	1 35
		1814.	Aug. 1.	2 25
			Oct 1.	3 00
Tin, per box		1812.	May 1.	28 00
			Aug. 1.	32 00
			Oct. 1.	33 00
		1814.	Aug. 1.	50 00
Plaster Paris, per ton		1812.	June 1.	12 37 ½
			Aug. 31.	14 50
			Oct. 5.	15 50
			Dec. 14.	17 50

Chapter XIV

1. New Harmony *[The progress to wealth and prosperity, therefore, has been far beyond any previous example in this country.]*

"In 1809, they built a fulling mill, which does a great deal of business for the country, a hemp mill, an oil mill, a grist mill, a brick warehouse, 46 by 36 feet, having a wine cellar completely arched over; and another brick building of the same dimensions. A considerable quantity of land was cleared. The produce of this year was 6000 bushels of Indian corn; 4500 bushels of wheat; 4500 bushels of rye; 5000 bushels of oats; 10,000 bushels of potatoes; 4000 lbs. of flax and hemp; 100 bushels of barley brewed into beer; and 50 gallons of sweet oil, made from the white poppy, and equal to the imported olive oil. Of this produce they sold 3000 bushels of corn, 1000 bushels of potatoes, 1000 bushels of wheat; and they distilled 1600 bushels of rye.

"In 1810, a wool-carding machine and two spinning jennies were erected, for the fabrication of broad cloth from the wool of Merino sheep. A frame barn was built, 100 feet long, and a brick house built, to accommodate 20 weavers' looms."[*]

"After breakfast, we visited the different branches of manufactures. In the wool loft, eight or ten women were employed in teazing and sorting the wool for the carding machine which is at a distance on the creek. From thence the roves are brought to the spinning house in the town, where we found two roving billies and six spinning jennies at work. They were principally wrought by young girls, and they appeared perfectly happy, singing church music most melodiously. In the weaving house sixteen looms were at work, besides several warpers and winders."[†]

"After dinner we visited the soap and candle works; the dye works; shearing and dressing works; the turners, carpenters, and machine makers; and, finally, we were conducted through the warehouses, which we found plentifully stored with commodities; among others, we saw 450 *pieces of broad and narrow cloth, part of it of Merino wool, and of as good a fabric as any that ever was made in England. We were told, that they could sell the best broad cloth, as fast as made, at ten dollars per yard.*"[‡]

"The society now [1811] consists of about 800 persons, and the operative members are nearly as follow: one hundred farmers; three shepherds; ten masons; three stone-cutters; three brickmakers; ten carpenters; two sawyers; ten smiths; two wagon makers; three turners; two nailors; seven coopers; three rope makers; ten shoemakers; two saddlers; three tanners; seven taylors; one soap boiler; one brewer; four distillers; one gardener; two grist millers; two oil millers; one butcher; six joiners; six dyers, dressers, shearers, &c.; one fuller; two hatters; two potters; two warpers; seventeen weavers; two carders; eight

---

[*]   Melish's Travels, II. 68.
[†]   Idem, 70.
[‡]   Idem, 71.

spinners; one rover; one minister of religion; one schoolmaster; one doctor; one storekeeper, with two assistants; and one tavern keeper, with one assistant.""*

2. *Additional thoughts on industry* *[for had the woollen manufacture been protected, the Merino sheep, in which such immense sums were invested, would have been preserved, instead of so large a portion of them being consigned to the slaughter-house.]*

Believing that the prejudices prevailing on this subject have done more injury to this country, and more retarded its progress than all the wars it ever carried on, from the landing of "the Pilgrims" to the present hour, I make no apology for adding another instructive quotation from the respectable writer who figures so largely at the commencement of it.[1] Would to heaven that those farmers and planters who form the majority of the legislature of the United States, were duly impressed with the soundness of his statements, and predicated the laws of their country on the useful lessons they furnish! The United States would then present a different spectacle from what they do at present to their friends and enemies—a spectacle of gratulation to the former, and of mourning to the latter.

"*A nation peopled only by farmers must be a region of indolence and misery.* If the soil is naturally fertile, little labour will procure abundance; but for want of exercise even that little labour will be burthensome and often neglected. Want will be felt in the midst of abundance; and the human mind be abased nearly to the same degree with the beasts that graze in the field. If the region is more barren, the inhabitants will be obliged to become somewhat more industrious and therefore more happy."

"*Those therefore who wish to make agriculture flourish in any country, can have no hope of succeeding in the attempt but by bringing commerce and manufactures to her aid; which, by taking from the farmer his superfluous produce, gives spirit to his operations, and life and activity to his mind.* Without this stimulus to activity, in vain do we use arguments to rouse the sluggish inhabitants. In vain do we discover that the earth is capable of producing the most luxuriant harvests with little labour. Our own abundant crops are produced as undeniable proofs of this in vain. *But place a manufacturer in the neighbourhood, who will buy every little article that the farmer can bring to market, and he will soon become industrious*—the most barren fields will become covered with some useful produce. Instead of listless vagabonds, unfit for any service—the country will abound with a hardy and robust race of men, fit for every valuable purpose: and the voice of festivity and joy be heard in every corner, instead of the groans of misery and the sighs of discontent." †

---

*   Melish's Travels, II. 77.

†   Anderson on National Industry, p. 61.

The vacancy in this page may be usefully filled with an extract from Parkes' Chemical essays[2], which bears cogently on this subject.

"If a line be drawn upon the map of England, across the country from Sunderland to Bristol, all the counties on the west of this line, will be found to contain coal. Formerly these were the least valuable districts, and the parts of the country which were the most thinly populated. Hence, when the constitution of the British parliament was established, the greatest weight of representation was given to the rich counties on the other side of that line. Whereas, now, *owing to the establishment of manufactures, the coal counties have become the most populous and wealthy*: and the agricultural districts have either been comparatively deserted, or at least have not much increased in population."

"This accounts in some measure for the inequality of our representation, and shows very distinctly the value of our mines of coal, and that *by the establishment of manufactures, even the most sterile and forbidding district may be rendered populous, flourishing and opulent.*"[*]

Chapter XV

Domestic exports 1803–14 *[Luxuries, which tend to introduce extravagance, and deprave our morals.]*

Domestic exports for fifteen years, from 1803 to 1817, inclusive.[†]

Cotton	$154,179,117
Vegetable food	192,564,368
Lumber, masts, &c.	52,796,000
Tobacco	74,768,000
Animal food and animals	34,712,560
Dried salt fish	16,915,256
Pickled fish	4,155,419
Whale oil and bones	2,819,528
Spermaceti oil and candles	1,658,320
Ginseng, peltry, &c.	8,130,305
Naval stores	6,579,931
Pearl and potashes	13,990,000
Manufactures	27,270,000
Uncertain	4,836,000
	$ 595,374,804
Average	$ 39,691,653

---

* Vol. II. p. 361.

† Seybert, 146–7.

Chapter XVII

[and the liberality and disinterestedness of the latter, are preached in long-winded speeches in, and memorials to, congress, and as long-winded newspaper essays, and are received as sacred and undeniable.]

Another contrast.

	Duty. Per cent.		Duty. Per cent.
Potatoes	15	Watches	7 ½
Butter	15	Jewelry	7 ½
Flour	15	Inkpowder	15
Malt	15	Printed books	15
Onions	15	Worsted shoes	15
Tobacco in the leaf	15	Linens and silks	15

Potatoes and tobacco—linens, silks, and printed books—subject to the same duty! What wonderful talents this tariff displays! How admirably it corroborates the fond "day dreams" in which we indulge ourselves, of our immense superiority over the benighted Europeans, who, *mirabile dictu*, according to Judge Story,[3] are studying lessons of political economy under congress—

"The statesmen of the old world, *in admiration of the success of our policy*, are relaxing the rigour of their own systems!!"

So says the celebrated Salem memorial, edited, according to public fame, by this learned judge.

APPENDIX TO *ADDRESSES OF THE PHILADELPHIA SOCIETY*

This material appears as a postscript to the Second Address.

Postscript, October 23, 1821.

The grand point, on which the political economists of the new and old school are at issue, is the unlimited freedom, or the qualified restriction of Commerce: the disciples of the new school contending for the former, as the best means of promoting national prosperity and happiness, and the adverse party contending for such restrictions as raised England to that height of power which she now possesses, and to that prosperity which she enjoyed till her wild and wasteful wars crippled her resources, impaired her prosperity, and entailed on her an enormous debt, with a most burdensome and oppressive taxation—such restrictions, in fine, as retrieved the desperate circumstances in which France was sunk, when subjugated by the Holy Alliance. In corroboration of the doctrines advanced on this vital topic in the preceding pages [written in March, 1819] I am happy to be able to adduce the powerful testimony and unanswerable arguments, of the Quarterly Review for January 1821; which are respectfully submitted to the consideration of the statesmen of the United States.

"Questions of commercial policy have been lately treated in so abstract a manner that their connection with common life and practice seems to be entirely forgotten. Speculative writers send forth from their closets general propositions and paradoxical dogmas upon matters relative to the common intercourse of the world, with the most confident affirmation of their universal applicability. They find supporters in persons of rank and influence, pleased with this sort of 'royal road to geometry;' while practical men, too much occupied to weigh theoretical notions of this difficult nature, or to examine their operation in the varied and conflicting movements of traffic and national interests, add their conclusive assent. The adopted opinions thus acquire general reception, and are promulgated as undisputed and unconditional truth, and the sole panacea for existing evils."

"Our forefathers could not maintain with greater zeal, that a favourable balance of trade and an abundant circulation of the precious metals were essential to prosperity, than has recently been manifested for the necessity of universal freedom of trade, with a view to the attainment of the same object."*

"In the conversion of unwrought into wrought commodities lies the great field in which legislators have endeavoured to appropriate by regulations— understood to operate as encouragements—the largest portion of skilful industry and production.

["It has been by means of complete prohibition, or the convenient expedient of taxes on importation, that governments have aimed to effect this appropriation of wealth. The duties imposed upon commodities which we cannot produce, as cotton, rice, coffee, are to be considered as merely financial: such as are laid upon productions common to the growth of this country, as flax, wool, deals, are protective as well as financial. The prohibition and duties laid upon some raw, and all wrought articles, are designed to advance the home production and manufacture; as in the instance of grain, wrought wool, linen, cotton, silk, refined sugar."†

"With regard to wrought goods, the manufacture of which requires small space and occupies a numerous and usually wealthy population, giving much value in a little bulk, it has been held the soundest policy to engross the largest possible portion of such productions. Either all foreign fabrics have been prohibited, or duties have been placed upon their introduction so heavy as to exclude the chance of an equal competition with the home manufacture."

"*These principles of restriction, exclusion, and encouragement, occurred at periods of the earliest application of the mind to the means of advancing the public wealth, and have been the rule of conduct for governments for centuries past.* They appear in the oldest enactments of the statute book, commencing with our first Edwards and Henrys; were long inculcated as incontrovertible, and at this day prevail in every stage of society:—in China and Turkey, in England, France, and the United States, the most ancient and the last instituted;—under every form, the freest and the most arbitrary governments alike act upon the system.

"This has been tenaciously adhered to in practice, though for more than half a century all writers upon commercial policy have held an opposite argument; every one, from the time of Quesnay and Smith, however differing on other points, agreeing in this one principle, that general freedom of trade is the surest and most rapid way to wealth. It is maintained that to force the consumer to pay dearer for home productions than he can purchase from abroad, is not to promote the national advantage, but the interest of the

---

*   *Quarterly Review*, No. 48, page 281.
†   *Quarterly Review*, No. 48, page 282.

producer at the expense of that of the consumer. It is asserted, that the freest admission of foreign products and manufactures will best assist, in the early stages of society, the progress of agriculture, till the accumulation of capital necessarily raises manufactures, foreign commerce, and navigation. In the advanced state, every individual, intent on the increase of his own advantage and fortunes, and left to the unrestrained pursuit of his interest, will follow it with most zeal and effect: and from prevalent private success results the general prosperity.

"A main principle insisted upon by the advocates of freedom of commerce, is, that no industry or source of wealth is lost by the declension or disappearance of a home manufacture, in consequence of the opening of the country to the admission of a like foreign fabric possessing a superiority; because something must be given in payment for the new importation, and the labourers in the declining manufacture will transfer themselves to the production of this other object required to effect the exchange.

"The truth of this position rests upon the power of the home manufacturer to find occupation in some other labour, which will afford the value wanted to give in exchange for the new foreign imports. We must retain yet in our possession a sufficient diversity of departments of industry, or some of so much magnitude as to receive the labourers dislodged from their usual employment by the introduction of foreign commodities. It can hardly be expected that any material new opening for labour can at this day be discovered; those remaining departments of industry, therefore, must be productive of objects, which will be received in other countries to an extent to pay for our new importations; and those increased in proportion to our transferred labour."*

"The transition from one description of labour to another would not be easy. *A man accustomed for a number of years to a particular kind of work, cannot readily pass over to another altogether different.* Persons, especially of the class of life of artizans and labourers, are slow to form and slow to change their habits; the skill which they tardily acquire, they tenaciously adhere to, and come with difficulty to learn any other. A farmer's labourer will not readily become a mechanic; a silk-weaver be made a cutler; a lace-maker or glover be converted into a maker of woollens."

"*Not only would a change of occupation be requisite, but also of the seat of industry.*" The Norfolk farming labourer might have to make hose in Leicester or Nottingham; the East Lothian cottager to weave muslins at Glasgow or checks at Carlisle; and the Spitalfields weaver to become a japanner at Birmingham or a cotton spinner at Manchester. Whole districts of Ireland might have to interchange residence with those of England and Scotland, the north with the south, and

---

*   *Quarterly Review*, No. 48, page 283.

the east with the west, with the rapidity of a horde of Tartars. *There must be a transference of the disengaged people to the seats of retained manufacture, or the retained manufacture must extend to their residence.* The latter is scarcely practicable, when the convenience or necessity is considered of concentration, in manufacturing industry, of the several connected processes and branches.

"The advocates of freedom of trade meet this objection by inculcating a gradual change, according to the nature of the industry which they see must be lost. If the silk and kerseymere weavers cannot convert their skill to a beneficial use in other employments, they are willing to allow a period equal to the probable lives of the silk and kerseymere weavers. Even then the opening of a foreign import of silk and kerseymere must overtake numbers of those exercising these trades; and it will be incumbent, first, to inquire whether this positive loss is likely to be accompanied with any commensurate benefit.

"While the peculiar skill of many trades cannot be turned to any other manufacture, the capital to a considerable extent, which employs that skill, and which is, in a great degree, fixed in machinery, buildings, implements, &c. *is applicable to no other object, and must be lost.* In the uncertainty, with all quarters of the world open, how far a manufacture may be affected, *the capital in many branches will be retained in a delusive hope till it decays within the hand.* The knowledge of a particular business which is frequently conjoined with capital, and leaves a double advantage in the remuneration of the skill and the interest of the money, causes an unwillingness to remove to other departments of industry, in ignorance of their nature and with but a chance of improvement. In such transitions, especially in the smaller, which, in the aggregate, form the most considerable portion of capital, more is wasted than transferred; and all is commonly wrecked in the gulf of bankruptcy."[*]

"Freedom of trade seems more peculiarly to favour the interests of merchants trading with foreign states, and most to prejudice certain branches of manufacture and agriculture; but of the labour constituting wealth,— *the commercial, which interchanges commodities, however useful and important,—is still subordinate to the manufacturing and agricultural, which produce those commodities*: and the greater the produce of agriculture and manufacture, which is raised and interchanged in a given country, the greater must be its affluence"[†]

"The slightest examination of the history of commerce shews *how many manufactures, and also natural productions of homogeneous climates, have owed their introduction amongst a people to special encouragement,* and have risen by protection till they flourished in self-supported excellence and extension. Because interference and encouragements may be carried to an extreme, are they, therefore, in all

---

[*]   *Quarterly Review*, No. 48, page 285.
[†]   *Quarterly Review*, No. 48, page 292.

cases, impolitic and injurious? Are governments to be considered as having done every thing, when, in fact, they have done nothing whatever?"*

"A superiority in a manufacture arises from skill, the result of manual dexterity, of chemical or mechanical ability, individual or co-operative. This, at times, will proceed from accident, or, when numbers are engaged in an employment, it will occur to the observing and reflecting: it becomes manifest in the qualities of finer texture, in brighter or more permanent colours, and in method of finishing. These are niceties and refinements, the effect of long labour and attention applied in a particular direction. *It may be the interest of a nation to preserve within itself, when at a moderate cost of restriction, the rudiments of all manufactures. Practice will confer skill, opportunity give rise to invention, and perseverance and the growth of wealth bestow importance and stability.*"†

"Florence owed her splendour to the woollen manufacture, with which she supplied the world." ***** "The spirit of the woollen manufacture, by a kind of Pythagorean transmigration, now resides in France, Flanders, and England. How has it escaped from Florence? *Can any reason be assigned but the absence of a sufficient safeguard from external intrusion and subversion?*"‡

"The favourite idea of our political economists is to banish regulations, and to leave every species of industry to its own direction. They dwell on the course which wealth naturally takes in its free progress to its greatest height, through the various stages of society, from the hunter, through the pastoral, agricultural, manufacturing, and commercial state. They hold every interruption to perfect freedom to be prejudicial to the speediest advance. *They beg the question of a never-failing activity and love of accumulation*; they count not on the disposition to indolence, the contentment with little, taught and actually practised by so many; the calls of religion; the love of pleasure; the passion for honour overcoming that for wealth: all which may arrest the advance of public opulence in its free course through the early and middle stages. We would call into action more motives than one. Individual exertion, on our adoption of liberty of trade, may not be allowed free play: if home regulations do not cramp it, external arts and rivalry will.

"If we endeavour to ascertain the result of freedom of trade in the commercial history of the world, it will, we believe, be found that *its effects have not been to create any material branches of manufactures, nor yet to retain those previously possessed.* It has, in fact, proved rather favourable to commerce than to manufactures. *Italy, once the seat of numerous manufactures, which admits all foreign goods upon moderate duties, has nothing remaining but some small fabrics of silk goods.* Switzerland receives foreign

---

*   Idem, page 293.
†   Idem, page 295.
‡   Idem, page 296.

manufactures, and possesses a few herself; but these have probably arisen from the forced situation of the war—she had none previously. Hume remarks 'that agriculture may flourish even where manufactures and other arts are unknown and neglected. Switzerland is, at present, a remarkable instance; where we find at once the most skilful husbandmen and the most bungling tradesmen that are to be met with in Europe.'* *Many small territories and islands are to be observed in different parts of the globe enjoying absolute liberty of commerce, Hamburgh, Lisbon, Malta, Guernsey, St. Thomas, &c. yet no manufactures have been found to mix amongst them;* and though possessed of certain portions of commerce, this may be ascribed more to favourable position, or vicinity to countries under restriction, than to any inherent virtue of an open commerce.

"The doctrine of free trade has something very generous in its professions. It aims to remove all impediments and obstructions on the intercourse of nations; to withdraw much complication in government with regard to legal enactments, to customs, and custom-house officers; to prevent the callous commission of vice in a profusion of oaths, of smuggling, and other encroachments on revenue; with endless jealousies and contentions of trade. In these feelings we participate: and *could the dreams of the theorists be verified, we would willingly enter into the adoption of that entire liberty of trade which was to lead to the realization of them.* But many of the evils enumerated are inseparable from the constitution of society; *laws are possibly as necessary to the protection of national industry as they are to that of individual property;* the safeguards and resources of the revenue must be maintained. If wealth be an essential part of power and a security of independence, we must admit and establish the system best fitted for its preservation. Narrow, malignant, or hostile feelings spring from the mind, and not from the existence of restrictions of self-defence or patriotic encouragement. If ill passions are bred by prohibitive regulations, their removal might lead to others of a nature not more benevolent—abjectness, sense of inferiority, and of inability to protect ourselves."†

"*It is a strong reason to doubt the practicability of these schemes, that statesmen have no where ventured upon them; not from ignorance, as has been petulantly pretended, but from extended knowledge.* Neither in old nor new states, do legislatures find the Utopian ideas of these philosophers to be feasible: yet Adam Smith, the great advocate for the most unrestricted trade, is read in all countries and languages, and his doctrines have been moulded into all shapes, *whether to inform youth or puzzle the learned!!!* Reflection and practice seem to show, that this valuable

---

*   Essay XI. On the populousness of Ancient Nations.
†   Quarterly Review, No. 48, page 300.

writer, in the zeal of his argument, *carried too far his views freedom of trade, as he assuredly did those of unlimited production and unrestrained parsimony.*"*

It is impossible attentively to read this reasoning, without a thorough conviction of the futility of the remedy proposed for the destruction of particular branches of industry by free importation, in Adam Smith's "*collateral branches*" and "*country labour.*"

---

*   Idem, page 301.

NOTES

The New Olive Branch (1820)

1 In the original title page, Carey quotes William H. Crawford's "Report on Currency Made to the House of Representatives of the United States 24 February 1820" and paraphrases a statement made by William Pitt, 1st Earl of Chatham (1708–1778). Malachi Postlethwayt (d. 1767), also quoted, was a British mercantilist economic thinker and author of *The Universal Dictionary of Trade and Commerce*.

2 Frederick Augustus Hervey, 4th Earl of Bristol and Bishop of Derry (1730–1803), was associated with the independence-minded Irish Volunteer movement, to which Carey belonged before being forced out of Ireland. This quotation refers to the Bishop's most notorious anti-government speech.

3 A reference to Patrick Colquhoun, *A Treatise on the Wealth Power and Resources of the British Empire* (1814).

4 Roman Playwright (c.195–159 BC). The quotation is from *Heauton Timorumenos*.

5 This portion vaguely echoes the language of the Declaration of Independence.

6 Carey appears to be confused here. These points do not occur in the second of the *Addresses of the Philadelphia Society for the Promotion of National Industry*, which was written by Carey and appears in this volume.

7 Carey refers to the ending of the Napoleonic Wars in 1815. During these wars the U.S. had prospered as a neutral carrier, but with the end of war that would no longer be the case.

8 The War of 1812.

9 Jerónimo de Uztariz (1670–1732) was a Spanish economist often associated with mercantilist thought.

10 James Monroe and William H. Crawford.

11 Alexander J. Dallas (1759–1817), treasury secretary 1814–16.

12 Jean-Baptiste Say (1767–1832).

13 David Ricardo (1772–1823).

14 The Edinburgh Review was an influential British serial that included a number of free trade essays in 1820.

15 The Encyclopedists, led by Denis Diderot, were the force behind the *Encyclopedie*, an important contribution to the Enlightenment which featured two influential essays by the physiocrat Francois Quesnay promoting free trade ideas.

16 This quotation from Wealth of Nations, book 4, chapter 2, is one which Carey addresses further in *Addresses of the Philadelphia Society for the Promotion of National Industry*, II.

17 Under the Articles of Confederation, in effect until 1789, Congress did not have the authority to lay duties.

18 Carey presumably refers to John Marshall's *Life of George Washington*, vol. 4 (1805), which includes a long description of Shays' Rebellion, which occurred in Massachusets from 1786–87.

19 James Bowdoin (1726–1790), governor of Massachusetts.

20 Several items have been excised here and moved to the appendix for chapter 2.

21 Carey is referring to the public securities purchased by individuals to support the American Revolution. These securities greatly depreciated during the financial insecurity following the war, leaving their original purchasers with large losses. Speculators (whom Carey describes as "deadly enemies" to the Revolution) purchased many of these certificates from the original holders and ultimately made large profits.

22 Thus do ye, but not for yourselves.

23 The War of 1812.

24 This is a rough paraphrase of Prospero's speech in Act IV, Scene I of *The Tempest*.

25 The severity of the crisis of the 1780s, the timing of the recovery, and the role of the constitution in the recovery are all debated by economic historians today as discussed in the introduction to this volume.

26 Carey refers to the first US tariff of 1789.

27 Thomas Jefferson (1743–1826), third president of the United States, 1801–1809.

28 Benjamin Austin, a Massachusetts state legislator and politician, had been a leader of the pro-manufacturing movement of the 1780s.

29 A reference to Adam Smith's work.

30 Carey refers to military campaigns in the War of 1812 fought in Washington, DC, Canada and the Chesapeake Bay.

31 Marquis de Condorcet (Marie Jean Antoine Nicolas de Caritat) (1743–1794).

32 The War of 1812 officially ended in December 1814 with the Treaty of Ghent, but word did not arrive in the United States until 1815.

33 John Taylor of Caroline (1753–1824).

34 Maximilien de Béthune, Duke of Sully, (1560–1641); Jean-Baptiste Colbert (1619–1683); and Frederick II (the Great) of Prussia (1712–1786) were all financial officials who advocated centralizing reforms and, in the latter two cases, were strongly protectionist.

35 Alexander J. Dallas (1759–1817), treasury secretary 1814–16.

36 See appendix for complete table.

37 An earlier iteration of *The New Olive Branch* was addressed to James Mercer Garnett (1770–1843), a free trade advocate and longtime president of the Fredericksburg (VA) Agricultural Society as well as a member of the US House of Representatives from 1805–1809. Pegram was probably James West Pegram, member of an influential Virginia agricultural family.

38 The Compensation Act of 1816 raised congressional pay from $6 per diem to $1,500 per year. It also raised a public outrage that forced Congress to repeal it.

39 The so-called First Seminole War of the mid-1810s culminated in Andrew Jackson's invasion of Florida in 1818.

40 The debate over slavery in Missouri that resulted in the Missouri Compromise of 1820.

41 John Stark (1728–1822).

42 Eligius Fromentin, (d.1822), was a Democratic-Republican US senator from Louisiana between 1813 and 1819.

43 Cuba.

44 Tench Coxe (1755–1824).

45 Tench Coxe was author of the 1814 Census of Manufactures.

46 Carey probably meant "charges" here.

47 Alexander Dirom (d. 1830) was a British general best known for his account of the war in India who also wrote *An Inquiry into the Corn Laws and Corn Trade of Great Britain, and Their Influence on the Prosperity of the Kingdom* (Edinburgh, 1796).

48 Patrick Coquhoun (1745–1820).

49 This quotation is from Jesus's *Sermon on the Mount*, Matthew 7:5.

50 This quotation is from Jefferson's letter to Benjamin Austin, which is inserted in the front matter of this book.

51 Albert Gallatin (1761–1849) was secretary of the treasury between 1801 and 1813.

52 A number of American ships were captured by Barbary pirates from 1784 to 1815, necessitating naval expenses and, in some cases, large ransoms for prisoners and tribute payments to the rulers.

53 Timothy Pitkin (1766–1847), *A Statistical View of the Commerce of the United States of America* (1816).

54 The total should be 28,030,672. The error is Carey's.

55 The "Indian's gun" was often said to "cost more than it comes to," i.e., it was not worth the investment.

56 Here Carey is mentioning a number of new American textile factories owned or managed by by E. I. Dupont in Wilmington, DE; Col. James Sheppard in Northampton, Mass.; William W. Young in Brandywine, DE, Abraham Schenk in Matteawan, NY, and Francis Cabot Lowell in Waltham.

57 Robert Morris, (1734–1806), was known as the "financier of the American Revolution." He was a signer of the Declaration of Independence and founder of the Bank of North America. Thomas Fitzsimons (1744–1811) was a US representative from 1789–1794 and a founder of the Bank of North America. George Clymer (1739–1813) was a signer of the Declaration of Independence and US representative from 1789–1790.

58 Rufus King (1755–1827) was a Federalist US senator from New York, 1789–1796 and 1813–1825. Carey appears to have mistakenly placed him in the House of Representatives.

59 John Forsyth, (1780–1841) was a US representative from Georgia, 1813–1818 and 1823–1827 and US Senator, 1818–1819 and 1829–1834.

60 Ædanus Burke (1743–1802) was a US representative from South Carolina from 1789 to 1790.

61 The congressional debates during this period reported speeches in the second person; thus Carey is quoting the debates quoting Burke.

62 Thomas Tudor Tucker (1745–1828), US representative from South Carolina, 1789–1792.

63 Apella was a Jew, possibly fictional, who was supposed to be particularly credulous according to the Roman poet, Horace.

64 Carey refers to the 1685 repeal of the Edict of Nantes of 1598, which had granted France's Protestant minority significant rights. The repeal caused many Protestants to flee the country.

Addresses of the Philadelphia Society for the Promotion of National Industry

1 Carey discusses the Harmony settlement more extensively in *The New Olive Branch*, chapter XIV.

2 This quotation, from a letter from Jefferson to Benjamin Austin of Boston, is a favorite of Carey's and also utilized in *The New Olive Branch*, chapter III.

3 The War of 1812.

4 Carey is arguing that, although the United States imposed some tariffs on imports, it was done in order to raise revenue to operate the government rather than to protect infant manufactures by keeping out foreign competition.

5 There was a Merino sheep fad in the 1810s as farmers and manufacturers hoped their wool would help to spur the textile industry.
6 Carey elaborates on this criticism of Adam Smith in the next two addresses.
7 Carey paraphrases Prospero in Shakespeare's *The Tempest*, Act IV, Scene I.
8 Carey lists a number of British merchant economists and American merchant politicians to make his point.
9 Jerónimo de Uztariz (1670–1732) was a Spanish economist often associated with mercantilist thought.

Appendix to *The New Olive Branch*

1 Carey refers to Adam Anderson (c. 1692–1765) a Scottish mercantilist economist who stressed the importance of manufacturing.
2 Samuel Parkes (1761–1825), author of *Chemical Essays*, was an English chemist and chemical manufacturer who opposed the onerous duties on salt.
3 Joseph Story (1779–1845) was a US Supreme Court justice from 1811 to 1845.

INDEX

Lightning Source UK Ltd.
Milton Keynes UK
UKOW02n2322151014

240144UK00003B/51/P